*Consta*

# *Constantinople*

## Edmondo De Amicis

Translated by Stephen Parkin

Foreword by Umberto Eco

With engravings by Cesare Biseo

ALMA CLASSICS

ALMA CLASSICS LTD
London House
243-253 Lower Mortlake Road
Richmond
Surrey TW9 2LL
United Kingdom
www.almaclassics.com

*Constantinople* first published in Italian as *Costantinopoli* in 1877
This translation first published by Hesperus Press Ltd in 2005
This revised translation first published by Alma Classics Ltd (previously
Oneworld Classics Ltd) in 2010
This new edition published by Alma Classics Ltd in 2013

Translation, Introduction and Notes © Stephen Parkin, 2005, 2010
Foreword © Umberto Eco, 2005
Cover © Marina Rodrigues

Printed and bound by CPI Group (UK) Ltd, Croydon, CR0 4YY

ISBN: 978-1-84749-266-1

# Contents

# Foreword

There's a short story by Borges ('The Story of the Warrior and the Prisoner') in which a barbarian from Lombardy called Droctulft arrives one day, together with his tribe, in front of the walls of Ravenna, with the plan of laying siege to the city and conquering it. Droctulft has come out of the forests of his native land; he is "brave, innocent and savage"; the only human dwellings he has ever known are forest huts, and it is the first time he has set eyes on a city. Try to imagine him as the walls and towers of Ravenna on the horizon grow clearer and larger as he approaches them and sees something he has never seen before. Borges describes it for us: he sees the cypresses and the marble monuments, a diverse yet not disorderly whole, an organism made up of statues, temples and gardens, columns and capitals, measured and open spaces. He sees a kind of complex mechanism: he doesn't yet understand its purpose, but he senses an immortal intelligence at work in its design. It is at this point that Droctulft kneels down, vanquished by the very thing he had come to conquer and destroy. The vision of the city amazes and changes him: he abandons his own people to fight (and eventually to die) for Ravenna.

The countless descriptions of arriving in Istanbul (from antiquity onwards the accounts of the journey to the city form a literary genre with its own rules, in which the enchantment of the first arrival is an essential element) constantly evoke the astonishment felt by Borges's legendary Lombard warrior. Perhaps this is because there are two types of cities: those you find yourself in suddenly, with no sense of approaching them from a distance (like London, Rome, Paris), and others which only emerge gradually in one's perception (New York is the obvious example, whether you arrive in the city by sea or along the motorway from the airport). Istanbul certainly belongs to the second type, at least for those who in the past came by sea. Whether the ship comes from the direction of the Bosphorus or the Dardanelles, it will always have to wind its way into the Golden Horn, revealing the city, as it does so, in a series of different angles, in a kind of fluid cinematic sequence.

The most cinematographic description of the arrival in Istanbul is by an Italian writer much less well known outside his own country than Nerval, Gautier, Flaubert or Loti: Edmondo De Amicis, the author of this book. In Italy every child – at least all those born between 1886 and my own generation – is familiar with his collection of stories *Cuore* (*The Heart of a Boy*), which is nowadays considered – with some justification – rather too sugary and moralistic for modern tastes, but De Amicis was also a very talented journalist, as is evident in *Constantinople*, a little-known but highly appealing account of the city which I took with me on my first journey to Istanbul.

Like De Amicis, I had put off visiting the city for years, for a variety of different, accidental reasons; I went on dreaming about it with the help of photographs and engravings, paintings and stories, and even old maps of the place. There are cities you find yourself in by chance and others which you prepare to visit over a long time, mixing fantasy and erudition. Perhaps I first arrived in Istanbul knowing too much, so that, in order to discover the real city which lay under the highly personal image I had created for my own use and enjoyment, I had to dig like an archaeologist.

But in Istanbul you also need to dig beneath the city others have created. Arriving there with De Amicis' account in my hand was certainly unwise, since the sight he saw and described no longer exists. For a start he arrives by sea after an eight-day voyage, a good mystical preparation for the moment when, on their last night at sea, the captain declares to the passengers: "Gentlemen, tomorrow at dawn we shall see the first minarets of Stamboul." De Amicis can hardly sleep: as soon as he sees a glimmer of light from the cabin's porthole, he goes up onto the deck, where he curses his luck, since they are surrounded by fog.

But the captain reassures him: the fog will make the entrance into the city even more beautiful. The ship is still heading towards the Princes' Islands in the Sea of Marmara, in those days of slow boats still two hours' journey away from coming into harbour in the Golden Horn. So the approach to the city is gradual, measured out, like taking small sips from a glass. After an hour the captain points to a white spot, the summit of a towering minaret, and slowly the shapes and colours of the houses at its base come into view, the tops of new minarets tinged with pink – and then, below the houses, the sombre city walls with their towers, but it's as if the city's on a plain, like a long one-dimensional frieze gradually unrolling in uniformity. And then, suddenly, out of the mist, "an enormous silhouette, a tall and weightless-seeming mass, still covered by mist, rose up from the summit of a hill and rounded gloriously into the air, in the midst of four slender and lofty minarets, whose silvery points glittered in the first rays of the sun". It is Hagia Sophia: how beautiful it must be to see it emerge suddenly out of nothing.

From that moment on De Amicis describes an unfolding revelation of new sights, as new towers and domes are seen through the morning mist, "patches of verdure, houses upon houses gleamed... her grand, irregular, fantastic roofscape... white, green, pink and glittering in the light". The entrance to the Bosphorus is still concealed by the fog, and the ship has to stop, giving the passengers a chance to look at the city which seems to move on its own, out of the mists which still envelop it. At last they can continue, passing under the hill of the Seraglio, "covered with cypresses, terebinths, spruces and huge plane trees... the roofs of kiosks, little pavilions crowned with galleries, silvery cupolas, small constructions of strange and graceful forms, with grated windows and arabesque portals... a maze of gardens, corridors, courts, recesses" which the passengers can imagine rather than see through their binoculars.

But I can't go on repeating the pages which De Amicis spends on his arrival: the sudden sight of Scutari in brilliant sunshine, Galata and Pera all at once before him, the small many-coloured houses, the forest of ships' masts, "little harbours, palaces by the water's edge, pavilions, gardens, kiosks, groves; and dimly seen in the mist beyond, the sun-gilded summits of yet more districts; a dazzle of colours, a green lushness, a sequence of views, a grandeur, a delight, a grace – enough to make one babble with incoherence". Alas, this was not the Constantinople I could see: I arrived by land and, even when I later crossed the Sea of Marmara on a ferry to the Asian shore in order to return and see the city from the water, it was in daylight and there was not a trace of fog (throughout my stay the sun shone every day so that the city seemed golden, even the greens of its gardens and wooded hills). Even if it had been foggy, the mist today would have cleared to reveal – alongside the minarets and domes – modern buildings and not the neighbourhoods and villages De Amicis saw. And yet, when I climbed to the top of the Galata tower a few hours after my arrival and saw the city at sunset, or on other days, when I approached it from afar, driving towards it along the shore of the Bosphorus or even just gazing at it from the bridges which cross the Golden Horn, I felt something of what De Amicis had felt.

Yet other travellers' accounts of cities can only help us up to a certain point. I certainly couldn't pretend that while walking over the Galata bridge I saw what De Amicis had seen, two endless streams of humanity crossing in contrary directions from dawn to dusk, the sedan chair, inlaid with mother-of-pearl, from which an Armenian lady peeped out, the elderly Turk wearing a muslin turban and a sky-blue kaftan walking beside a Greek on horseback followed by his dragoman, the dervish with his tall conical hat, the group of Persians with their astrakhan fur caps shaped like pyramids, the barefoot gypsy woman, the aged Jew, the eunuch marching in front of the harem carriage, the African slave carrying a monkey, a storyteller dressed like a necromancer (but the thought occurs: did De Amicis really see all these people, all together, or did he make up a collage of different sights seen over different days?). Whatever the case, I had to let go of others' accounts of Istanbul and discover the city I could call my own.

– Umberto Eco

# Introduction

The posthumous reputation of Edmondo De Amicis has suffered from the huge success he enjoyed while he was alive in two ways. The first is a general phenomenon: the popularity of many nineteenth-century authors with what was the first mass reading public quickly subsided after their death, as fashions moved on and their books were forgotten, often unjustly. This has been the case with De Amicis's works, and only quite recently has a new interest been shown in them. And yet it is not entirely true to say that De Amicis's name was forgotten: he has remained known, within Italy at least, as the author of the children's book *Cuore*, a story written in the form of a diary of a year in the life of a boys' class in a Turin school in the 1880s, shortly after the country's unification. This classic is skilfully written and still affecting, despite its numerous and notorious platitudes and sentimentalities; moreover, steeped in its author's patriotic and political ideals, it has been invested with an iconic significance in the national culture beyond its purely literary merit. Yet once again, De Amicis's success has done him a disservice: not only has *Cuore*'s disproportionate celebrity thrown his other books into the shade, the critical and ideological reaction against that particular work has damaged his general reputation as an author.

For there are many other books: De Amicis was a varied writer, who wrote to make a living from his pen – novels and short stories, poems and essays, journalism and political tracts, and travel books. He worked professionally and inventively at a time when the growth of the reading public and new developments in publishing meant that genres were open to transformation and innovation. Just as *Cuore* can be seen as an ingenious variation within a tradition of moralistic and didactic literature for children dating back to the eighteenth century, so his travel writing, with which he made his early reputation, mixes old and new ingredients to come up with a formula which is recognizably close to the genre as we know it today: topographical and historical information, often in the form of extended imaginary evocations, lyrical description, social observation and amusing anecdote, with the traveller/writer present as the focus of all these varied elements. Yet what makes his book on Constantinople so distinctive and impressive is something quite different and personal: the encounter of an exuberantly talented young writer with a subject which fascinates and challenges him. This is the dynamic at the heart of the book which makes it, despite its obvious flaws, one of the best accounts of the city ever written. By the time of the publication of *Constantinople* in 1877, De Amicis was already widely admired for his descriptive powers (his numerous detractors found him *merely* descriptive): the capital of the Ottoman Empire, with all its spectacular beauty and colour, its teeming life and startling contrasts, puts these to the test as De Amicis himself makes clear in repeated passages. "I see, I speak, I write, all at once, with no hope of success..." – the wonderful opening chapter of the arrival by boat, with its cinematic sweep and movement (towards the end of his life De Amicis showed an interest in the new art form and was among the first writers to attempt to copy its techniques in writing, but in this chapter he is anticipating what the movie camera could do), sets the terms of the contest between the writer trying to describe, to fix the spectacle in words, and the vast city changing all the time. But he is not only in competition with his subject, but with other writers who have described the city before him – and painters as well (the rather perfunctory role played in the book by his travelling companion Enrico Junck, whose job it was to provide the illustrations for De Amicis's text, is perhaps an indication of this additional artistic rivalry). Indeed, in his travel writing De Amicis worked rather like a painter: during the visit itself he would jot down observations and notes, while on his return and at his desk he would by dint of wide reading and reflection work these rapid sketches up into a full-scale canvas, allowing himself a painter's licence in altering perspectives and details in order to construct a better artistic effect. *Constantinople* in fact had a long and difficult gestation. De Amicis's visit to the city took place in 1874, three years before the book was finally published; there are occasional references in the text to this lapse of time. Although any reader of the book would assume, and not just because of its length, that he must have been in the city for at least a month, it appears that he was there for little more than a week and possibly less. His original intention seems to have been to write a much shorter work, like the essay he had published on London

– *Ricordi di Londra* – in 1874; it was apparently his publisher who put pressure on him to write a work in two consecutively published volumes, the sales of which would capitalize on his popularity (an accurate calculation as it turned out – the book went through several editions in the space of a year). Yet the best parts of the book retain the freshness and spontaneity of observation of the young writer jotting down impressions as he strolls about the city, the passages which convey what the contemporary Turkish novelist Orhan Pamuk has described as De Amicis's attention to the random texture of the city's daily life (he singles out as one of the best examples the chapter on the packs of dogs which roam the streets).

Pamuk contrasts this attention with other writers' standard evocation of the exotic, the "oriental", in describing Constantinople, but it has to be admitted that there is also a good deal of this in De Amicis's text, which all too often reveals the crudely assimilated influence of the previous writers on the city whose books he studied when he was working on it, notably Théophile Gautier's classic *Constantinople*, which had appeared thirty years before. The assumptions of nineteenth-century "orientalism" can be unsettling, and modern readers will doubtless be made uneasy by, for example, De Amicis's persistent racial stereotyping – of Turks, Greeks, Armenians, Jews – and his frequently facile and jejune comments on Islam. It is perhaps best to understand these attitudes and opinions as a historical idiom – although it is sobering to see to what extent the same assumptions are still implicit in, for example, the current debate on Turkey's accession to the European Union – and necessary if we are to take the measure of the significance of the work as a whole. Nor should they blind us to some of the insight and acuity of De Amicis's impressions – he was after all a talented journalist – of the struggle taking place between conservatism and reform, Ottoman tradition and European modernization in a period of transition for Turkish society – to which as an Italian from the newly unified state he may have been particularly sensitive – and which would only reach a resolution in the creation of the modern Republic in the traumatic aftermath of Ottoman defeat in the First World War.

Finally, a word on the text. The only previously English translation, published in a heavily abridged form in 1878, has been consulted. De Amicis was of course writing long before the romanization of the Turkish alphabet in the 1920s: almost all the place names and personal names have been modernized to their present-day Turkish or standard forms (e.g. Fındıklı, Beşiktaş, Mehmet for the Sultans, Mohammad for the Prophet, etc.), largely to make it easier to continue to use the volume as what it was certainly intended to be in part when it was first published: a guide book to the city and its past. As De Amicis himself predicts, since the time he was writing Istanbul has changed enormously – like almost every other modern metropolis, almost entirely for the worse (perhaps the saddest loss which strikes a reader now is that of the vast parklike cemeteries, so often referred to in the text, where the Turks would visit their dead and picnic by their tombs) – but not beyond recognition. The city described by De Amicis can still be seen by today's visitors and, where the physical reality has disappeared, with his eloquent help, evoked.

This translation benefited from the patient research work and intelligent suggestions of Christian Müller: my thanks to him.

– Stephen Parkin

Edmondo De Amicis (1846–1908)

Shoe bazaar

Cemetery in Pera

Exterior of a Turkish café in
the Golden Horn quarter

Dogs eating

View from the tower of Galata

At the Sweet Waters of Europe

The walls

The Sultan on his way to the mosque

Cemetery in Scutari

Eyüp

# Constantinople

Amigos, es éste mi último libro de viaje;
desde adelante no escucharé más que las
inspiraciones del corazón.
— *Luis de Guevara, Viaje en Egipto**

# The Arrival

THE EMOTION I FELT ON ENTERING CONSTANTINOPLE almost made me forget everything I had seen in my ten days' voyage from the straits of Messina to the mouth of the Bosphorus. The blue Ionian Sea, motionless as a lake, the distant mountains of the Morea tinted rose-pink by the first rays of the sun, the islands of the Greek archipelago glowing in the sunset, the ruins of Athens, the Gulf of Salonika, Lemnos, Tenedos, the Dardanelles, and many persons and events that had amused and interested me during the voyage, all faded at the sight of the Golden Horn; and now, if I wish to describe them, I must work more from imagination than from memory. But in order that my first page starts out warm and alive, I must begin on the last night of the voyage, in the middle of the Sea of Marmara, at the moment when the captain of the ship approached me and my friend Junck,* and putting his hands on my shoulders said, in a thick Sicilian accent, "Gentlemen, tomorrow at dawn we'll see the first minarets of Stamboul."

Ah! Reader, full of money and ennui – you who, a few years ago, when on a whim you felt like visiting Constantinople, filled your wallet and packed your case and within twenty-four hours had left as if taking a short trip to the countryside, uncertain up to the last moment whether you shouldn't go to Baden-Baden instead! If the captain had said to you, "Tomorrow morning we shall see Stamboul," you would have answered phlegmatically, "I'm glad to hear it." But you need to have nursed this wish for ten years, to have passed many winter evenings sadly studying the map of the East, have inflamed your imagination with the reading of a hundred books, have wandered over one half of Europe in the effort to console yourself for not being able to see the other half, have been nailed for one year to a desk with that purpose only, have made a thousand small sacrifices, calculated and recalculated, built many castles in the air and gone through many domestic battles; finally you need to have passed nine sleepless nights at sea with the immense and luminous image of the city before your eyes, so happy that you even feel a pang of remorse at the thought of the dear ones you've left behind at home; and then you might understand what these words mean, "Tomorrow at dawn we'll see the first minarets of Stamboul"; and instead of answering quietly, "I'm glad to hear it," you would have done as I did and struck the ship's rail with your fist in excitement.

One great pleasure for me and for my companion was our profound conviction that our huge expectations could not be disappointed. There is no doubt about Constantinople; even the wariest traveller can be certain they won't experience disappointment there. And it's not a case of nostalgic memories or conventional admiration. It is one of universal and sovereign beauty, before which poets and archeologists, ambassadors and shopkeepers, princesses and sailors, sons of the north and of the south, are all alike overcome with wonder. All the world thinks it is the most beautiful place on earth. Once they've arrived, travel writers are overwhelmed. Pertusier stammers, Tournefort declares that human speech is incapable, Pouqueville thinks he's on another planet, La Croix is intoxicated, the Vicomte de Marcellus ecstatic, Lamartine gives thanks to God, Gautier doubts the reality of what he sees, and one and all pile image upon image, make their style as brilliant as possible, and torment themselves in vain to find expressions that do not miserably fall short of their thoughts. Chateaubriand alone describes his entrance into Constantinople with a remarkable air of calm, but even he does not fail to remark that the sight is the most beautiful in the world, while Lady Mary Wortley Montagu passes the same judgement, interpolating a "perhaps", as if tacitly leaving the first place to her own beauty, of which she had such a high opinion.* There is even a reserved German who says that the loveliest illusions of youth and even the dreams of first love grow pale in the presence of the sweetness which pervades the soul at the sight of these enchanted places; and an erudite Frenchman asserts that the visitor's first reaction is one of terror. Let the reader imagine the brain-fever produced by such words, perused over and over again, in two young men, a good painter and a bad poet! But even such illustrious praises were not enough, and we sought the opinion of our ship's crew. Even these poor rough fellows, in trying to describe such beauty, felt the need of some expression or comparison out of the ordinary, and kept looking round to find it, rubbing their hands together, and making attempts at description with faraway-sounding voices and those slow, expansive gestures with which such men express their wonder when words fail them. "To come into Constantinople on

4

a fine morning," said the head steersman, "that – believe you me, sirs – well, *that's a great moment in a man's life*."

Even the weather smiled on us; it was a warm, serene night; the sea lapped the sides of the vessel with a gentle murmur; the masts and spars and rigging were outlined sharp and still against the starry night sky; the ship did not appear to move. On the prow lay a large group of Turks peacefully smoking their narghiles with their faces turned up to the moon, their white turbans shining silvery in her rays; at the stern, there were people from every nation, among them a famished-looking company of Greek actors who had embarked at Piraeus. I can still see, in the midst of a bevy of small Russian girls going to Odessa with their mother, the sweet little face of Olga, quite astonished that I could not understand her language and provoked by the fact that the questions she repeated three times received no intelligible answer. On one side of me there is a fat and dirty Greek priest wearing what looks like an upside-down top hat, who is looking through a telescope to see if he can make out the archipelago of Marmara; on the other side, an Evangelical English clergyman, as cold and as stiff as a statue, who for three days has not uttered a word or looked a living soul in the face; in front of me are two pretty Athenian sisters with red caps and hair falling in tresses over their shoulders, who the moment anyone looks at them turn in tandem towards the sea in order to show off their profiles; a little further on an Armenian merchant fingers the beads of his oriental rosary, a group of Jews in traditional costume, Albanians with their white petticoats, a French governess who puts on melancholy airs, a few of those ordinary-looking travellers with nothing about them to indicate their country or their trade, and in the midst of them a small Turkish family, consisting of a father in a fez, a mother in a veil and two children in baggy pantaloons, all four of them huddled together under an awning upon a heap of mattresses and cushions, and surrounded by belongings of every shape and colour.

Everyone became more than usually lively as we approached Constantinople. Almost all the faces that were visible by the light of the ship's lanterns were cheerful and bright. The Russian children jumped up and down around their mother, shouting out the old Russian name for Stamboul, *"Zavegorod! Zavegorod!"** Here and there you could hear the names of Galata, Pera, Scutari, Büyükdere, Therapia, like the first sparks of a great firework which was just about to explode. Even the sailors were happy to arrive where, as they told

us, they'd be able to forget their troubles for a while. There was even a perceptible agitation on the prow among that white sea of turbans; even those idle and impassive Muslims were already anticipating the extraordinary silhouette of *Umm al-Dunia*, the mother of the world, swaying gently on the horizon, the city, in the words of the Koran, "where one side looks upon the land and the other two upon the sea".*
It almost seemed as if the steamer were moving ahead fuelled by all the anticipation and impatience on its decks. Every now and then I leant upon the rail and gazed at the sea and seemed to hear a hundred voices mingling with the sound of the waves. They were the voices of those who loved me, saying, "Go on, go on, my son, my brother, my friend! Go and enjoy your Constantinople. You have earned it, be happy, and God be with you."

Only towards midnight did the passengers start to go down to their cabins. My friend and I went in among the last, reluctantly, unwilling to confine the joy we felt within four walls – it was too large for the horizons of the Propontis to contain. About halfway down the stairs we heard the voice of the captain inviting us to come up in the morning to the bridge. He poked his head through the hatch and called, "Be up before sunrise. And the last one up on deck walks the plank!"

No warning was ever needed less. I didn't sleep a wink all night. The young Mehmet II himself, on that famous night in Adrianople,* when he was kept awake by his vision of the city of Constantinople, cannot have twisted and turned in his bed as many times as I did in my berth during those four hours of waiting. In order to calm my nerves, I tried counting up to a thousand or staring at the sprays of water which constantly splashed around the porthole of my cabin, or humming tunes to the monotonous beat of the engines; but it was all in vain. I was feverish and breathless, and the night seemed to go on for ever. At the first sign of dawn I rose. Junck, my companion, was up already. We dressed in haste and in three bounds were on deck.

Curse it!

It was foggy!

The horizon was completely covered on every side; it threatened rain; the great spectacle of the entrance into Constantinople was lost, our most ardent hopes were dashed – in a word, our voyage was ruined! I was devastated. At this point the captain appeared with his habitual smile. We didn't need to say anything: he saw and understood, and, clapping me on the shoulder, said in a tone of consolation, "It's nothing. Don't get worked up, gentlemen. You can thank the fog. Because of it, we'll make the finest entrance into Constantinople you could hope for. In two hours we'll have clear weather, take my word for it!" I felt life returning to me. We climbed up to the officers' deck; at the prow all the Turks were already seated with crossed legs upon their carpets, their faces turned towards Constantinople. In a few minutes all the other passengers came out, carrying telescopes of all sizes, and leant over the port-side railing in a long row, as in a theatre gallery. A fresh breeze was blowing; no one spoke. All eyes and every telescope gradually fixed on the northern shore of the Sea of Marmara; but as yet, there was nothing to be seen. The fog now formed a whitish band along the horizon; above, the sky shone clear and golden; directly in front of us, ahead of the prow, the nine Princes' Islands – the Demonesi of the ancients – could dimly be made out, a pleasure resort of the court in the time of the late Byzantine Empire and still frequented for the same purpose by the present-day inhabitants of Constantinople.

The two shores of the Sea of Marmara were still completely hidden; only after an hour had gone by could we see them. But it is impossible to understand a description of the entrance into Constantinople without first having clear in your mind the layout of the city. Imagine you are facing the mouth of the Bosphorus, the stretch of water which divides Asia from Europe and joins the Sea of Marmara to the Black Sea. On your right is the Asian coast, and the European shore on your left; here ancient Thrace, and there ancient Anatolia; moving into the channel, the entrance is scarcely passed before there appears, on the left, a bay and a narrow roadstead, which lies at an almost exact right angle to the Bosphorus and penetrates for several miles into the European part, curving like the horn of an ox, from which it derives its name: the Golden Horn, or Horn of Abundance, through which the wealth of three continents flowed when it was the port of Byzantium.

At the angle formed by the European shore, with the Sea of Marmara on one side and on the other the Golden Horn, where Byzantium once stood, the Turkish city of Stamboul now rises upon its seven hills. At the other angle, between the Golden Horn and the Bosphorus, stand Galata and Pera, the European cities. Facing the entrance to the Golden Horn, upon the hills of the Asian side, is the city of Scutari. What is called Constantinople then is in fact made up of three great cities, divided by the sea but placed one opposite the other, with the third facing the other two, and so near to each other that their buildings can be seen distinctly from every shore, as in Paris or London at the wider parts of the Seine or the Thames.

The point of the triangle upon which Stamboul stands curves toward the Golden Horn: this is the famous Seraglio Point which, when you are approaching the city by the Sea of Marmara, conceals up to the last moment the view of the two shores of the Golden Horn, the most beautiful part of Constantinople.

It was the captain of the ship with his mariner's eye who first spotted Stamboul.

The two Athenian sisters, the Russian family, the English clergyman, Junck and I, and others who were all going to Constantinople for the first time were standing round him, silent and straining our eyes in vain to see through the fog, when he pointed to the left, towards the European shore and called out, "Ladies and gentlemen, see the fog lifting over there."

It was a white point, the summit of a very high minaret, the lower part of which was still hidden. Every telescope turned in its direction and every eye stared at that small aperture in the fog as if hoping to make it larger. The ship advanced swiftly. In a few moments a dim outline appeared beside the minaret, then two, then three, then many, which little by little took the form of houses, stretching out in a row. In front and to the right of us everything was still shrouded in fog. What we saw gradually appearing was that part of Stamboul which extended in a curve of about four Italian miles along the northern shore of the Sea of Marmara, between Seraglio Point and the Castle of the Seven Towers. But the hill of the Seraglio was still covered. Behind the houses, tall white minarets gleamed out one after another, with their pinnacles tinged with rosy light from the rising sun. Below the houses began to emerge the old dark crenellated walls – reinforced with regularly spaced towers – which encircle the city in an unbroken chain, the sea waves breaking upon them. In a short time a tract about two miles in length of the city was visible; and, to tell the truth, the sight fell short of my expectations. We were off the point where Lamartine had asked himself, "Is this Constantinople?" and exclaimed, "What a disappointment!" The hills were all hidden, only the shore with its long row of houses was visible: the city looked entirely level. "Captain," I called out, "Is this Constantinople?" The captain grabbed me by the arm and pointed with his hand. "Oh, man of little faith!" he cried – "Look up there!"

I looked and exclaimed in amazement. An enormous silhouette, a tall and weightless-seeming mass, still covered by mist, rose up from the summit of a hill and rounded gloriously into the air, in the midst of four slender and lofty minarets, whose silvery points glittered in the first rays of the sun. "Hagia Sophia!" shouted a sailor; and one of the two Athenian girls murmured to herself, "Hagia Sophia!" (The Holy Wisdom). The Turks on the prow stood up. But already other enormous domes and minarets – packed and mingled like a grove of gigantic palm trees without branches – shone dimly through the mist in front of and around the great basilica. "The Mosque of Sultan Ahmet," called out the captain, pointing; "the Mosque of Beyazit, the Mosque of Osman, the Mosque of Laleli, the Mosque of Süleyman." But no one was paying any more attention to him; the fog parted on every side, and through its rifts mosques, towers, patches of verdure, houses upon houses gleamed; and as we went on the city rose higher, and her grand, irregular, fantastic roofscape could be seen more and more distinctly, white, green, pink and glittering in the light, while the gentle slopes of the Seraglio hill could already be made out against the receding fog. Four miles of city, all that part of Stamboul that faces the Sea of Marmara, lay spread out before us, and her dark walls and many-coloured houses were reflected in the clear and sparkling water as in a mirror.

Suddenly the ship came to a halt. Everyone gathered round the captain to ask why. He explained that we needed to wait for the fog – which still lay like a thick curtain across the entrance to the Bosphorus – to lift. Yet after only a few moments we started to move on cautiously.

We drew near to the hill of the Old Seraglio.

At which everyone's curiosity, mine included, became uncontrollable.

"Look the other way," said the captain, "and only turn round to see when the whole hill is facing us."

I duly turned away and fixed my eyes on a stool, which seemed to bob up and down.

After a moment, the captain exclaimed, "We're here!" I turned round; the ship had stopped. We were close in front of a great hill, covered with cypresses, terebinths, spruces and huge plane trees, projecting their branches far beyond the crenellated walls and casting shadows on the water, while in the midst of all this foliage could be seen, distinct but disordered, as if scattered here and there at random, the roofs of kiosks, little pavilions crowned with galleries, silvery cupolas, small constructions in strange and graceful forms, with grated windows and arabesque portals; all white and small, half concealed, leaving the fancy to conjure up a maze of gardens, corridors, courts, recesses; an entire town surrounded by a wood and set apart from the world, imbued with mystery and melancholy.

Although it was still slightly obscured with mist, the sun was now shining full upon it. Not a living soul could be seen, no sound broke the silence. We stood with our eyes fixed upon those heights crowned with the memories of four centuries of glory, pleasure, love, conspiracy and bloodshed – the throne, the citadel, the tomb of the great Ottoman Empire – and no one spoke or moved.

Suddenly the mate called out: "Ladies and gentlemen, there's Scutari ahead!" and all eyes turned to the Asian shore. There lay Scutari, the golden city, stretching out of sight over the slopes of her hills, veiled in the luminous morning mists, as flourishing and fresh as if it had just been created by the wave of a wand. Who can describe that spectacle? The language we use to describe our cities would give no idea of that immense variety of colour and of prospect, that marvellous confusion of building and landscape, of gaiety and austerity, of Europe and the Orient, bizarre, charming and grandiose! Imagine a town made up of ten thousand little purple and yellow houses, of ten thousand lush green gardens, of a hundred mosques as white as snow; above the town there's a forest of towering cypresses; the largest cemetery in the East, at either end interminable white barracks, more clusters of houses and cypress trees; villages grouped upon heights, behind which others half hidden in verdure peep out; and everywhere the tops of minarets and white domes shining halfway up the slope of a hill that closes off the horizon like a great curtain; a vast city scattered over an immense garden, along a shore broken by steep, sycamore-covered gullies in some places, and sloping into verdant levels which open into shady flowery inlets; and the whole beautiful sight reflected in the blue mirror of the Bosphorus.

While I stood gazing at Scutari, my friend nudged me to announce he had just discovered another city. I turned in the direction of the Sea of Marmara, and there it was indeed, on the same Asian side, beyond Scutari: a long line of houses, mosques and gardens, which the ship had already left behind, and which had until now been hidden by the fog. With our telescopes we could distinctly see the cafés, bazaars, the

European-style houses, the landing stages, the orchard walls, and the small boats scattered along the shore. It was Kadiköy – "the village of the Judges" – built upon the ruins of ancient Chalcedon, once the rival of Byzantium, founded in 685 BC by the Megarians,* who were called blind by the oracle of Delphi for choosing that site instead of the opposite shore where Stamboul stands. "That makes three towns so far," said the captain, "and keep counting because you'll see the others before long."

The ship was still unmoving between Scutari and the hill of the Seraglio. The fog still hid the Bosphorus beyond Scutari as well as Galata and Pera in front of us. Large vessels and steamers, caiques and small sailing boats passed alongside us, but no one paid them any attention. Everyone was looking at the grey curtain which hid the European city from our eyes. I was shaking with impatience and pleasurable anticipation. Only a few more seconds, and then the wonderful spectacle would be revealed to cries of amazement. My hand was trembling so much I could hardly hold the telescope still. The captain looked at me, enjoying my plight, and rubbing his hands exclaimed, "Now we're there!"

At last patches of white started to emerge through the mist, then the dim outline of a great height, then the scattered and vivid glitter of window panes shining in the sun, and finally Galata and Pera in full light, a hill of many-coloured houses, one above the other; a lofty city crowned with minarets, cupolas and cypresses; upon the summit the monumental palaces of the embassies, and the great tower of Galata; at its foot the vast arsenal of Tophane and a forest of ships' masts; and as the fog receded, the city lengthened rapidly along the Bosphorus, and neighbourhood after neighbourhood became visible, stretching from the hilltops down to the sea, jostling with houses and dotted with white mosques; rows of ships, little harbours, palaces by the water's edge, pavilions, gardens, kiosks, groves; and dimly seen in the mist beyond, the sun-gilded summits of yet more districts; a dazzle of colours, a green lushness, a sequence of views, a grandeur, a delight, a grace – enough to make one babble with incoherence. On the ship everyone stood agape; passengers and crew, Turks, Europeans and children, no one spoke a word or knew which way to look. We had Scutari and Kadiköy to one side and on the other the hill of the Seraglio; in front of us Galata, Pera, the Bosphorus. To see them all we had to keep whirling round, eagerly looking on every side,

11

laughing and gesticulating, speechless with delight. By God, what an extraordinary moment!

And yet the grandest and loveliest sight still awaited us. We were motionless off Seraglio Point; only once we were past the Point would we see the Golden Horn, the most wonderful view of Constantinople. "Now, ladies and gentlemen, pay attention please," the captain called out before giving the order to move on, "the *critical moment* has arrived. In three minutes we shall see Constantinople." A cold shiver ran through me, my heart was beating wildly. I waited for the order to start moving again with feverish impatience. Then the captain shouted: "Forward!" The ship moved, we were off! Kings, princes, potentates, all you who are blessed with wealth and good fortune, how I pitied you: at that moment my place on the ship's deck was worth all your treasures put together. I wouldn't have sold the view I saw for an empire.

A minute, then another minute, as we steamed past Seraglio Point... I glimpse a vast space filled with light and colour... We've passed the Point... and here is the city of Constantinople! Endless, sublime, superb! The glory of creation and of the human race! So such beauty had not been a dream after all!

And now, poor wretch, try to describe, to profane with your words that divine vision! Who would dare to describe Constantinople? Chateaubriand, Lamartine, Gautier – all mere stammering! And yet images and words rush to my mind and flow from my pen. I see, I speak, I write, all at once, with no hope of success but in a kind of drunken haze of delight. Let me at least try. The Golden Horn directly in front of us like a broad river; and on either shore two lines of hills on which two parallel cities stretch away into the distance, eight miles of hills, valleys, bays and promontories; a hundred slopes covered with buildings and gardens; a vast double terrace of houses, mosques, bazaars, seraglios, baths, kiosks, in an infinite variety of colours; among them thousands of minarets with shining pinnacles rising into the sky like tall ivory columns; groves of cypress trees descending in long dark lines from the heights to the sea, encircling residential districts and harbours; and a lush vegetation springing up everywhere, cresting the summits, weaving round the roofs and hanging down into the water. To the right Galata, with a forest of masts and pennants in front; above Galata, Pera, the great outlines of her European palaces clear against the sky; in the foreground, a bridge connecting the two shores, crossed in each direction by two colourful streams of people; to the left Stamboul upon her broad hills, each of which is surmounted by a vast mosque with lead dome and golden pinnacles; Hagia Sophia, coloured white and rose; Sultan Ahmet, flanked by six minarets; Süleyman the Great crowned with ten domes; Sultana Valide mirrored in the waters; on the fourth hill the Mosque of Mehmet II; on the fifth the Mosque of Selim; on the sixth the Seraglio of Tekir; and rising above them all the white tower of the Seraskerat which overlooks the shores of both continents from the Dardanelles to the Black Sea. Beyond the sixth hill of Stamboul and beyond Galata nothing but vague outlines can be seen, patches of city or suburb, glimpses of harbours, fleets, groves – pale in the azure air, unreal, like tricks of the light and atmosphere. How will I ever grasp the details of this extraordinary picture? The eye fixes a moment upon the nearer shore, upon a Turkish house or gilded minaret; but immediately darts off into that luminous depth, randomly roaming down and across the two shores and the two cities, with one's bewildered understanding painfully trying to keep up. All this loveliness has an air of serene majesty; there is something youthful and amorous about it which revives a thousand memories of childhood fairy tales and dreams; something ethereal, mysterious, sublime, carrying the imagination off beyond the real world. The sky, misted delicately with opal and with silver, forms a backdrop on which everything is drawn with marvellous clearness and precision; the sapphire-coloured sea, dotted with crimson buoys, mirrors the minarets in long rippling reflections; the domes glitter; the trees sway and shimmer in the morning breeze; flocks of doves swoop over the mosques; a thousand gilded and painted caiques dart about the waters; the breeze from the Black Sea wafts the fragrance from ten thousand gardens; and when, drunk with the beauty of this paradise, and forgetful of all else, you turn away, you see behind you with renewed wonder the shores of Asia closing the panorama with the grandeur of Scutari and the snowy peaks of Mount Olympus, the Sea of Marmara sprinkled with islets and white with sails; and the Bosphorus covered with ships winding their way between the endless rows of kiosks, palaces and villas to vanish mysteriously among the fertile hills of the East. This is the most beautiful sight on earth and whoever denies it shows a lack of gratitude to both God and Nature! Our senses could not bear a greater beauty.

Once my first emotions had died down, I looked at my fellow travellers: all their expressions had changed. The two Athenian ladies had wet eyes; the Russian in that solemn moment had clasped the little Olga to her breast; even the cold English clergyman was heard to speak for the first time as he exclaimed, "Wonderful, quite wonderful!"*

The ship had stopped not far from the bridge; in a few moments it was surrounded by a crowd of boats, and a throng of porters – Turks, Greeks, Armenians and Jews – who, cursing in barbarous Italian, took possession of our persons and effects. After he had made a vain attempt at resistance, I embraced the captain, kissed the little Olga, said goodbye to everyone, and with my companion got down into a four-oared caique, which took us to the custom house, from where we climbed through a maze of narrow streets to the Hotel Byzantium at the top of the hill of Pera.

## Five Hours Later

The vision of this morning has vanished. The Constantinople of light and beauty has given place to a monstrous city, scattered about over an infinity of hills and valleys; it is a labyrinth of human anthills, cemeteries, ruins and solitary places; a confusion of civilization and barbarity which presents an image of all the cities upon earth, and gathers to itself all aspects of human life. It is really only the skeleton of a great city – the walls, which form only a small part – while the rest is an enormous agglomeration of shacks, an interminable Asiatic encampment swarming with peoples of every race and religion who have never been counted. It is a great city in the process of transformation, composed of ancient cities that are in decay, new cities which emerged yesterday, and other cities now being born; everything is in confusion; on every side can be seen the vestiges of gigantic works, mountains bored through, hills cut down, entire districts levelled to the ground, great streets laid out; an immense mass of debris and remains of conflagrations upon ground forever tormented by the hand of man. The most incongruous objects are all jumbled together, an endless procession of bizarre and unexpected sights that make your head spin. You walk along a fine residential street to find it ends in a gorge; you come out of the theatre to find yourself surrounded by tombs. You climb to the top of a hill to discover a forest under your feet and another city on the opposite slope;

you turn back on a sudden to look at the area you have just crossed and you find it at the bottom of a deep valley, half-hidden by trees; you turn the corner of a house and come across a harbour; you go down a street and you've left the city behind – you're in a deserted defile from which nothing but the sky is visible. Towns spring up, hide themselves, rise above your head or behind your back or sink under your feet, far off, nearby, in the sun, in the shade, among groves, by the sea. Take a step forward – a wide panorama opens before you; take a step back – nothing to be seen; lift your eyes, a thousand minarets; lower them a little, they are all gone. An endless maze of streets wind about among small hills, rise on embankments, skirt ravines, pass under aqueducts, break into alleys, run down steps, through bushes, rocks, ruins, sand dunes. Here and there, the great city draws breath, so to speak, for a quiet spell in the countryside, and then begins again, even more crowded and bustling than before; here it is a plain, there it climbs, further on it rushes downwards, fans out, and again crowds together; in one place it is all smoke and noise, in another it goes to sleep; now it is all red, now all white, and then gold dominates, and still further on it is like a mountainside pasture in spring. The elegant city, the village, the open country, the gardens, the port, the desert, the market, the necropolis, alternate, without end, rising one above the other on terraced slopes, so that at some points you can take in with one glance all the diversities of an entire region. An infinite variety of bizarre outlines stands out everywhere against the sky or the water, crowded together in such a crazy confusion of architectural styles that the eye cannot focus on them as they shimmer and merge. European palaces rise in the midst of Turkish houses; behind the minaret stands the bell tower; above the terrace, the dome; beside the dome, a crenellated wall; the Chinese roofs of kiosks hang over the façades of theatres; the grated balconies of harems face on to large plate glass windows; Moorish lattices look out onto balustraded terraces; niches with statues of the Madonna are set beneath Arabian arches; tombs lie in the courtyards, and towers rise among workers' hovels; mosques, synagogues, Greek and Catholic and Armenian churches jostle each other for position; and from every nook and cranny the branches of cypresses, umbrella pines, fig and plane trees stretch over the roofs. Indescribable makeshift buildings follow every twist and turn, rise and fall of the land – houses wedged like slices together, three-sided towers, like upside-down pyramids, surrounded with bridges, ditches, props, all piled up like rocks in a landslide.

15

Every hundred yards everything changes. Here you are in a suburb of Marseilles; turn round, and it is an Asian village; turn the corner – a Greek quarter; turn once more – a suburb of Trabzon. By the language, by the faces, by the look of the houses, you can tell you've changed country. There are pieces of France and strips of Italy, flecks of England and offshoots of Russia. Across the entire face of the city, in its streets and in their bustling activity, over this sacred soil, a great struggle is being waged between the Christians who try to reconquer it and the children of Islam who defend it with all their might. Stamboul, once entirely Turkish, is now assailed on every side by Christian quarters, which are gradually making inroads into it along the shores of the Golden Horn and the Sea of Marmara; on the opposite shore the conquest proceeds apace: churches, palaces, hospitals, public gardens, factories, schools tear through Muslim quarters, overturn the graveyards, and march onwards from hill to hill. Already you can see the outlines of a great city rising upon this battleground which will one day cover the European shore of the Bosphorus, as Stamboul now covers the shore of the Golden Horn.

But the mind is constantly distracted away from these general observations by a thousand new sights; there is a dervish monastery in one street, a Moorish barracks in another, and Turkish cafés, bazaars, fountains, aqueducts at every turn. In a quarter of an hour you have to change your pace ten times. You descend and then ascend, you jump down a slope, climb up rocks, sink in the mud and clamber over a hundred obstacles, make your way now through crowds, now through bushes, now through ragged washing hung out to dry; now you stop your nose against the smell and now you breathe in fragrant air. From a dazzling height where you can see the Bosphorus, Asia and the open sky above, you go down a few steps into the gloom and obscurity of a maze of alleys lined with dilapidated houses and littered with stones like the bed of a stream. From cool shade you step into suffocating dust and blinding sunlight; from street crossings full of noise and movement into sepulchral recesses, where human voices are never heard; from the divine Orient of our dreams into another Orient, gloomy, dirty and decrepit beyond our worst imaginings. After a few hours spent in this way, you're in a state of complete bewilderment. Should anyone suddenly ask you: "What is Constantinople like?" you could only grasp your head in your hands and try to still the storm of thoughts. Constantinople is a Babylon, an entire world by itself, a chaos. Beautiful? Wonderfully beautiful. Ugly? It is horrible! Did you like it? Passionately. Would you live in it? Who knows! Who could say that he would willingly live on another planet? You go back to your hotel, full of enthusiasm and disillusion, enchanted, nauseated, dazzled, stunned, with your head whirling with a brain-fever, which gradually quietens down into a state of utter exhaustion and complete inertia. Years have gone by in a few hours and you feel like an old man.

And the inhabitants of this monstrous city? What of them?

## The Bridge

To see the population of Constantinople, it's a good idea to go upon the floating bridge, about a quarter of a mile in length, which extends from the most advanced point of Galata to the opposite shore of the Golden Horn, facing the great Mosque of the Sultana Valide. Both shores are part of Europe, but the bridge may be said to connect Asia to Europe because in Stamboul only the ground you walk on is European – even the few Christian suburbs on the hill above are Asian in character and atmosphere. The Golden Horn, which looks like a river, separates the two worlds like an ocean. News of events in Europe circulates in Galata and Pera clearly and in detail, and is much discussed, but arrives on the other shore confused and garbled, like a distant echo; the fame of great men and important happenings in the West are stopped by that narrow waterway as by an insuperable barrier; and over that bridge, which a hundred thousand people cross every day, not a single idea passes in ten years.

Standing there, one can see all Constantinople go by in an hour. There are two never-ending currents of human beings that meet and mingle from sunrise to sunset, presenting a spectacle compared to which the marketplaces of India, the fair of Nizhni Novgorod and the festivals of Peking fade into nothingness. To see anything at all, you must choose a small portion of the bridge and fix your eyes on that alone; otherwise in the attempt to see everything one ends up seeing nothing. The crowd goes by in great multicoloured waves, and each new group represents a new populace. The most extravagant types, costumes and social classes that can be imagined may there be seen in the space of fifty yards and within ten minutes. Behind a crowd of Turkish porters who run past, bending under enormous burdens, a sedan chair comes along, inlaid with ivory and mother-of-pearl, with an Armenian lady looking out; on either side of it a Bedouin wrapped in a white mantle and a Turk in muslin turban and sky-blue kaftan, beside whom canters a young Greek gentleman followed by his dragoman in an embroidered jacket and a dervish with his tall conical hat and camel-hair tunic, who makes way for the carriage of a European ambassador, preceded by a footman in livery. All this is glimpsed rather than seen. Before you've had time to turn round, you find yourself in the middle of a crowd of Persians, in pyramid-shaped hats of astrakhan fur, who are followed by a Jew in a long yellow coat, open at the sides; a frowzy-headed gypsy woman carrying her child in a sling on her back; a Catholic priest with breviary and staff; while through a confused throng of Greeks, Turks and Armenians a fat eunuch rides on horseback, crying out "Make way!" in front of a Turkish carriage, painted with flowers and birds, and filled with the ladies from a harem, dressed in green and purple, and wrapped in large white veils; behind the carriage come a Sister of Charity from one of the hospitals in Pera, an African slave carrying a monkey, and a professional storyteller wearing a necromancer's robe. What is quite natural, but appears strange to the newcomer, is that all these different people pass each other without a second glance, like a crowd in London; no one stops for a moment, everyone is in a hurry; and you won't see one smiling face in a hundred. The Albanian in his white petticoat and with pistols in his belt, beside the Tartar dressed in sheepskins; the Turk on the back of a richly caparisoned mule trots quickly between rows of camels; behind the twelve-year-old adjutant of an imperial prince, mounted upon his Arab steed, sways a cart filled with all the odd domestic clutter of a Turkish household; the Muslim woman on foot, the veiled female slave, the Greek with her long plaits and red cap, the Maltese hooded in her black *faldetta*,* the Jewish woman in traditional dress, the Negress wrapped in a many-coloured shawl from Cairo, the Armenian from Trabzon, swathed funereally in black, are sometimes seen in single file, as if they had taken up their positions deliberately for the sake of contrast. It is a changing kaleidoscope of races and religions that forms and disperses continually with a rapidity the eye can scarcely follow. It is amusing to look down at the passing feet and see all the footwear in the world go by, from that of Adam down to the latest fashion in Parisian boots – yellow Turkish babouches, red shoes for Armenians, turquoise for

Greeks, and black for Jews; sandals, great boots from Turkistan, Albanian gaiters, low-cut shoes, richly coloured gambados worn by horse merchants from Asia Minor, slippers embroidered with gold thread, Spanish *alpargatas*, shoes made of satin, rope, rags, wood, so many that while you look at one you catch a glimpse of a hundred more. You need to be on the alert not to be jostled and pushed to the ground at every step. Now a water-carrier with a huge jar upon his back goes by; now a Russian lady riding a horse, now a squadron of imperial soldiers in Zouave dress, who look as if they're about to launch an attack; now a crew of Armenian porters, two by two, carrying on their shoulders immensely long bars, from which great bales of merchandise are suspended; and now a crowd of Turks who dart off both sides of the bridge to board the steamers lying alongside. You hear the clacking and shuffling of many feet, exotic voices, guttural exclamations, incomprehensible interjections, among which the few French or Italian words that reach the ear gleam out like sudden flashes in the pitch dark. The figures that most attract the eye in all this mass of humanity are the Circassians, who mostly go around in groups, walking along slowly; big bearded men with frightening faces, wearing bearskin caps like the old Napoleonic Guard and long black kaftans, with daggers at their belts, and silver cartridge-boxes on their chests: real brigands, who look as if they had come to Constantinople to sell a daughter or sister and have their hands steeped in Russian blood. Then the Syrians, with robes like a Byzantine dalmatic, and their heads wound round with gold-striped kerchiefs; Bulgarians, dressed in coarse gowns and wearing hats topped with fur; Georgians in varnished leather caps, with their tunics tightly bound round the waist with a metal belt; Greeks from the Archipelago, covered from head to foot with embroidery, little tassels and gleaming buttons.

From time to time the crowd thins out a little; but immediately other groups come forward, waves of red skullcaps and white turbans, amid which the top hats, umbrellas and elaborate hairstyles of European men and women seem to float, as if borne along on that Muslim torrent. Simply the variety of religions you see is amazing. Here a Capuchin friar with his shining tonsure and there an ulema's tall turban like a janissary's; further on an Armenian priest in a black veil, imams in white tunics, nuns in wimples, Turkish military priests dressed in green, with sabres at their side, Dominican friars, pilgrims back from Mecca sporting a talisman round their necks, Jesuits, dervishes – who, it is curious to note, in the mosques torment their own flesh in expiation of their sins, yet cross the bridge protected by a parasol – all pass by. If you are attentive, you notice a thousand amusing incidents. Here is a eunuch, glaring ferociously at some foppish Christian youth, who has glanced too curiously into the carriage of his mistress; there is a French cocotte, dressed in the very latest fashion, who trips behind a pasha's begloved and bejewelled son; or a lady from Stamboul, pretending to adjust her veil so that she can get a better look at the train of a lady from Pera; or a cavalry sergeant in full ceremonial rig, stopping in the middle of the bridge to launch an explosive and terrifying sneeze, or a quack, taking some poor wretch's last penny while making a cabbalistic gesture over his face, which will supposedly cure his bad eyesight; or a family of travellers who have just arrived and have lost each other in the bustling crowd of Asiatic ruffians, with the mother searching for her screaming children, and the men pushing a way through. Camels, horses, sedan chairs, oxen, carts, barrels on wheels, bleeding donkeys, mangy dogs cut a long line through the massed crowds.

Sometimes a mighty pasha, wearing three horsetails, passes by, lounging in a splendid carriage followed by his pipe-bearer on foot, his guard and one black slave: then all the Turks salute him, touching their foreheads and chest, and the beggar-women, horrible witches with muffled faces and naked breasts, run after the carriage begging for charity. Off-duty eunuchs, with cigarettes dangling from their lips, stroll by in twos and threes; their soft pudginess, long arms and black clothes make them instantly recognizable. Little Turkish girls dressed like boys, in baggy green trousers and pink or yellow waistcoats, run and jump about with feline agility, making way for themselves with their henna-tinted hands. Bootblacks with gilded boxes, street barbers carrying their stool and basin, sellers of water and sweetmeats weave through the crowd in every direction, shouting in Greek and Turkish. At every step a military uniform advances glitteringly: officers in fezzes and scarlet trousers, their chests decked with medals; grooms from the Seraglio, grand as army generals; gendarmes, with a whole arsenal at their belts; Zeybeks, or irregular soldiers, in huge baggy trousers that make them resemble in profile the Hottentot Venus;* imperial guards with long white plumes upon their casques and gold-braided chests; the watchmen of Constantinople carrying handcuffs (their job must be like trying to hold back the Atlantic breakers). The contrasts between all this gold and all those rags, between people loaded down with garments, who look like walking bazaars, and people who are almost naked, are very striking. The display of so much nudity is itself remarkable. Here all shades of skin colour can be seen, from the milky-white of Albania to the raven-black of Central Africa and the bluish-black of Darfur; chests which look as though they'd resound like a bronze vase or shatter like earthenware if you hit them; backs glistening, bony and hard, hairy like the shank of a wild boar; arms tattooed in red and blue with crude images of ships and pierced hearts or designs of flowers and inscriptions from the Koran. But it is impossible to take all this in on your first walk across the bridge. While you are examining the tattoo on one arm, your guide tells you that a Wallachian, a Serbian, a Montenegrin, a Cossack from the Don or the Ukraine, an Egyptian, a Tunisian, a prince of Imeritia have just walked by. You hardly have time to look at all the passing races and nations. It appears that Constantinople is what it always has been: the capital of three continents, and the queen of twenty kingdoms. But even this description can't give an adequate idea of the spectacle, which resembles vast overlapping tides of emigration, produced by some enormous cataclysm which has overturned the old continent.

An experienced eye can discern among the waves of that great sea faces and costumes from Karaman and Anatolia, Cyprus and Candia, Damascus and Jerusalem; the Druze, the Kurd, the Maronite, the Taliman, the Pomak,* the Croat, and others, innumerable varieties of all the anarchic confederations which stretch from the Nile to the Danube, and from the Euphrates to the Adriatic. Seekers after the beautiful or the grotesque will find their most far-fetched desires fulfilled here: Raphael would be in ecstasies, and Rembrandt would tear his hair out. The purest types of Greek and Caucasian beauty are mingled with flat noses and narrow heads; queens and harridans pass alongside you; faces beautified with cosmetics and deformed by disease and wounds; monstrously large feet and tiny Circassian ones no longer than your hand; gigantic porters, corpulent Turks, and black men who are merely bones, the sight of whom fills you with pity and dismay – all the physical forms in which asceticism or the excess of pleasure, extreme labour, domineering opulence and dying poverty can be displayed. And yet the variety of dress is even more marvellous than the variety of person. If you love colours you can have your fill of them here. No two figures are dressed alike. Here are shawls twisted around the head like primitive fillets or a crown of rags, skirts and undervests chequered and striped like a Harlequin, belts stuck full of long knives reaching from the hips to the armpits, Mameluke trousers, short drawers, kilts, togas, trailing sheets, coats trimmed with ermine, waistcoats like golden cuirasses, sleeves puffed and slashed, monkish habits and brazen décolletage, men dressed like women, and women who look like men, beggars who seem to be princes, an elegant fashion show of rags in a crazy profusion of colours, frills and flounces and fringes, childish and theatrical trinketry, like a party in a madhouse for which all the rag-and-bone men in the world have ransacked their stores. Over the hollow murmur that comes from this multitude you can hear the shrill cries of the Greek boys selling newspapers printed in every language; the stentorian shouts of the porters, the boisterous laughs of Turkish women, the squeaking voices of eunuchs, the falsetto trill of blind men chanting verses of the Koran, the low creaking of the bridge as it moves upon the water, the whistles and bells of a hundred steamers, from whose funnels dense smoke is often blown by the wind over the crowd, blotting out for a moment the whole scene. This carnival crowd of different races embarks in the small steamboats that leave all the time for Scutari, for the villages along the Bosphorus, and for the suburbs of the Golden Horn; they spread through Stamboul, in the bazaars, in the mosques, in the neighbourhoods of Fener and Balat, to the furthermost parts of the city along the Sea of Marmara; they swarm upon the European shore, to the right towards the Sultan's palaces, to the left up to the heights of Pera, from where they come down once more to the bridge through a warren of narrow streets that wind about the sides of the hills, so forming a link between Asia and Europe, ten different towns and a hundred neighbourhoods, in one vast net of daily chores, intrigues and mysteries, the mere thought of which leaves your brain reeling. The spectacle should be a cheerful one, but it is not. Once your initial astonishment is over, the festive colours fade; it is no longer a grand carnival procession passing by, but humanity itself with all its miseries and follies, with all the infinite discord of its beliefs and its laws; it is a pilgrimage of debased peoples and fallen races; an immensity of suffering needing help, of shame to be purged, of chains to be broken; an accumulation of tremendous problems written in characters of blood, which can only be solved by the shedding of blood; the sense of vast and utter disorder is depressing. And then curiosity is blunted rather than assuaged by this

Galata Bridge

Entrance to the Sultan Ahmed Mosque, Stamboul

endless variety of strange objects. What mysterious changes occur in the human soul! Not a quarter of an hour had gone by since my arrival on the bridge when I found myself leaning on the parapet, absent-mindedly scribbling with my pencil upon a beam and thinking to myself, between two yawns, that there was some truth in Madame de Staël's famous assertion: "Travelling is the most melancholy of pleasures."*

## Stamboul

To recover from this mood of stupefaction, you have only to make your way into one of the thousand narrow streets that wind about the hillsides in Stamboul. Here a profound peace holds sway, and one can contemplate in tranquillity that mysterious and reticent East in all its facets, which on the other side of the Golden Horn can only be glimpsed fleetingly amid the noisy confusion of European life. Here everything is indisputably oriental. A quarter of an hour's walk leaves behind all the passers-by and their noise. The houses on either side are all of wood, painted in a thousand different colours, their upper storeys projecting over the lower and the windows protected in front by a sort of glazed balcony, with closely latticed wooden shutters, like small houses attached to the main one, giving to the streets a singular appearance of mystery and melancholy. In some places the streets are so narrow that the projecting parts of opposite houses almost touch each other, and you may walk for a long distance under the shadow of these human cages, under the very feet of the Turkish women who spend most of the day there, with only one thin strip of sky above you. The doors are all shut, the windows of the ground floor grated; everything suggests jealousy and suspicion; it is like going through a city of monasteries. As you walk on you might hear a laugh, and, lifting your eyes, catch a glimpse through some small aperture of a tress of hair and a sparkling eye that instantly vanish. Here and there you may come across a lively, low-voiced conversation going on across the street, but it stops abruptly at the sound of your footsteps. Who knows what web of gossip and intrigue you have momentarily disturbed? You see no one, but a thousand eyes see you; you are alone, but you feel as though you were surrounded by a crowd; and involuntarily you quicken your pace and walk along demurely, not

looking around you, wishing to pass unobserved. An opening door or
a window shutting startles you like a loud noise. These streets might
appear dull, but that's far from being the case. You see a green grove
with a white minaret in the middle; a Turk dressed in red coming down
the hill towards you; a black slave-woman standing still in a doorway;
a Persian carpet hanging from a window; and each is a small picture
so full of life and harmony that you could gaze at it for an hour. Of
the few people who pass by, not one looks at you. Only now and then a
voice behind you calls out *"Giaour!"* ("Infidel!") and, turning, you see
a boy's head just disappearing behind a shutter. Sometimes the door of
a house opens, and you stop short, expecting to behold some beauty
of the harem, when out trips a European lady in her hat and train, who
with a murmured "adieu" or "au revoir", walks quickly away, leaving
you gaping. In another street, utterly Turkish and completely silent,
you are startled by the sound of a horn and horses' hooves. What can
it be? You turn and can hardly believe your eyes. A large tram rolling
forward on two iron rails, which had escaped your notice, and full
of Turks and Europeans, with its conductor in uniform and a list of
fares, just like a tram in Vienna or Paris. The incongruity of such an
apparition in one of these streets can hardly be expressed; it seems
like a joke or a mistake, you want to laugh as you stare at the vehicle
as if it's the first time you'd seen one. It's like an image of Europe, and
once it has gone by you find yourself back in Asia, as if the scenery
has been changed in a theatre. Some of these solitary streets open into
squares, shaded by one widespreading plane tree. On one side there
is a fountain, where camels are drinking; on the other a café, with a
row of mattresses before the door and some Turks reclining on them,
smoking; next to the door a huge fig tree is growing, round which
there is a twisting vine with its tendrils trailing nearly to the ground.
Between their leaves the distant blue of the Sea of Marmara and two
or three white sails can be seen. Brilliant light and deep silence invest
these places with so solemn and melancholy an atmosphere that once
they have been seen you can never forget them. On you go, drawn as
by some hidden charm in the quiet, which enters little by little into the
soul like a dreamy reverie, and after a while you lose all sense of time
and space. You come to wide spaces with traces of a recent outbreak
of fire; sudden slopes with only a few houses scattered here and there,
the grass growing round them and goat tracks winding among them;
high points from which the eye can take in streets, alleys, gardens,

hundreds of houses, but with not a human creature in sight, no puff of smoke or door ajar, nor the least sign of habitation or life – so that you might think you were alone in that immense city, and the very thought fills you with fear. But once you go down the slope and arrive at the end of these narrow streets, everything changes. You find yourself back in one of the great thoroughfares of Stamboul, flanked by magnificent buildings. You walk among mosques, kiosks, minarets, galleried arcades, fountains in marble and lapis lazuli, mausoleums of the sultans, resplendent with arabesques and gold inscriptions, walls covered with mosaics under porches of carved cedar wood, in the shadow of lush blossoming plants that cascade over the walls and gilded gates of the gardens and fill the air with perfume. With every step you come across carriages with pashas, officials, aides-de-camp, eunuchs from great households, a procession of servants and parasites all coming and going between the different ministries. Here you behold and admire the metropolis of a great empire in all its magnificence. There is graceful architecture, murmuring water, cool shade, caressing the senses like soft music and filling the mind with pleasant images. These streets lead to the great squares where the imperial mosques are situated, and you stand amazed before their immense forms. Each of these mosques is the nucleus of a small town, as it were, of colleges, hospitals, schools, libraries, warehouses, baths, which almost pass unnoticed in the shadow of the great dome round which they are clustered.

The architecture, which you had imagined to be very plain, presents instead an extraordinary variety of detail which attracts the eye on every side. Here are domes covered with lead, strangely formed roofs that rise one above the other, aerial galleries, enormous porticoes, windows with columns, arches with festoons, fluted minarets surrounded by small terraces with stone tracery; monumental doors and fountains covered with lacelike stone carving; walls spangled with gold and a thousand other colours; the whole chiselled and daringly worked with the lightest of hands, and shaded by oak trees, cypresses and willows, from which flocks of birds fly out to circle slowly round the domes, filling every corner of the immense building with their song. One is conscious of a feeling stronger and deeper than that of mere aesthetic appreciation. These great buildings are a colossal affirmation in stone of an order of ideas and emotions different from those in which we have been brought up; they are like the framework of a race and a religion which are hostile to us, and their proud lines and soaring pinnacles pay witness to the glories of a God who is not our God and of a people who struck fear into our ancestors; on first seeing them they evoke a feeling of respect in us, a mixture of diffidence and fear, which dampens our natural curiosity and keeps us at a distance.

Within the shady courtyards a few Turks are performing their ablutions at the fountains, beggars are crouching at the foot of columns, veiled women are walking slowly under the arcades; everything is calm, imbued with a kind of voluptuous melancholy which both attracts and puzzles the mind like an enigma. Galata and Pera seem far away. You are alone in another world and in another age, in the Stamboul of Süleyman the Great and Beyazit II, and when you emerge from these stupendous works of the Ottomans and find yourself again in that other Constantinople, meanly built of wood, falling into decay, full of filth, misery and squalor, you feel bewildered. As you walk on, the houses become shabby, the trellises are falling to pieces, the basins of the fountains are covered with moss; tiny mosques with cracked walls and wooden minarets stand in the midst of weeds and nettles; ruined mausoleums, broken steps, passages choked with rubble, whole neighbourhoods fallen into a dreary decrepitude, where no sound is heard, save the flutter of a stork or falcon, or the guttural cry of the muezzin, as he chants the word of God from the top of some hidden minaret.

No city represents the nature and philosophy of its inhabitants better than Stamboul. All grand and beautiful things are from God, or from the Sultan, image of God on earth; everything else is transitory and bears the mark of a profound disdain for worldly affairs. The pastoral tribe has become a nation, but its instinctive love for rural nature, for contemplation and indolence has preserved in its metropolis the semblance of an encampment. Stamboul is not a city; she neither labours, nor thinks, nor creates; civilization beats at her gates and assaults her in her streets, but she dreams and slumbers on in the shadow of her mosques, and takes no heed. It is disconnected, scattered, formless, more like the resting place of a nomadic people than the embodiment of the power of an established state; like a vast sketch of a metropolis; a great spectacle rather than a great city. And it is not possible to form any just conception of it unless one sees it as a whole. One must start from the first hill, which is the apex of the triangle and surrounded by the Sea of Marmara. Here is what might be called the head of Stamboul: a monumental neighbourhood, rich in memories, in majesty, and in light. Here is the Old Seraglio, on the site where Byzantium and its Acropolis were first built, and the temple of Jove, and the palace of the Empress Placidia, and the baths of Arcadius; here are the Mosques of Hagia Sophia and Sultan Ahmet, and the Atmeydanı which occupies the site of the ancient Hippodrome, where, upon an Olympus of bronze and marble, and amid the roar of the spectators robed in silk and purple, the golden four-horsed chariots raced before the Emperors glittering with pearls. From this hill you descend into a shallow valley, where the western walls of the Seraglio extend, marking the outer limits of ancient Byzantium, and here is the Sublime Porte,* by which you enter the palace of the Grand Vizier and the Ministry of Foreign Affairs: an austere and silent part of the city where all the melancholy of the empire's destiny seems to have collected. You go up the second hill, on which the marble Mosque of Nuruosmaniye – the Light of Osman – stands, and where there is the burnt column of Constantine, on which once stood a bronze statue of Apollo with the head of the Emperor; here one stood right in the middle of the ancient Forum, surrounded by colonnades, triumphal arches and statues. Beyond this hill opens the valley of the bazaars, which extends from the Mosque of Beyazit to that of the Sultana Valide, and contains a vast labyrinth of covered streets or arcades, full of noise and people, from which you emerge with glazed eyes and deafened ears. On the third hill, which dominates both the Sea of Marmara and the Golden Horn, looms the enormous Mosque of Süleyman, the rival of Hagia Sophia and "the joy and splendour of Stamboul", as the Turkish poets write, as well as the wonderful tower of the Ministry of War, which stands upon the ruins of the ancient palaces of the Constantines, once inhabited by Mehmet the Conqueror and later converted into a seraglio for the dowager sultanas. From the third to the fourth height the great Aqueduct of Valens, with its rows of graceful arches, extends like some bridge in the sky, its pendent vines swaying above the houses in the populous valley. Passing under the aqueduct, you climb up the fourth hill. Here, upon the ruins of the famous Church of the Holy Apostles, founded by the Empress Helena, and rebuilt by Theodora, stands the Mosque of Mehmet II, surrounded by hospitals, schools, and caravanserais; next to the mosque are the slave market, Mehmet's Baths and the granite column of Marcian, still resting on its marble plinth decorated with the imperial eagles; and near the column, the place where the famous massacre of the janissaries* occurred, then called the square of the Atmeydanı. Then you cross another valley and another town to reach the fifth hill. Here there is the Mosque of Selim, near the ancient cistern of St Peter, now transformed into a garden. Below, along the Golden Horn, extends Fener, the Greek quarter, the seat of the patriarchate, where what remains of old Byzantium has taken refuge, with the descendants of the Paleologus and the Comnenus families, and where the horrid massacres of 1821 took place.* Down into a fifth valley and up onto the sixth hill. This was the part occupied by the eight cohorts of Constantine's forty thousand Goths; it lies outside the circuit of the first walls, which only encircled the fourth hill; the space occupied by the seventh cohort still bears the name of Hebdomon. On the sixth hill there are still the remains of the walls of the Palace of Constantine Porphyrogenitus,* where the emperors were crowned, now called by the Turks Tekfur Sarayı or Palace of the Princes. At the foot of the sixth hill lies Balat, Constantinople's Jewish ghetto, a filthy place, running along the shore of the Golden Horn as far as the walls of the city, and beyond Balat, the ancient suburb of Blachernae, once graced by palaces with gilded roofs, the favourite residences of the emperors, famous for the great Church of the Empress Pulcheria, and for its sanctuary of relics, but now full of ruins and sadness. At Blachernae the battlemented wall begins that runs from the Golden Horn to the Sea of Marmara, encircling the seventh hill, where the Forum Bovis once stood, and where the base of the column of Arcadius can still be found; the easternmost and the largest of the hills of Stamboul, between which and the other six flows the narrow river Lycus, that enters the city near the Charisius Gate, and flows into the sea not far from the ancient gate of Theodosius. From the walls of Blachernae can be seen the suburb of Ortaköy, sloping gently down towards the sea and crowned with gardens; beyond Ortaköy, the district of Eyüp, the holy site of the Ottomans, with its pretty mosque, and its vast cemetery, white with tombs and mausoleums and shaded by a grove of cypresses; beyond Eyüp is the plain of the ancient military camp, where the legions raised the new emperors upon their shields; and beyond this there are other villages, whose vivid colours glow amid the green trees bathed by the last waters of the Golden Horn. Such is Stamboul. It is divine, but the heart swells at the thought that this endless Asian village stands upon the ruins of that second Rome, that immense museum of treasures plundered from Italy, Greece, Egypt and Asia Minor, the mere recollection of which dazzles the mind like some heavenly vision. Where are now the grand colonnades that crossed the city from the sea to the walls, the gilded cupolas, the colossal equestrian statues that rose upon giant pillars in front of amphitheatres and baths; the bronze sphinxes couched upon porphyry pedestals, the temples and palaces that reared their granite façades among an aerial company of marble gods and silver emperors? All gone or transformed. The bronze statues have been melted down into cannon; the copper sheathing of the obelisks turned into coinage; the emperors' sarcophagi have become fountains; the church of St Irene is an arsenal, the cistern of Constantine a workshop, the pedestal of Arcadius's column a blacksmith's forge, the Hippodrome a horse market; ivy and rubble cover the foundations of the imperial city, grassy cemeteries cover the amphitheatres, and only a handful of inscriptions blackened by fire or smashed by the invaders' scimitars record that upon this hill once stood the extraordinary capital of the Empire of the East. Stamboul sits upon the vast ruins, like a concubine upon a tomb, awaiting her own end.

## At the Hotel

And now may it please my readers to follow me back to my hotel and take a short rest.

A great part of what I have described so far was seen by my friend and myself on the day of our arrival; let the reader imagine what a state our heads were in when we returned to our hotel as evening fell. In the street we had not exchanged a word, and we were hardly in our room before we sank down on the sofa, and, looking at each other, asked at the same moment and in one voice:

"What do you think of it?"

"To think I came here to paint!"

"And I to write!"

And we laughed in each other's faces with brotherly compassion. Indeed, on that evening, and for several days after, His Majesty Abdülaziz* might have offered me as a reward an entire province in Asia Minor, but I could not have succeeded in putting ten lines together about the capital of his empire, so true is it that, to describe great things you must be at a distance from them, and to remember them well, you must have forgotten them a little first. And then how could anyone write in a room from which he could see the Bosphorus, Scutari, and the summit of Mount Olympus? The hotel itself was a spectacle. Every hour of the day the staircases and corridors swarmed with people from every country. Twenty nationalities sat down every day to dinner: I used to imagine that I was a delegate from the Italian government and would be expected to rise as soon as the fruit was served to discuss some great international question. There were ladies with pink complexions, wild-haired artists, adventurers whose grim-set faces you could hammer out coins with, or those of Byzantine virgins round which only a golden nimbus was missing, strange and sinister visages; and every day they changed. When everyone was talking over dessert it was a veritable tower of Babel. On our first day I had made the acquaintance of several Russians who were infatuated with Constantinople. Every evening we met, on our return from the furthest parts of the city, and each of us had a story to tell of his travels that day. One had climbed to the top of the tower of Seraskerat, another had visited the cemeteries of Eyüp, a third had come from Scutari, a fourth from a sailing trip down the Bosphorus; our conversation was pervaded by colour and light, and when words failed us, the sweet and perfumed wines of Greece came to our aid and prompted us. There were also some of my own fellow countrymen, wealthy dandies, whose continual carping about Constantinople from first course to last made me bite my tongue in vexation: there were no pavements, the theatres were dark, and there was nothing to do in the evening. They had come to Constantinople to find ways of passing their evenings! One of them had made the journey up the Danube. I asked him if he had enjoyed his trip along the great river. He replied that nowhere in the world could they cook sturgeon as well as they did on the steamers belonging to the Royal and Imperial Austrian Company. Another was a pleasant Don Juan-like character, one of those men who travel to seduce and who keep a notebook in which they jot down their conquests. He was a lanky fair-haired aristocrat, abundantly endowed with the eighth gift of the Holy Spirit,* who inclined his head with a mysterious smile whenever the conversation came round to Turkish women, and only contributed short remarks to the conversation, which he continually interrupted with sips of his wine. He always arrived for dinner out of breath and a little later than everyone else, and seated himself with the air of someone who has just played a successful trick on the Sultan a few minutes ago, and between one dish and another he toyed with small folded notes, that doubtless we were supposed to think were billets-doux from ladies of the harem, but were certainly only hotel bills. But the kind of people you bump into in hotels in cosmopolitan cities – they have to be seen to be believed! There was a young Hungarian, about thirty years of age, tall, nervous, with a diabolical expression, and a hasty, feverish way of talking, who after having been secretary to a rich gentleman in Paris, had joined the French Zouave troops in Algeria, was wounded and taken prisoner by the Arabs, escaped to Morocco, and returning to Europe, went off to the Hague in the hope of getting an officers' brevet to go and fight the Aceh pirates; he was rejected so decided to enlist in the Turkish army, but, passing through Vienna on his way to Constantinople, got a bullet in his neck in a duel about a woman (and here he displayed the scar). He was also turned down at Constantinople – "What am I to do?" he said. "*Je suis enfant de l'aventure*;* I must fight somewhere. I've already found someone who will take me to India" – and here he produced his boat ticket – "I'm going to be an English soldier; in the interior there's always something doing; I only want to fight; what does it matter whether I get killed or not? One of my lungs is kaput already."

Another real character was a Frenchman, whose whole life seemed to pass in a perpetual battle with various postal administrations. He was in ongoing dispute with the Austrian, French and British post offices; he wrote letters of complaint to the *Neue Freie Presse*;* sent off rude telegrams to all the post offices on the continent, and every day had an argument with one of the post-office clerks, never received a letter on time, and never posted one which arrived at its correct address: he related all his misfortunes and all his altercations at table, always concluding by assuring us that the mail services had shortened his life. I also recall a Greek lady, oddly dressed, with a haunted look, and always alone, who each evening rose from the table in the middle of dinner and left, after having made a cabbalistic sign over her plate the meaning of which no one ever succeeded in divining. Nor have I forgotten a Wallachian couple, a handsome young fellow of five and twenty, and a girl in the first flush of youth, who appeared on one evening only, and who had undoubtedly eloped; he had taken the lead and she had followed him: you had only to fix your eye upon them

31

for an instant to make them both blush crimson, and every time the door opened they jumped out of their skins. There were a hundred others whom I might recall. It was a magic lantern show. On the days when a steamer arrived, my friend and I used to amuse ourselves by watching the new arrivals as they came in at the main entrance, tired and bewildered, some of them still excited by the spectacle they had seen on entering the harbour, and with an expression on their faces as if they were saying to themselves, "What world is this? Where are we?" One day there arrived a young lad who was quite mad with delight in finding himself finally in Constantinople, a childhood dream of his, and he held his father's hand in both of his, while the father said in a voice full of emotion: "*Je suis heureux de te voir heureux, mon cher enfant.*"* We passed the hot hours of the day at our window, and looked at the Tower of the Maiden, which rises, white as snow, on a solitary rock in the Bosphorus, opposite Scutari, and while we wove our own fancies around the legend of the Persian prince who sucked the poison from the arm of the beautiful sultana which an asp had bitten, every day at the same hour a little boy appeared at a window in the house across the road and made rude signs at us. Everything was curious in this hotel. Among other things, as we went out each evening we encountered at the entrance two or three shady-looking characters, who we presumed ran an agency for artists' models and seemed to think that everyone they saw was an artist since they sidled up to all comers and whispered in their ear: "A Turk? – A Greek? – An Armenian? – A Jewess? – A Negress?"

## Constantinople

But let us return to Constantinople, and rove about like the birds of the air. Here even the slightest whim is allowed. One can light one's cigars in Europe, and drop the ash in Asia. On getting up in the morning, we can enquire: "What part of the world shall I visit today?" We have a choice of two continents and two seas. We have at our command horses standing saddled in every square, sailboats in every cove, steamboats at a hundred landing stages; the darting caique, the flying *talika*,* and an army of guides speaking all the languages of Europe. Do you wish to hear an Italian comedy? To see the dancing dervishes? Or the antics of Karagöz* in the Turkish

Street in Stamboul

Armenian and Turkish market sellers

The exterior of a Turkish café on the Golden Horn

puppet show? Do you want to hear saucy songs from Parisian music halls? Or see gypsy acrobats? Or listen to a storyteller telling an old Arabian tale? Or would you prefer a Greek theatre? To hear an imam preach or watch the Sultan pass by? All you need to do is ask. Every nation is at your beck and call: the Armenian to shave you, the Jew to polish your boots, the Turk to show you to your boat, the Negro to rub you down in the bath, the Greek to bring you your coffee – and all of them to cheat you. If you are thirsty on your walks you can refresh yourself with ices made from the snows of Olympus; if you have expensive tastes in food and drink, you can drink the water of the Nile, like the Sultan; or if your digestion is bad, the water of the Euphrates; or if you're highly strung, the water of the Danube. You can eat like a desert Arab, or like a gourmand at the *Maison Dorée*.* Should you wish to take an afternoon nap, there are the cemeteries; for distraction, the bridge of the Sultana Valide; for a dreamy reverie, the Bosphorus; for a Sunday outing, the Princes' Islands; to see Asia Minor, you can climb the mount of Bulgurlu; to see the Golden Horn, the tower of Galata; and to see everything, the tower of the Seraskerat. But this is a city even more bizarre than it is beautiful. Objects which you'd never associate in your normal thoughts can here be seen alongside each other. The caravan leaving for Mecca, and the stopping train for the old city of Bursa,* both start from Scutari. Under the mysterious walls of the Old Seraglio there's the railway line to Sofia. Turkish soldiers escort the Catholic priest as he carries the Holy Sacrament to the dying; people picnic in the cemeteries; life, death and all the pleasures mix and merge. There is all the bustle of London with the lethargy of the Orient, a teeming street life together with an impenetrably mysterious privacy; absolute government and freedom without bounds. For the first few days you can't make it out; you think that at any moment all this confusion will either die down or break out into a revolution; every evening you return to your hotel feeling you've just been on a long journey; every morning you ask yourself: "But is this really Stamboul?" You're completely bewildered. One impression cancels out another, desires crowd upon you, time hurries by; you would like to stay here all your life; you want to leave tomorrow. And when you try to describe this chaos in words – then you're tempted to bundle up all the books and papers on your table and throw the whole lot out of the window.

# Galata

My friend and I did not really recover our habitual presence of mind until the fourth day after our arrival. We were on the bridge early one morning, wondering what we should do that day, when Junck suggested we go on a very long walk with a set destination, for the purpose of tranquil observation and study. "Let us walk," said he, "along the northern shore of the Golden Horn, and do the whole of it, even if we have to walk till nightfall. We'll have lunch in a Turkish tavern, take our siesta under the shade of a plane tree, and come home in a caique." I accepted the proposal; we equipped ourselves with cigars and small change, and after briefly perusing a plan of the city set off in the direction of Galata.

Let the reader who wishes to know Constantinople well do us the kindness of accompanying us.

We arrived in Galata, from where our excursion was to begin. Galata is built upon a hill that forms a promontory between the Golden Horn and the Bosphorus, where the great necropolis of ancient Byzantium once stood. Today it is the financial district of Constantinople. The streets are almost all narrow and twisting, lined with taverns, confectioners, pastry-cooks, butchers and barbers, Greek and Armenian cafés, merchants' offices, workshops and booths; the whole area is dark, damp, muddy and clammy like the slum quarters in London. A dense and busy crowd fills the streets, constantly making way for carriages, porters, donkeys and omnibuses. Almost all the trade of Constantinople passes through Galata. Here is the stock exchange, the custom house, the offices of the Austrian Lloyd and the French Messageries; churches, monasteries, hospitals and warehouses. An underground railway connects Galata to Pera. If it were not for the turbans and fezzes in the street, you wouldn't think you were in the Orient. On all sides you hear French, Italian and Genoese dialect being spoken. For the Genoese it's like another homeland; they still have the air of masters, as in the time they used to close the port whenever they chose, and answered the Emperors' threats with cannon fire. But little remains of the monuments of their former power apart from some old houses supported by great pillars and heavy arches, and the ancient edifice which was once the *podestà*'s residence. Old Galata has almost entirely disappeared. Thousands of small houses have been cleared to make room for two long streets, one of which climbs the hill towards

Pera, and the other which runs parallel to the seashore from one end of Galata to the other.

My friend and I chose the latter for our ramble, continually having to step into shops to let great omnibuses pass, preceded by bare-chested Turks who cleared the way with strokes of a whip. Street cries sounded around us all the way: the Turkish porter shouted *"Sakın ha!"* ("Clear the way!"), the Armenian water-carrier, *"Var mi su?"*, the Greek water-seller, *"Krio nero!"*, the Turkish donkey boy, *"Burada!"*, the sweetmeat-seller, "Sherbet!", the newspaper vendor, *"Neologos!"*, the European coachman, "Watch out! Watch out!"* After about ten minutes' walking we were deafened. At a certain point we discovered, to our astonishment, that the street was no longer paved: the paving stones appeared to have been removed only very recently. We stopped and looked about for an explanation; an Italian shopkeeper satisfied our curiosity. That street led to the Sultan's palaces. A few months previously, as the Imperial cortège was passing through it, the horse carrying His Majesty Abdülaziz slipped and fell, and the good Sultan, in his annoyance, ordered that the offending pavement should be taken up, from the point where his horse fell as far as his palace.

## The Tower of Galata

At this memorable spot we fixed the easternmost point of our wanderings, and turning our backs on the Bosphorus, directed our steps through various dark and dirty alleyways towards the tower of Galata. The district of Galata has the form of an unfurled fan, with the tower at the summit of the hill as its handle. It is round and very tall, built of dark stone, terminating in a conical copper roof, under which runs a row of large glazed windows, a kind of covered terrace where night and day a guard watches for the first sign of any conflagration that may break out in the city. The Galata of the Genoese extended as far as this tower, which rises in fact upon the line of the wall that once separated Galata from Pera; no traces of the wall are now to be found. Nor is the tower itself – which was erected in honour of the Genoese who fell in battle – the original one, for it was rebuilt by Mehmet II and before that had been restored by Selim III; nonetheless it is a monument crowned with Genoese glory, and no Italian can look upon it without proudly remembering that small band of merchants, sailors and soldiers, haughty and bold and heroically stubborn, who for centuries held the banner of their republic aloft and negotiated on equal terms with the emperors of the East.

## The Cemetery of Galata

Hardly had we got beyond the tower than we found ourselves in a Muslim graveyard, the cemetery of Galata; a great forest of cypress that from the summit of the hill of Pera descends steeply to the Golden Horn, shading a myriad of little stone and marble columns, leaning in all directions and scattered in disorder all down the slope. Some of these little columns are surmounted by a turban, and retain traces of colour and inscriptions; others end in a point; many are overturned; and some are broken off, the turbans knocked clean away: these are supposed to have been the tombstones of the janissaries, whom Sultan Mahmut wanted to humiliate even in death. The majority of the graves are marked by a prism-shaped mound with a stone at either end, upon which, according to Muslim belief, the two angels Nakir and Munkar will seat themselves when they come to judge the souls of the dead. Here and there are to be seen small mounds of earth surrounded by a low wall or balustrade, in the middle of which stands a column surmounted by a large turban, with other small columns grouped around it: it belongs to a pasha, or some great noble, buried in the midst of his wives and children. Narrow paths wind all about the wood; a Turk sits in the shade smoking his pipe; some children run and jump among the graves; a cow is grazing; hundreds of turtle doves coo in the cypresses; groups of veiled women stroll by; and in the distance between the trees shine the blue waters of the Golden Horn striped by the white minarets of Stamboul.

## Pera

Leaving the cemetery we enter the main street of Pera. Pera is one hundred metres above sea level, is airy and lively, and looks down upon the Golden Horn and the Bosphorus. It is the "West End"* of the European colony; the centre of pleasure and elegance. The street we follow is bordered by English and French hotels, elegant cafés, glittering shops, theatres, consulates, clubs and ambassadors' mansions; among which the stone-built Russian embassy is the largest and most conspicuous, dominating Pera, Galata and the district of Fındıklı like some great fortress.

Here is a crowd which is very different from that found in Galata. Almost all the men wear top hats while the ladies have feathered and flowered bonnets. There are dandies from Greece, Italy and France; important merchants, embassy officials, officers from foreign ships, ambassadorial coaches, and shady characters of every nationality. Turkish men stop to admire the wax heads in the barbers' shops, and Turkish women stand open-mouthed before the milliners' window displays; Europeans talk in loud voices, joking and laughing in the street; the Muslim feels himself to be in a foreign country and walks on holding his head a little less high than he does in Stamboul. Suddenly my friend made me turn and look back at Stamboul, which lay behind an azure veil in the distance, with the Seraglio, Hagia Sophia and the Mosque of Sultan Ahmet gleaming through; another world from the one we stood in. "And now," said he, "look here." I dropped my eyes and read in a shop window: "*La Dame aux camélias – Madame Bovary – Mademoiselle Giraud ma femme*."* I too felt the force of that sudden contrast and had to stand awhile mulling it over. Presently it was my turn to stop my companion and show him a marvellous café, where, at the end of a long dark corridor, a large open window gave on to – at what seemed an immense distance – a magnificent view of Scutari in the sunlight.

We walked on and had nearly reached the end of the great street of Pera, when we heard a thundering voice declaiming in French, "I love thee, Adèle – I love thee more than life itself!" We looked at each other in amazement. Where could it come from? Turning round we saw through the gaps in a fence a garden with rows of seats, a stage and a company of actors rehearsing. A Turkish lady nearby was also looking through the gaps and shaking with uncontrollable laughter. An old Turk passed by and shook his head pityingly. Suddenly the lady gave a shriek and fled; other women standing nearby screamed and turned their backs. What had happened? It was only a Turk, a man of about fifty, familiar to everyone in Constantinople, who is used to walking about the streets in the state to which once, under the reign of Mehmet IV, a famous Turkish dervish had wanted to reduce everyone: namely, naked from head to toe. The poor wretch jumped along over the cobblestones, yelling and sniggering, while a crowd of boys followed him, making the most infernal racket. "He'll be arrested, I trust?" said I to the doorkeeper of the theatre. "Of course not," he replied; "He's been going about like that for months, just as he likes." All down the street of Pera we could see people coming out of their shops to look, women running away, girls covering their eyes, doors being closed, heads leaning out of windows suddenly disappearing inside. This happens every day and no one gives it a second thought.

Leaving the street behind us, we found ourselves near another Muslim cemetery, shaded by a cypress grove and enclosed by a high wall, obviously newly built. We should never have guessed the reason for the wall if we had not been told later: the sacred grove intended for the repose of the dead was being used as a kind of pleasure garden for soldiers and their girls! Further on, in fact, we found the enormous artillery barracks built by Halil Pasha; a solid rectangular edifice, in the Moorish style of late Turkish architecture, with a door flanked by slender columns and surmounted by the crescent and golden star, with projecting galleries, and windows emblazoned with heraldic arms and arabesques. In front of the barracks there is the street of Dgiedessy, which is a continuation of the thoroughfare in Pera, with a vast parade ground on the other side and beyond that more residential areas. On weekdays the place is utterly silent, but on Sunday evenings long lines of carriages and people out for a stroll pass by, and all the fashionable world of Pera comes to while away the evening in the cafés and beer gardens beyond the barracks. We made our first stop at the *Bella Vista* café, where the elite of Pera society gathers: it is aptly named, for from its garden jutting like a terrace over the hillside, you have a view below of the Muslim suburb of Fındıklı, the Bosphorus swarming with vessels, the Asian shore sprinkled with gardens and villages, Scutari and her white mosques: a dreamlike vision of green and azure and sunlight. We got up to go with regret, and felt ourselves wretched skinflints as we left eight small coins for our two cups of coffee and that vision of an earthly paradise.

## A Vast Cemetery

Leaving the *Bella Vista* café we found ourselves in a vast cemetery made up of separate sections, where the dead of each religion, excluding the Jews, are interred. It is a thick forest of cypresses, acacias and sycamores, among which glimmer thousands of white tombstones, looking from a distance like the scattered ruins of some vast former edifice. Between the trees shines the Bosphorus with the Asian shore. Wide paths wind about it, where Greeks and Armenians are walking. Upon some of the tombs Turks are sitting cross-legged, admiring the view. The shade and coolness and peace give one the sensation of entering some great cathedral in the summer heat. We stopped in the Armenian cemetery. The sepulchral stones are all large and flat, and covered with inscriptions in the regular and elegant Armenian script, and on nearly all of them is carved some emblem of the trade or profession of the deceased. There are hammers and saws, pens, jewel boxes, necklaces; the banker is represented by a pair of scales, the priest by a mitre, the barber by a basin, the surgeon by a lancet. On one stone we saw a head severed from the trunk with blood spurting from the neck: it was the tomb either of a murdered man, or of one who had been judicially executed. An Armenian lay beside it in the grass, asleep, with his face turned to the sky. We entered the Muslim cemetery. Here too there was an infinite number of small columns scattered about in rows and disorderly groups, some with the tops gilded and painted; those for women had an ornament in relief representing flowers; many were surrounded by shrubs and flowering plants. As we stood looking at one of these, two Turks came up, leading a child between them, and, seating themselves upon a tomb slightly further on, opened a bundle they were carrying under their arm and began to eat. When they had finished, the elder of the two wrapped up something in a sheet of paper – it looked like a fish and a piece of bread – and with a respectful gesture, placed the little packet in a hole near the head of the grave. This done, they both lit their pipes and smoked peacefully, while the child played about among the tombs. It was explained to us afterwards that the fish and bread were left as a mark of affection for their relative, probably recently deceased; and the hole in which they placed it is to be found in every Muslim tomb, near the head, so that through it the dead may hear the lamentations of their friends, and may receive from them a few drops of rose water or the perfume of a flower. Having finished their smoke by the graveside, the two pious Turks took the child between them, and vanished among the cypresses.

## Pancaldi

Proceeding on our way, we soon found ourselves in another Christian quarter – Pancaldi, with spacious streets and new buildings, surrounded by villas, gardens, hospitals and barracks. Of all the suburbs of Constantinople it is the furthest from the sea, and after visiting it, we turned back towards the Golden Horn. In the last street, we witnessed a new and solemn spectacle: a Greek funeral procession. A silent crowd filled the street on both sides; first came a group of Greek priests, in embroidered robes; then the archimandrite with a crown upon his head, and a long gown richly decorated with gold; some young clerics in brilliant-coloured gowns; a quantity of friends and relations in their richest costumes, and in the midst of them a bier, wreathed with flowers, on which lay the body of a girl of fifteen, with uncovered face, and resplendent in satin and jewels. The little snow-white face had an expression of pain about the contracted mouth, and two beautiful tresses of black hair lay over the shoulders and bosom. The bier passed by, the crowd closed in, and we remained alone and saddened in the deserted street.

## St Dimitri

Climbing the hill of Pancaldi, and crossing a dried-up river bed, we went up another hill and found ourselves in another neighbourhood, St Dimitri. Here the population is almost all Greek. Black eyes and thin aquiline noses are to be seen on every side; old men of patriarchal aspect; slender, bold-looking young men; small women with plaited hair; boys with shrewd little faces, romping in the middle of the street among the hens and pigs, and filling the air with the sound of their silvery and harmonious speech. We approached a group of these, who were playing with stones and chattering all together, when one, a child of about eight years old, and the wildest of them all, every moment throwing his little fez into the air and yelling, "*Zito! Zito!*" ("Hurrah!"), suddenly turned to another young lad who was seated on a doorstep, and called out in Italian: "Cecchino! Throw me the ball." I seized him by the arm like a gypsy about to abduct him and asked, "Are you Italian?" – "No, sir," he replied, "I'm from Constantinople."

"And who taught you to speak Italian?" I asked.

"Why, mamma, of course," he said.

"And where is mamma?" At that moment a smiling woman came up, carrying a baby in her arms, who told me that she was from Pisa, the wife of a Livorno marble-cutter, that she had lived eight years in Constantinople, and this was her son. If this good woman had been a handsome matron, with a turreted crown upon her head, and a mantle over her shoulders, she could not have represented Italy more vividly to my heart and eyes. "How did you come to be here?" I asked. "And what do you think of Constantinople?"

"What shall I say?" she answered, with an open smile. "It's the kind of place… to tell the truth, it always seems to me like the last day of carnival here." And launching into broad Tuscan, she told me that "as for the Muslims, their Jesus is Mohammad", that a Turk may marry four wives, that you need to be very clever to understand a word of Turkish, and other such novel opinions; but spoken in that tongue, in that Greek neighbourhood, it was dearer to me than any more unusual news could be, and I went away leaving a few coins in the boy's hand, and murmuring to myself, "Ah! A breath of Italy every now and then does one a world of good."

## Tatavla

We retraced our steps across the small valley and arrived in another Greek quarter, called Tatavla, where, as our stomachs were beginning to rumble in protest, we took the opportunity to go inside one of those innumerable taverns, all unusual in appearance but all identically fashioned. An immense room, big enough for a theatre, surrounded by a high wooden gallery with a balustrade and where the only source of light is the open door. On one side there is an enormous stove, at which some brigand in his shirtsleeves is frying fish, turning roasts, mixing sauces, and generally occupied in devising ways of shortening human existence; on the other side a serving counter where another evil-looking bandit is distributing red and white wine in goblets with handles; in the middle and in front some stools and some small tables which are only a little higher than the stools, like a cobbler's bench. We entered with some hesitation because we feared a group of rough-looking Greeks and Armenians might show a mocking interest in us, but they did not even deign to glance at us. The inhabitants of

41

Constantinople are, I think, the least curious of any populace in the world; one must either be the Sultan or walk about naked like the madman of Pera to attract the slightest notice. We seated ourselves in a corner and waited. No one came. Then we realized that in a Constantinople tavern, the custom is to serve yourself. First we went to the stove and demanded some roast meat – God only knows from what quadruped it came – and then to the counter to get a goblet of the resinous wine of Tenedos, and carrying everything back to the table that only just reached to our knees, we bent over and consumed the burnt offering. With an air of resignation we settled the bill and issued forth in silence, afraid that if we opened our mouths we would start to bark or bray, and resumed our journey towards the Golden Horn.

## Kasımpaşa

After ten minutes walk, we are once more in the heart of Turkey; in the great Muslim suburb of Kasımpaşa, a veritable city thickset with mosques and dervish monasteries, full of flower and vegetable gardens, which occupies a hill and a valley, and spreading down to the Golden Horn, encircles the whole of the ancient bay of Mandrakia, from the cemetery of Galata to the promontory that overlooks Balat, on the opposite shore. From the heights of Kasımpaşa, the spectacle is enchanting. Below, upon the shore, you see the immense arsenal of Tersane; a labyrinth of docks, factories, squares, storehouses and barracks, extending for a mile along that part of the Golden Horn which is used as a naval base; the graceful, elegant building of the Naval Ministry, which seems to float upon the water, stands out white against the dark green of the Galata cemetery; the harbour is busy with small steamboats and caiques filled with passengers, darting about among the battleships lying at anchor and old frigates dating from the Crimean war; and on the opposite shore, Stamboul, the Aqueduct of Valens raising its lofty arches against the blue sky, the great Mosques of Süleyman and Mehmet II, and a myriad houses and minarets. To savour the spectacle at more leisure we sat down in a Turkish café, and sipped the fourth or fifth of those twelve daily cups of coffee which everyone in Constantinople needs to take, whether he wants to or not. It was a mean little place, but like all Turkish cafés, very striking; not very different, probably, from the first cafés in the time of Süleyman the Great, or from those into which Murat IV used to burst clutching his scimitar, when he went on his nightly rounds to find out and punish the vendors of the prohibited beverage. How many imperial edicts, how many theological disputes and how much bloodshed have been occasioned by "this enemy of sleep, and of fertility" as the more austere ulemas used to call it, or "this genius of dreams and exciter of the imagination" as their colleagues with rather broader opinions preferred to describe it; today, after love-making and tobacco, it is the poorest Turk's sweetest consolation. Coffee is drunk on the tops of the towers of Galata and the Seraskerat, in all the steamboats, in the cemeteries, in barbers' shops and baths and bazaars. No matter what part of Constantinople you find yourself in, you have only to shout without turning your head: "*Kahveci!*" ("Coffee-seller!"), and in three minutes a cup is steaming in front of you.

## The Café

Our café was a whitewashed room, wainscoted with wood to the height of a man, with a low divan running all round it. In one corner there was a stove at which a Turk with a cleft nose was making coffee in small copper coffee pots, and pouring it out as it became ready into tiny cups, adding the sugar at the same time; for, in Constantinople, the coffee is made fresh for every customer, and is brought to him already sugared, together with a glass of water that every Turk drinks before bringing the cup of coffee to his lips. Upon the wall hung a small mirror, and beside it a sort of rack holding some cut-throat razors, since most cafés are also barbers' shops, and not infrequently the café owner is also a dentist and a blood-letter, and operates upon his victims in the same room where the other customers are taking their coffee. Upon the opposite wall hung another rack full of crystal narghiles with long flexible tubes, twisted like serpents, and chibouks of earthenware with cherry-wood stems. Five pensive Turks were seated upon the divan smoking the narghile, while three others sat in front of the door on low straw stools in a row, one beside the other, pipes in their mouths, leaning against the wall; in front of the mirror sat a fat dervish in a camel-hair gown, having his head shaved by one of the shop boys. No one looked at us when we sat down, no one spoke, and, except for the owner and his assistant, no one made a movement. The only sound was the bubbling of the water in the narghiles, which was like the purring of a cat. Each one looked straight before him expressionlessly, with fixed eyes. It was like a small waxwork display. Many of such scenes remain forever impressed upon my memory. A wooden house, a seated Turk, a lovely distant view, a great light and a vast silence. Such is Turkey. Every time I think of the country, these images come into my mind, just as whenever someone speaks to me of Holland, I instantly see a canal and a windmill.

## Piyalepaşa

From there we skirted a large cemetery, which stretched from Kasımpaşa down the hill to Tersane, then climbed north again, and came down into the small valley of Piyalepaşa, a little neighbourhood half hidden among gardens and orchards, and stopped before the mosque which gives it its name. It is a white mosque, surmounted by six graceful domes, with a courtyard surrounded by an arched colonnade set on pretty columns, a slender minaret, and a circle of immensely tall cypresses. At that hour all the small houses round about were closed, the streets deserted, the court of the mosque itself in perfect solitude; the dazzle and torpor of midday lay over everything, and no sound broke the silence save the buzzing of flies. We looked at our watches: three minutes to twelve; one of the five canonical Muslim hours, when the muezzins appear upon the terraces of the minarets to chant to the four quarters of the horizon the ritual phrases of Islam. We were well aware that in all Constantinople there is not a minaret upon which there does not appear, at the appointed time, punctual as clockwork, the announcer of the Prophet. And yet it seemed to us strange that also in that remote area of the vast city, upon that solitary mosque, in that deep silence, the figure should appear and the voice ring out. I held my watch in my hand, and both of us watched intently the small door – as high up as the third storey of an ordinary house – upon the balcony of the minaret. The minute hand touched the sixtieth mark, and no one emerged. "He's not coming!" I said. "He's here!" replied Junck. And there he was. The parapet of the balcony concealed all of him apart from his face, which couldn't be seen clearly from below. He stood silent a moment: then, covering his ears with his hands and lifting his face to the sky, he chanted in a slow, high, tremulous voice, with a solemn and mournful rhythm, the sacred words which were then resounding from every minaret in Africa, Asia and Europe: "God is great! There is but one God! Mohammad is the Prophet of God! Come to prayer! Come and be saved! God is great! God is one alone! Come to prayer!"

He chanted the same words towards each of the four points of the compass, and then vanished. At the same instant, there came to our ears faintly the last notes of another distant voice that sounded like the cry of some creature in distress, and then everything fell silent again, and we too did not speak for several minutes, conscious of a vague sadness, as if those two phantasmal voices had counselled prayer to us alone, and then left us to ourselves in the valley, like two souls abandoned by God. No tolling bell has ever touched my heart like this; and on that day I understood for the first time why Mohammad, calling the faithful to prayer, had preferred the human voice to the trumpet of the Israelites, or the tocsin of the early Christians. He took a long time to decide, and it was a close thing that the Orient did not take on an entirely different atmosphere, because, had he chosen the tocsin, which later became a bell, the minaret too would have been transformed, and one of the most original and graceful features of an oriental city and landscape would have been lost for ever.

## Okmeydanı

Reclimbing the hill from Piyalepaşa towards the west, we found ourselves in a large open space of bare earth, from which we could see the whole of the Golden Horn, and all of Stamboul, from Eyüp to the Seraglio hill; four miles of gardens and mosques, a prospect of such grandeur and grace that it should be contemplated on one's knees, like a celestial vision. The desolate spot on which we stood was the Okmeydanı, or square of arrows, where the sultans used to go to practise archery, as the kings of Persia did too. A few small inscribed marble columns are still standing, at irregular distances, marking the points where the imperial arrows fell. The elegant kiosk, with its tribune, from which the sultans took aim, is also still there. In the fields to the right, a long line of admiring beys and pashas would stretch out, enabling the Padishah to pay homage to his own dexterity, while to the left stood twelve pages of the imperial household, who ran to pick up the arrows and to mark the points where they fell; hiding behind the trees and bushes, a few adventurous Turks looked on at the august figure of the *Grand Signor*; and upon the tribune the most vigorous archer in the empire stood in a proud athletic pose: Mahmut with his glittering eyes which made all onlookers drop their own in obeisance, and whose famous beard, black as a crow from the Taurus Mountains, stood out from afar against his white cloak spattered with the blood of the janissaries. Now everything is more prosaic; the Sultan fires at a target with a revolver in a palace courtyard, and the Okmeydanı is given over to infantry soldiers and rifle practice. There is a dervish monastery on one side, a solitary café on the other; and the whole place is as desolate and as melancholy as a steppe.

## Piripaşa

We walked down into another small Turkish suburb, called Piripaşa, perhaps after the famous Grand Vizier of Sultan Selim, who educated Süleyman the Great. Piripaşa faces the Jewish quarter of Balat, on the opposite shore. We met no one but a few old beggars and dogs. But the solitude enabled us the better to consider the plan of the place. It is a remarkable fact: there, as in every other area of Constantinople, once you have entered it, having seen it first from the sea or from the neighbouring heights, you have the same impression as when you watch the performance of a ballet from the stage wings after seeing it from the stalls; you are astonished that such an assemblage of mean and ugly things should produce such a brilliant illusion. I believe there is no city in the world where beauty is so purely appearance, as in Constantinople. Seen from Balat, Piripaşa is a charming little place, glowing with colour and garlanded with green, reflected in the waters of the Golden Horn like some nymph, evoking a hundred images of love and pleasure. Once you are in its streets all this beauty vanishes. A few small shabby houses, painted in garish colours like fairground booths, a few narrow dirty courtyards looking like witches' covens; dusty fig trees and cypresses, gardens littered with rubbish, deserted alleyways, poverty, squalor and wretchedness. But go down a few steps, jump into a caique, and after four or five strokes of the oars, you can look back and see again your former fantasy, in all its grace and beauty.

## Hasköy

Continuing along the shore of the Golden Horn, we went down into another large and densely populated district, with a strange atmosphere; after only a few steps we realized that we were no longer among Muslims. The ground seemed to swarm with dirty dandruffed children; misshapen and ragged old women were seated in the doorways, sewing with their bony hands on the front steps of houses full of junk and old iron; men wearing long, dirty garments and with a ragged kerchief bound round their heads sidled furtively along; emaciated faces appeared in the windows; ragged washing was hanging between the houses; there is litter and filth at every step. It is Hasköy, the Jewish ghetto on the northern shore of the Golden Horn, opposite the ghetto on the other shore. During the Crimean war they were connected by a wooden bridge of which no trace remains. From this part onwards there is a long line of arsenals, military schools, barracks and drill grounds, extending almost to the end of the Golden Horn. But of all this we saw nothing, because by this time both our legs and our heads had given out. Already everything that we had seen was confused in our minds; we felt as if we had been journeying for a week; we thought of distant Pera with a slight sensation of homesickness, and would have turned back there and then were it not for the solemn vow we had made upon the bridge; and if Junck had not revived my spirits, in his usual way, by singing the grand march from *Aida*.*

## Halıcıoğlu

And so on we went. Crossing another Muslim cemetery, and ascending another hill, we entered the suburb of Halıcıoğlu, inhabited by a mixed population; a small town, where at every turn, one encountered a new race and a new religion. We went up, we went down, we climbed, we wound about among tombs, mosques, churches and synagogues; we skirted round graveyards and gardens; we met handsome Armenian matrons and light-footed Turkish women who gave us sidelong glances under their veils; we heard Greek, Armenian and Spanish spoken – the Spanish of the Jews – and we walked and walked. "This city must come to an end somewhere!" we said to ourselves. "Everything on earth has a limit!" Already there were fewer houses, kitchen gardens appeared, we passed through one last group of cottages, at last we reached our journey's end...

EDMONDO DE AMICIS

## *Sütlüce*

But no! We had only arrived in another district of the city. The Christian quarter of Sütlüce is situated upon a hill surrounded by orchards and graveyards. At the foot of this hill there used to be the only bridge across the Golden Horn. But we *have* in fact come to the end, for this neighbourhood is the last and our excursion is finished. Looking about for a place to rest, we climbed up a steep bare slope above Sütlüce and found ourselves in the largest Jewish cemetery of Constantinople: a huge area covered with myriads of overturned stones, looking like a town destroyed by an earthquake, without trees or flowers, a blade of grass or trace of a path; a desolate solitude that oppresses the heart, like the spectacle of some great disaster. We sat down to rest on a tombstone facing the Golden Horn, and admired the magnificent panorama that lay spread out before us. Below us could be seen Sütlüce, Halıcıoğlu, Hasköy, Piripaşa, a succession of different districts between the azure of the sea and the green of gardens and cemeteries; to the left the solitary Okmeydanı, and the hundred minarets of Kasımpaşa; further on Stamboul, chaotic and interminable; beyond Stamboul the lofty lines of the Asian mountains reaching to the heavens; directly facing us, on the other side of the Golden Horn, the mysterious quarter of Eyüp, where we could clearly distinguish each splendid mausoleum and marble mosque, the tree-shaded slopes scattered with tombs; the solitary pathways and graceful melancholy retreats; to the right of Eyüp other villages reflected in the water, and then the last curve of the Golden Horn, disappearing between two high shores covered with trees and flowers.

As we gazed upon this spectacle, weary, almost half-asleep, we set all the beauty to music, and unconscious of what we were doing hummed some tune; we wondered about the dead man on whose tomb we were resting; we poked an ants' nest with a straw; we talked about a hundred foolish things; and from time to time we asked each other: are we really in Constantinople? And then we thought that life is brief and all is vanity; and then we quivered with happiness; but deep down we felt that no earthly beauty can give us perfect joy unless we contemplate it hand in hand with the woman we love.

Landing dock on the Golden Horn

The Towers of Galata and ferries on the Bosphorus

Shoe bazaar

## In a Caique

The sun was about to set when we walked down to the shore and took a four-oared caique; we had hardly given the order – "Galata!" – when the little boat had already pushed off far into the water. The caique is certainly the prettiest boat that ever floated on water. It is longer than the gondola, but narrower and lighter; it is carved and painted and gilded; it has neither rudder nor benches; you sit upon a carpet, or cushion, and only your head and shoulders appear above the side; it is so designed as to be able to move in either direction; it loses its balance at the slightest movement, darts from the shore like an arrow shot from a bow, seeming to skim the water like a swallow; and weaving in and out everywhere, it glides and flies with its many colours reflected in the water like a pursued dolphin. Our two rowers were handsome young Turks, bare armed and legged, with blue shirts, white baggy britches and red fezzes; two twenty-year-old athletes, bronzed, clean, cheerful and lively, who sent the boat its own full length ahead at every stroke; we passed other caiques so swiftly as scarcely to distinguish them; flocks of ducks went by, and birds flew over our heads; we skirted great covered barges full of veiled women, and here and there the seaweed covered the surface of the water completely. Seen from the water at that hour, the city took on an entirely new appearance. The Asian shore was invisible because of the curving channel; the hill of the Seraglio closed in the Golden Horn, making it seem like a very long lake; the hills of the opposing shores seemed to grow in size, and Stamboul in the far distance, melting into soft gradations of blue and ash-grey tints, seemed like some vast enchanted city, lightly floating on the sea and fading ethereally. The caique darted, the two banks receded rapidly, inlets and groves and villages sped by; and as we sailed on everything seemed to rise and grow larger before us; the colours of the city grew faint, the horizon caught flame, the water sent back reflections of purple and gold. A deep amazement entered our souls, together with an indescribable sweetness: we smiled but could not utter a word... When the caique drew up at the landing stage in Galata, one of the boatmen had to yell "Meester! Ees come!" in our ears, before we woke from our dream and stepped on shore.

# The Grand Bazaar

After making a rapid survey of the whole of Constantinople and exploring both shores of the Golden Horn, it is time to enter into the heart of Stamboul, and see that universal never-ending fair, that dark and hidden city full of marvels, treasures, and memories, which stretches from the hill of Nuruosmaniye, to that of the Seraskerat, and is known as the Grand Bazaar.

We start from the Mosque of the Sultana Valide. Here perhaps some epicurean reader would wish to stop and give a glance at the Balık Pazarı, the fish market, famous since the time of that old Andronicus Paleologus, who, as is well known, earned from the fisheries alone, along the walls of the city, enough to meet the culinary expenses of his entire court. Fish, indeed, is still abundant in Constantinople, and the Balık Pazarı on its best days could provide the author of the *Ventre de Paris** with a subject for an extravagant and appetizing description, like the great banquets depicted in old Dutch paintings. The vendors are almost all Turks, and stand ranged around the square, with their fish piled up on mats spread on the ground, or upon long tables, around which crowds of buyers and packs of dogs push and shove. There you will find the delicious mullet of the Bosphorus, four times as large as those caught in our waters; oysters from the island of Marmara, which only the Greeks and Armenians know how to grill to perfection; pilchards and tunny-fish, the salting of which is carried out almost exclusively by Jews; anchovies, which the Turks learnt how to prepare from the people of Marseilles; sardines, with which Constantinople supplies the Greek Archipelago; the *lüfer*, the most flavoursome fish in the Bosphorus, which is always caught by moonlight; the mackerel of the Black Sea, which makes seven incursions one after the other into the waters of the city, creating a noise which the inhabitants of the villas along the shore can hear distinctly; giant *istavrit*, enormous swordfish, turbot, or as they are called in Turkey, *kalkan balıği*, or "shield-fish", and a thousand smaller fishes that swim between the two seas, pursued by dolphins and *falianos*, and chased by innumerable seagulls whose prey is often snatched from their beaks by kingfishers.* Cooks from the kitchens of pashas, elderly Muslim gourmets, slaves and tavern assistants approach the stalls, look at the merchandise with a meditative air, make their bargains in monosyllables, and depart with their purchase dangling by a string, grave and taciturn, as if they were carrying the head of an enemy; by midday the place is empty, and the vendors have all dispersed to the neighbouring cafés, where they remain until sunset, leaning against the wall and daydreaming, with the narghile between their lips.

To reach the Grand Bazaar, you take a street leading off the fish market which is so narrow that the upper stories of the houses almost touch one another, and walk on between two rows of low, dark shops, where tobacco is sold, "the fourth column" – after coffee, opium and wine – "of the canopy of voluptuousness", or "the fourth sofa of enjoyment". As with coffee, sultans' edicts and muftis' pronouncements have fulminated against it, but the problems and penalties it has provoked have only made it more delicious. The entire street is occupied by tobacco merchants. The tobacco is displayed on trestles in pyramids or round heaps, each one topped by a lemon. There is the Latakia of Antioch, the Seraglio tobacco, yellow and silky-fine, tobacco for cigarettes and for the chibouk, of all grades of strength and flavour, from that smoked by brawny Galata porters to that which soothes bored concubines in the kiosks of the imperial gardens. *Tömbeki*, a very strong tobacco that would go to the head of the oldest and most seasoned smoker, if its fumes did not reach the lips purified by the water of the narghile, is kept in closed glass jars, like a medicine. The tobacconists are almost all Greeks or Armenians, ceremonious in manner, affecting gentlemanly airs; their customers stand in groups and chat; here you may see employees from the Foreign Ministry or the Seraskerat; some great man might give you an occasional nod; politics, the latest piece of news or most recent scandal are discussed; it is a small, private, aristocratic bazaar, which invites you to repose, and even if you're only passing through leaves you with a sense of the pleasure of conversation and smoking.

Going on, you pass under an old archway, festooned with vines, and arrive in front of a vast stone edifice, through which runs a long, straight, covered street, flanked by dark shops, and crowded with people, chests, sacks and heaps of merchandise. You are met by so strong an aroma of spices that it almost knocks you backwards. It is the Egyptian bazaar where foodstuffs from India, Syria, Arabia and Egypt are gathered and afterwards reduced to essences, pastes, powders and ointments, which go to paint the faces and hands of the concubines, to perfume rooms and baths and breaths and beards and dishes, to reinvigorate exhausted pashas, to calm unhappy wives, to

51

stupefy smokers, to spread dreams, intoxication and oblivion over the endless city. After a few steps your head begins to swim and you have to go outside, but the sensation of that warm, heavy atmosphere, and those inebriating perfumes, accompanies you a long time in the open air, and remains vivid in the memory as one of the most intimate and charged impressions of the East.

Coming out from the Egyptian bazaar, the way passes through a street of noisy coppersmiths, Turkish taverns that fill the air with nauseous smells, and a thousand obscure nooks and niches of shops where quantities of nameless objects are manufactured, and finally arrives at the Grand Bazaar. But long before reaching it you are assailed and have to defend yourself. At a hundred paces from the great entrance gate are stationed, like so many bandits, the merchants' middlemen, together with the middlemen's middlemen; they recognize a foreigner at first glance, have at once divined that he is coming to the bazaar for the first time, and in general can guess pretty well from what country he comes so that they're rarely wrong in choosing which language to use with him. They approach, fez in hand, and smilingly offer their services. Then follows a dialogue which almost invariably goes like this:

"I'm not planning to buy anything," you say.

"No matter, sir; I only want to show you the bazaar."

"I don't want to see the bazaar."

"But my services are free."

"I do not wish to have your services, even for free."

"Well, then, I'll just accompany you to the end of the street, to give you some information that will be useful when you do come and buy."

"I don't even wish to talk about buying."

"Then we will talk of other things, sir. Have you been in Constantinople long? Are you satisfied with your hotel? Have you got a permit to visit the mosques?"

"I'm telling you that I do not wish to talk. I wish to be alone."

"Well, I will leave you alone; I'll just follow on behind you."

"Why do you want to follow me?"

"To prevent you from being cheated in the shops."

"But I'm not going into the shops!"

"Just to make sure no one gives you any bother in the street."

In short, either you go on wasting your breath or you let him accompany you.

The outside of the Grand Bazaar has nothing to attract the eye, or give an idea of its contents. It is an immense stone edifice, built in the Byzantine style, irregular in form, surrounded by high grey walls, and surmounted by hundreds of little cupolas, covered with lead and perforated with holes to give light to the interior. The principal entrance is an arched doorway of no particular architectural distinction; in the streets outside you hear no noise from within at all – even when you're standing just in front of the door it still seems that there's only silence and solitude within those fortress walls. But once inside you stand bewildered. You find yourself not in a building, but a labyrinth of streets under vaults and flanked by carved columns and pillars; a veritable city, with its mosques, fountains, crossroads and little squares, dimly lit like a thick forest into which no ray of sunlight penetrates; and filled by a dense throng of people. Each street is a bazaar and almost all lead out of one main street, with an arched roof of black and white stone, decorated with arabesques like the nave of a mosque. In these dimly lit thoroughfares, carriages, horsemen and camels are constantly passing through the middle of the crowds with a deafening noise. Words and gestures beckon the visitor on all sides. The Greek merchants call out loudly and gesture imperiously. The Armenian, quite as cunning, but more humble in manner, solicits you obsequiously; the Jew whispers his offers in your ear; the silent Turk, seated cross-legged on a cushion at the entrance to his shop, just catches your eye and resigns himself to what will be. A dozen voices call you: "*Monsieur!* Captain! *Caballero! Signore! Eccellenza! Kyrie!* My Lord!" At every turn, you glimpse arches and pillars stretching away through every side door, long corridors, narrow alleys, distant and confused views of the bazaar, and everywhere there are shops, merchandise piled up or hanging from wall and ceiling, busy merchants, loaded porters, groups of veiled women, noisy throngs coming and going, forming and dispersing, a confusion of people and objects which is enough to make one's head spin.

The confusion, however, is only apparent. This immense bazaar is ordered like a barracks, and it only needs an hour or two to enable you to find anything you want without a guide. Each kind of merchandise has its own particular quarter, its street, its corridor and its public square. There are a hundred little bazaars contained in one great one, and opening one into the other like the rooms of a vast apartment; and each bazaar is at the same time a museum, a passageway, a market and a theatre, where you may look at everything without buying anything, drink coffee, enjoy the coolness, chatter away in ten languages, and make eyes at the prettiest women in the Orient.

You might choose a bazaar at random and spend half a day there without being aware of the passage of time, for example, in the textiles and clothes bazaar. It's an emporium of such beauty and such abundance that it is enough to ruin your eyes, your brains and your pocket; you must be on your guard, for the slightest whim might mean you need to telegraph home for a loan. You stroll in the midst of towering heaps of brocades from Baghdad, carpets from Karaman, silks from Bursa, linens from Hindustan, muslins from Bengal, shawls from Madras, cashmeres from India and Persia, cloths of many dyes from Cairo; cushions arabesqued in gold, silk veils woven with silver threads, gauze scarves with blue and crimson stripes, so light and transparent they seem like air; materials of every fabric and every pattern, in which red, blue, green, yellow – all the colours it is most difficult to match with taste – are brought together and interwoven, with a boldness and a harmony which make you gasp; tablecloths of all sizes, with red or white backgrounds embroidered with arabesques, flowers, verses from the Koran, and imperial ciphers, which you could gaze at for hours, like the walls of the Alhambra. Here, as in the wardrobes of the harem, all the different items of clothing in a Turkish lady's wardrobe may be identified and admired: from the green, orange or purple mantles that cover the whole person, down to the silk chemise, the gold-embroidered handkerchiefs and the satin girdle, which only the husband or the eunuch are allowed to see. Here are kaftans of red velvet, bordered with ermine, and covered with sequins; corsets of yellow satin, trousers of rose-coloured silk, undervests of white damask embroidered with golden flowers, bridal veils sparkling with silver spangles; short velvet capes trimmed with swansdown; Greek, Armenian and Circassian garments, of the oddest cuts, overloaded with ornament, hard and gleaming like cuirasses; and alongside all these, the prosaic, dingy-looking cloths of France and England, like a tailor's bill marking the pages of a book of poems. No man in love with a woman can walk through this bazaar and not curse fate for not making him a millionaire, or without being overcome for a moment by an overwhelming urge to sack and pillage.

To free yourself of such ideas, you have only to turn into the pipe bazaar. Here the imagination is led back to calmer desires. The eye dwells fondly upon bundles of chibouks with stems of cherry, jasmine, maple and rosewood; cigarette-holders made of yellow amber from the Baltic, polished and lustrous as crystal, set with rubies and diamonds, and of innumerable shades of colour or transparency; pipes from Kayseri, their stems wound round with silk and gold threads; tobacco pouches from Lebanon, lozenged in various colours and gleamingly embroidered in arabesques; narghiles in Bohemian crystal, or made of steel and silver, of beautiful antique shapes, damascened, enamelled, encrusted with precious stones, with tubes of morocco leather sparkling with golden rings; wrapped in cotton wool and perpetually watched over by two fixed eyes, that at the approach of any curious browser dilate like the eyes of an owl, and stifle, when it's on the tip of your tongue, the question: "How much?" – unless you happen to be a vizier or a pasha at the very least, who's bled a whole Asian province dry over several years. Only a messenger from the Sultana who wishes to give a token of her gratitude to a complaisant Grand Vizier comes here to buy, or a high court dignitary, who has just been promoted, and is obliged, for the sake of decorum, to spend fifty thousand lira on a rackful of pipes, or one of the Sultan's ambassadors, who wishes to take to some European monarch a splendid souvenir of Stamboul. The Turk of modest means gives a wistful glance and walks on by, paraphrasing the Prophet's sentence to console himself: "The fires of hell shall groan like the growl of a camel in the belly of the man who *smokes a gold or silver pipe…*"*

One falls once more into temptation upon entering the perfume bazaar, which is one of the most completely oriental, and one of the dearest to the Prophet who named his three favourite pleasures as women, children and perfumes. Here can be found the famous Seraglio pastilles for perfuming kisses, the capsules of aromatic gum which the robust girls of Chios pluck from the mastic trees, and which weak Muslim women use to strengthen their gums; the exquisite essences of jasmine and bergamot, and that most potent essence of roses, sealed in boxes of gold-embroidered velvet, and sold at a price to make your hair stand on end; here is *kohl* for the brows and lashes, antimony for the eyes, henna for the fingernails, soaps that soften the skin of the lovely Syrians, pills that remove facial hair from the masculine Circassian women, citron and orange waters, little bags of musk, oil of sandalwood, grey amber, aloes to perfume pipes and coffee cups, a myriad of powders, waters and pomades with fantastic names and mysterious uses, each representing a lover's whim, a plan for seduction, a refinement of pleasure, and which together emit a sharp and sensual fragrance, which evokes a vision of languid eyes and caressing hands, and a low murmur as of sighs and kisses.

These fancies all vanish as you enter the jewellers' bazaar, a dark, deserted alley, flanked by mean-looking shops, which no one would think contained the fabulous treasures which are hidden there. The jewels are shut up in oaken coffers, bound and plated with iron, and placed in front of the shops immediately under the eyes of the merchant: elderly Turks or Jews with long beards and piercing eyes which seem to penetrate to the very bottom of your purse and pocket. Sometimes one of them is standing in front of his lair, and as you pass by, he first fixes his eye intently upon yours, and then with a rapid gesture holds up before you a diamond from Golconda, or a sapphire from Hormoz, or a ruby from Jamshid, which at the slightest sign of demur on your part is withdrawn as quickly as it appeared.* Others circle you slowly, stop you in the middle of the street, and after looking round them with an air of suspicion, draw out a dirty rag, and unfolding it, display a fine Brazilian topaz, or a beautiful Macedonian turquoise, staring at you all the time with a look of demoniacal temptation. Others merely give you a piercing look and, deciding you don't have the appearance of a likely customer, don't deign to show you anything. Not one makes a motion to open the coffer, even if you have the face of a saint, or seem as rich as Croesus.* The necklaces of opals, the flowers and stars of emeralds, the crescents and diadems set with pearls of Ophir,* the dazzling heaps of aquamarines and chrysoprase, of agates, garnets, and lapis lazuli, these remain firmly hidden from the eyes of an impecunious browser, especially if he happens to be an Italian writer. The utmost he dares is to ask the price of some *tesbih** made of amber, coral, or sandalwood, to click through his fingers as Turks do, and kill time when he's not working to a deadline.

It is more amusing to go into the shops of the European merchants who sell haberdashery, where there are things to suit all purses. You have scarcely entered before you are surrounded by a circle of people sprung from who knows where. It is not possible to deal with one person alone. What with the merchant himself and his partners, the middlemen, and all their hangers-on, there are always half a dozen people. If you escape one, you are sure to fall into the clutches of the others: there is no help for you. The artfulness, the patience, the obstinacy, the diabolical cunning which they show in making you buy what they please defy description. They begin by asking an absurdly inflated price; you offer a third; they drop their arms disconsolately or strike their foreheads with a gesture of despair, and make no reply; or else they burst into a torrent of passionate words intended to touch your heart. You are a cruel man, you're forcing them out of business, you want to reduce them to poverty, you have no pity on their children, they cannot understand what they have done to you to be treated in such a manner. At the same time as they're telling you the price of an item, a middleman from a neighbouring shop whispers in your ear: "Don't buy it – they're cheating you." You think he's sincere, but he's really in cahoots with your merchant; he tells you they are cheating you over the shawl only to win your confidence and secure your downfall the next minute by advising you to buy the carpet. While you examine it, they exchange signs, nudges, winks and whispers. If you know Greek, they speak Turkish; if you can follow Turkish, they speak Armenian; if you understand Armenian, they'll talk in Spanish; in one way or another they'll make sure they understand each other while you don't have a clue what they're saying. If you are hard to convince, they flatter you; tell you that you speak their language admirably, that you have the air of a perfect gentleman, and that they will never forget your handsome face; they talk about your country, which they have visited, since they have been everywhere; they give you coffee, and offer to accompany you to the custom house when you leave, ostensibly to prevent you being charged too much duty, but actually to cheat you, the custom house and your travelling companions, if you have any. They turn the whole shop upside down and are not at all put out if you buy nothing; if not now you will buy some other day; you are sure to come back to the bazaar and their hunting dogs will smell you out again; if you do not fall into their hands, you will fall into those of their associates; if they don't fleece you as merchants, they will skin you as middlemen; if they don't settle you in the shop, they will finish you at the custom house: they are certain to get you. Who are these people? No one knows. By dint of speaking many languages they have lost their original accent; because they put on an act all day long, they have changed the physiognomical features of their race; at any given moment they can be from any country they please, follow any trade they choose, be interpreters, guides, merchants, usurers; but above all, they are past masters at cheating the world and his wife.

The Muslim merchants offer a very different field of observation. Among them are still to be found those old Turks, now rare in the streets of Constantinople, who are like living personifications of the age of Mehmet and Beyazit; the flesh and bone vestiges of that old Ottoman edifice that first began to disintegrate under the reforms of Mahmut, and which continues day by day and stone by stone to crumble and change. Go to the Grand Bazaar and gaze into the depths of the little dark shops in the more remote streets, and there you will find the enormous old turbans of Süleyman's time, shaped like the cupola of a mosque; the impassive faces, glazed eyes, hooked noses, and long white beards; the antique orange and purple kaftans, the great pleated trousers tied round the waist with long sashes; the haughty, grave demeanour of the old master race, their faces dulled by opium, or glowing with ardent religious faith. They are there at the back of their dark narrow shops, sitting with folded arms and crossed legs, motionless and solemn as graven images, silently awaiting the arrival of the predestined purchaser. If things go well, they murmur "*Maşallah!*" ("God be praised!"), if they go badly, "*Olsun!*" ("Let it be!") and bend their heads in resignation. Some are reading the Koran, others finger their rosaries, listlessly muttering the hundred names of Allah; others who have just concluded a successful deal *drink their narghile*, as the Turkish expression has it, gazing round with a sleepy, voluptuous look; and others bend forward, with half-closed eyes, frowning as if in deep thought. What are they thinking? Perhaps of their sons who died under the walls of Sebastopol, or of their caravans which have been lost, or of their past pleasures, or the gardens of eternity promised by the Prophet, where under the shade of palms and pomegranate trees, they will wed the dark-eyed virgins untouched by man or genie.

Each one of them is odd and picturesque in his own way; every shop door is the frame of a picture full of colour and invention, which fills the mind with stories of adventure and romance. That lean, bronzed man with bold features is an Arab, who himself led his camels laden with gems and alabaster out of his own faraway country, and has more than once heard the desert robbers' bullets whistling over his head. This one in the yellow turban, with a lordly mien, has crossed the Syrian desert on horseback, bringing silk from Tyre and Sidon. The black man with his head wrapped in an old Persian shawl, and his forehead seamed with scars from incisions made by necromancers to protect him from death, who holds his head high, as if he were still looking at the Colossi of Thebes and the tops of the Pyramids, comes from Nubia. That handsome Moor with his pale face and black eyes, wrapped in a snow-white mantle, has brought his carpets from the furthermost ends of the Atlas mountains. The haggard-looking Turk in the green turban has just returned from the great pilgrimage, where he saw his friends and relations die of thirst in the never-ending plains of Asia Minor, and, arriving in Mecca half dead, dragged himself seven times round the Kaaba, and swooned as he covered the Black Stone with ardent kisses. The giant of a man with a white face, arched eyebrows and glaring eyes, who looks more like a warrior than a merchant, and whose whole bearing evokes pride and ambition, has brought his furs from the northern Caucasus, where in his youth he struck off many a Cossack's head from his shoulders; and this poor wool merchant, with his flat face and small oblique eyes, his body muscular and hard as an athlete's, was saying his prayers not so long ago under the shadow of the great dome that protects the tomb of Tamerlane;* he started out from Samarkand, crossed the deserts of Bukhara, journeyed through Turkoman hordes, sailed across the Dead Sea, escaped the bullets of the Circassians, gave thanks to Allah in the mosques of Trabzon, and came to seek his fortune in Stamboul, from where he will return, in his old age, to Tartary, which has kept a place for ever in his heart.

One of the most splendid bazaars is for shoes, and it is perhaps the one which excites the imagination most. There are two rows of glittering shops, making the street look like a room in a palace, or like one of those gardens in Arabian tales, where the trees have golden leaves and blossoms of pearl. There are enough shoes for all the little feet in all the courts of Asia and Europe. The walls are stacked with slippers; in velvet, in leather, in brocade, in satin, in the most startling colours and the oddest shapes, embroidered with filigree, glittering with sequins, decorated with swansdown and silk tassels, starred with flowers in gold and silver, completely covered with intricate arabesques, and sparkling with sapphires and emeralds. There are shoes for bargees' wives at five lira a pair and for sultans' mistresses costing a thousand. There are morocco-leather boots which will tread the cobbles of Pera, and pumps which will shuffle over the carpets of the harem, pattens that will echo on the marble floor of the imperial baths, small white satin slippers on which an amorous pasha will plant his kisses, and perhaps a pair of pearled ones which will wait beside the Sultan's bed for some beautiful Georgiana* to slip her feet into when she gets up. But where are the feet that can get into them? There are some that appear to have been made for houris or fairies; about as long as a lily leaf and wide as a rose petal, so small even the women of Andalusia would despair of getting them on, and so pretty you start to dream; these are not slippers but jewels to keep on your dressing table, boxes for sweets or billets-doux. It is impossible to believe you could find a foot small enough to fit into them – and I doubt you could resist the temptation of fondling such a foot for an entire month in your hands, showering it with questions and caresses. This bazaar is much frequented by foreigners. Young men from Europe can be seen there, holding a piece of paper with the size of some French or Italian foot of whose daintiness they are proud, and exclaiming in annoyance or amazement when they find it's far too big for some tiny slipper which has attracted their attention; others on asking the price take to their heels without a further word as if they'd heard a gun go off. Many Muslim women also come to buy here: *hanims* in large white veils, and often one can catch a fragment of their long conversations with the merchant, some harmonious words in their beautiful language, in their clear, sweet voices that caress the ear like the sound of a mandolin. *"Bunu kaça verirsin?"* ("How much is this?") *"Pahalıdır."* ("It is too much.") *"Ziyade veremem."* ("I won't pay any more.") And then a girlish ringing laugh that makes one want to pinch their cheeks and chuck them under the chin.

The richest and most picturesque of all the bazaars is the one which sells weaponry. It is a museum rather than a bazaar, brimming with treasures, the sight of which carries the imagination off into the realms of history and legend, and arouses an indescribable sentiment of wonder and dismay. All the cruellest, strangest, most frightening weapons that have ever been brandished in the defence of Islam, from Mecca to the Danube, are displayed here, bright and sharp, as if they had just been hung up on the wall by the fanatical soldiery of Mehmet or Selim: you can almost see glittering among them the bloodshot, fiery eyes of those formidable Sultans, those wild janissaries, those ruthless, fearless spahis, azabs, *silahtars*, who scattered severed heads and torn corpses over Asia Minor and Europe. Here can be found those famous scimitars that could cut a feather in the air, and slice off the ears of an insolent ambassador; those massive khanjars that with a single blow could split a man open and spill his innards; those maces that have battered Serbian and Hungarian helmets; yataghans with handles of carved ivory, encrusted with amethysts and rubies, whose blades are still notched with the number of heads they've lopped off; daggers with silver, velvet and satin sheaths, and handles of agate and ivory, set with garnets, coral and turquoises, inscribed with verses from the Koran in gold letters, and with curved and twisted blades that look as if they were searching for a heart to stab. Who knows if in this terrible and inexhaustible armoury Orhan's scimitar is to be found, or the wooden sabre with which the dervish warrior Abdal Murat sheared off a head with one stroke of his powerful arm, or the famous yataghan that Sultan Mussa used when he split Hassan from shoulder to chest, or the enormous sabre of that giant Bulgarian who planted the first ladder against the walls of Constantinople, or the mace with which Mehmet II struck dead the plundering soldier under the dome of Hagia Sophia, or the great damask-sheathed blade wielded by Skanderbeg* when he cut Firuz in two below the walls of Svetigrad? The most terrible blows and the most horrible deaths in all Ottoman history rise up before the mind's eye: those weapons seem still to drip with blood; no doubt the old Turks lurking in their shops have gathered up weapons and corpses on the battlefield and still keep the skeletons stashed in some dark corner. Among the weapons can also be seen great saddles of blue and crimson velvet, embroidered with stars and crescents in gold and pearl, with plumed frontals, and inlaid silver bits, and caparisons as splendid as royal mantles; objects out of the *Arabian Nights* made for the triumphal entry of a king of the genii into a golden city of dreams. On the walls above these treasures are hung ancient muskets with flint and wheel, great Albanian pistols, long Arabian rifles, worked like jewels, antique shields of tortoiseshell and hippopotamus hide, Circassian mail, Cossack targes, Mongol visors, Turkoman bows, assassins' daggers, horrid blades in sinister shapes: each one seems to reveal a crime and makes one think of the contortions of the death agony. In the midst of all this threatening and magnificent array the most obviously Turkish merchants in all the Grand Bazaar sit cross-legged: for the most part old and dour-looking, pale as anchorites and haughty as Sultans, figures out of the past, dressed in the fashion of the first Ottomans, looking as if they had been resuscitated from the tomb to recall their unworthy descendants back to the austerity of the ancestral race.

Another bazaar to be seen is the old-clothes bazaar. Here Rembrandt would have taken up residence and Goya would have spent his last peseta. If you have never seen an old-clothes shop in the Orient you cannot imagine the abundance of rags, the riot of colour, the piquant contrasts, the spectacle at once dreary, dirty and carnivalesque presented by the bazaar, this common sewer of rags, in which all the cast-offs from harems, barracks, courts and theatres are waiting for a painter's invention or a beggar's need to bring them back to the light of day. Dangling from long poles inserted in the walls are old Turkish uniforms, swallow-tailed jackets, lordly dolmans, dervish tunics, Bedouin cloaks, all grease-stained and tattered and torn, looking as if they had been pierced by poniards, and reminiscent of the sinister belongings of murder victims which are displayed on the tables of the assize courts. Here and there among the rags a scrap of gold embroidery glitters; old silk girdles, loosened turbans, rich shawls in tatters, velvet bodices from which it looks as if both pearls and the nap with them have been ripped off by a robber's hand, drawers and veils that perhaps belonged to some faithless beauty who now sleeps in a sack at the bottom of the Bosphorus, and other women's garments and ornaments, in delicate colours and textures, held captive among coarse Circassian kaftans with rusty cartridge belts, long black Jewish gowns, rough cassocks and heavy mantles that may have once concealed the bandit's gun or the cut-throat's dagger. Towards evening, in the mysterious light that falls from the holes pierced in the vaulted ceiling, all these pendent garments take on the appearance of bodies hanging from the gallows; and when in the darkness of a shop you see the glittering cunning eyes of some old Jew, scratching his forehead with his crooked fingers, you could believe it was the hand which tightened the noose, and you glance back over your shoulder to check the outer door of the bazaar is still open.

One day is not enough if you want to see all the ins and outs of this strange place. There is the fez bazaar, where fezzes from every country are sold, from Morocco to Vienna, adorned with inscriptions from the Koran that ward off evil spirits; those which the beautiful Greek women of Smyrna wear above the knot of their black tresses braided with coins; the red skullcaps of Turkish women; fezzes belonging to soldiers, generals, Sultans and dandies, in all shades of red and all shapes, from the earliest ones worn in the time of Orhan to the large and elegant fez of Sultan Mahmut, the emblem of reform, abhorred by elderly Muslims. There is the fur bazaar, where you can find the sacred black-fox pelt, which once could only be worn by the Sultan or his Grand Vizier; marten fur, which lined ceremonial kaftans; white bear and black bear, blue fox, astrakhan, ermine, and sable on which the Sultans would lavish fabulous sums. You should visit the cutlers' bazaar, if only to handle a pair of those enormous Turkish scissors with bronzed and gilded blades, engraved with fantastic designs of birds and flowers, which slice together in the most ferocious manner and open wide enough even for the head of a malignant critic. Then there are the bazaars of the gold-thread makers, of the embroiderers, sellers of knick-knacks, tailors, potters – all different in layout, some gloomy, some bright, but all alike in one respect: no woman ever sells or works there. Very occasionally some Greek woman, seated for a moment before a tailor's counter, will shyly offer you a handkerchief which she has just finished embroidering. Oriental jealousy forbids women to serve in shops, regarding them as schools of coquetry and intrigue.

But there are other parts of the Grand Bazaar where a stranger cannot venture unless he is accompanied by a merchant or a middleman; and these are the areas within each of the small quarters into which this singular city is divided, the interior of the buildings round which the crowded streets wind. If it is difficult not to lose your way in the street, here it is impossible. From corridors only a little wider than a man and so low that you can scarcely walk upright you come out into dimly lit courtyards no bigger than a cell, crammed with chests and bundles, to grope your way down some wooden steps, pass through other courtyards lit by lanterns, descend below ground level, emerge again into daylight, walk keeping your head down through long winding passages, under damp vaults, between black walls and mildewed floorboards, which lead to secret doors by which you find yourself unexpectedly at the point where you started; everywhere you see shadows coming and going, motionless spectral figures standing in corners, people moving merchandise or counting money; lights appear and disappear, the sound of voices and hurried steps comes from you know not where; unidentifiable black objects obstruct your path, strange gleams of light, odd textures and unfamiliar smells assail your senses, until you feel you're wandering in some sorcerer's cave and long to find the way out.

In general the middlemen take strangers into these places in order to lead them to those out-of-the-way shops where a little of everything is sold, a kind of Grand Bazaar in miniature, a sort of superior second-hand shop, curious to see but dangerous for the purse, for they contain such rare and fascinating objects that even a dyed-in-the-wool miser would not be able to resist them. These merchants deal in a little of everything and are of course confirmed rascals and cheats, and polyglot like the rest of their kind; they have a certain theatrical way of attracting clients which is entertaining to watch, and rarely fails. Their shops are almost all small and dark, full of presses and cupboards; you need to light a lamp and there is hardly enough room to turn round in. After showing you some small cabinet in carved ivory and mother-of-pearl, some Chinese porcelain or Japanese vase, the merchant says that he has something specially for you, and draws forth a casket from which he empties a heap of trinkets out onto the table: a fan of peacocks' feathers, for example, a bracelet made from old Turkish coins, a little camel-hair cushion with the Sultan's cipher embroidered in gold, a small Persian mirror painted with a scene from the *Book of Paradise*; a tortoiseshell spoon of the kind used by the Turks to eat cherry jam; an old ribbon of the Ottoman chivalric order. There is nothing here that pleases you? He opens another casket, and this time there can be no doubt it is meant for you alone. There is a broken elephant's tusk, a bracelet from Trabzon that looks like a tress of silver hair, a little Japanese idol, a sandalwood comb from Mecca, a large Turkish spoon carved in openwork and inlaid, an antique narghile in engraved silver gilt, fragments of mosaic from Hagia Sophia, a heron's plume which – the merchant swears on his honour – comes from the turban of Selim III. Is there nothing here that takes your fancy? And he opens another casket, and pulls out an ostrich egg from Sennar, a Persian inkhorn, a damascened ring, a Mingrelian bow, with its quiver of elk-skin, a Circassian double-pointed cap, a jasper *tesbih*, an incense burner of enamelled gold, a Turkish talisman, a camel driver's knife, a phial of attar of roses – is there nothing that tempts you yet, in Heaven's name? Haven't you got gifts to buy? Have you no thought for your relations? No remembrance of your friends? But perhaps you have a passion for cloths and carpets, and here too he can be of help. Here, my Lord, is a striped mantle from Kurdistan; here is a lion's skin, here is a carpet from Aleppo with steel nails, here is a carpet from Casablanca, three fingers thick, which is guaranteed to last for four generations; here, your excellency, are old cushions, old brocade, and old silk foot-muffs, a little faded and moth-eaten,

Cloth vendors at the Grand Bazaar

Scutari

but the embroidery! You won't find its like today, not even for a small fortune. For you, *caballero*, who have been brought here by a friend of mine, *you* shall have this sash for five napoleons, even if it means I have to live on bread and garlic for a week.

If you remain staunch against temptation, he will whisper in your ear that he can sell you the very rope with which the terrible mutes of the Seraglio strangled Nasuh Pasha, the Grand Vizier of Mahmut III; if you laugh in his face and tell him you won't fall for that story, he will drop it like the intelligent man he is and make one final attempt by throwing down in front of you a horsetail like those which are carried before and behind a pasha; or a janissary's helmet, carried off by his father, all stained with blood, on the very day of the famous massacre; or part of a flag from the Crimea, with the crescent and silver stars; or an agate washbasin; or a brazier in carved copper; or a dromedary's halter hung with shells and bells; or a eunuch's whip of hippopotamus hide, or a Koran bound in gold, or a scarf from Khorasan, or a pair of kadin's slippers with pointed toes, or a candlestick made from an eagle's talon, until at last your imagination catches fire and you are seized by a wild desire to throw down your wallet, watch, overcoat and cry out: "I'll take the lot!" And indeed you need to have the wisdom of Solomon to be capable of resisting. How many artists have come out of this place as naked as Job, and how many rich men have squandered away their heritage!

But before the Grand Bazaar closes, we should take one more turn and see it in the hour before it shuts. The movement of the crowd is more frenetic, the merchants' appeals more imperious, Greeks and Armenians run about with shawls and carpets over their arms, crying their wares; clusters of people gather, thin out, break up and gather together again further on; horses, carriages and beasts of burden file towards the exit. In that hour, all the merchants with whom you have bargained and quarrelled without coming to an agreement flit about you in the twilight like bats; they peep out at you from behind columns, come round corners so they can bump into you, cross your path at every turn, or step on your toes in feigned distraction, in order to remind you by their presence of that piece of cloth or that jewel, and re-awaken your desire for it. Sometimes you have a whole train of people shadowing you; if you stop, they stop, if you move to one side, they move to one side; and if you turn back you meet the stare of ten pairs of wide eyes fixed on you as if they'd like to eat you alive. But the light wanes, and the crowd is thinning; under the long vaulted roofs the voice of some invisible muezzin can be heard from some wooden minaret, announcing the close of day; some Turks spread their carpets and murmur their evening prayer in front of their shops; others perform their ablutions at the fountains. The elderly guardians in the weapons bazaar have already closed the great iron doors; the small bazaars are empty, the corridors are lost in darkness, the openings of streets gape like caverns, camels come upon you suddenly, the voices of the water vendors die away under the distant arches, Turkish women quicken their steps and eunuchs narrow their eyes, visitors leave hurriedly, the shutters are closed, the day is over.

* * *

And now I hear questions on all sides: "But what about Hagia Sophia? And the Old Seraglio? And the palaces of the Sultan? And the Castle of the Seven Towers? And Abdülaziz? And the Bosphorus?" I will readily describe everything in turn, but before I do, please allow me to continue to roam freely about Constantinople, changing my subject on every page, just as when I was there, my thoughts changed with every step I took.

## The Light

And first of all, the light! One of my most vivid pleasures in Constantinople was to see the sun rise and set from the bridge of the Sultana Valide. At dawn, in autumn, the Golden Horn is almost always covered by a light fog, behind which the city is seen vaguely, like those gauze curtains that descend upon the stage to conceal the preparations for a spectacular scene. Scutari is quite hidden; nothing can be made out but the dark uncertain outline of her hills. The bridge and the shores are deserted, Constantinople sleeps; the solitude and the silence make the sight more solemn. The sky begins to glow golden behind the hills of Scutari. Upon that luminous strip are drawn, one by one, black and sharply outlined, the tops of the cypress trees in the vast cemetery, like an army of giants ranged upon the heights; and from one end of the Golden Horn to the other, a tremulous light is gleaming, like the first shiver of the great city waking up. Then behind the cypresses on the Asian shore an eye of fire appears, and suddenly the white tops of the four minarets of Hagia Sophia are flushed with pink. In a few moments, from hill to hill, from mosque to mosque, down to the end of the Golden Horn, all the minarets, one after the other, turn rose colour, all the domes, one by one, are silvered, the flush descends from terrace to terrace, the tremulous gleam spreads, the great veil dissolves, and all Stamboul appears, rosy and resplendent upon her heights, blue and violet along the shores, clean and fresh, as if just risen from the waters. As the sun rises the delicacy of the first tints vanishes in an immense brightness, and everything remains bathed in brilliant light until twilight begins to fall. Then the divine spectacle begins again. The air is so limpid that from Galata one can see distinctly the distant trees beyond Kadiköy. The whole of Stamboul stands outlined against the sky with such clarity of form and vividness of colour, that each single minaret, obelisk, and cypress tree on the hills can be counted from Seraglio Point to the cemetery of Eyüp. The Golden Horn and the Bosphorus take on a wonderful ultramarine colour; the heavens, the colour of amethyst in the east, are flaming behind Stamboul, tinting the horizon with infinite gleams of rose and carbuncle that make one think of the first day of creation; Stamboul darkens, Galata becomes golden, and Scutari, struck by the last rays of the setting sun, with every pane of glass giving back the glow, looks like a city on fire. This is the best hour of day to contemplate Constantinople. There is one rapid succession of the softest tints, pale gold, rose and lilac, which quiver and float over the hillsides and upon the water, each moment awarding the prize of beauty to a different part of the city then taking it away, revealing a thousand modest graces of the landscape that have not dared to show themselves in the full light of day. The great melancholy suburbs are lost in the shadow of the valleys; little purple towns smile upon the heights; the light ebbs away from villages as if they are about to expire; some disappear at once like extinguished flames; others, that seemed already dead, suddenly revive and glow and quiver for a few more moments under the last rays of the sun. Then there is nothing left but two resplendent points upon the Asian shore; the summit of Mount Bulgurlu, and the extremity of the cape that guards the entrance to the Propontis; at first they are two golden crowns, then two purple caps, then two rubies; then all Constantinople is in shadow, and ten thousand voices from ten thousand minarets proclaim the close of day.

EDMONDO DE AMICIS

# The Birds

Constantinople has one grace and gaiety peculiar to itself: its infinite number of birds of every kind, for which the Turks nourish a warm sentiment of sympathy and regard. Mosques, groves, old walls, gardens, palaces, all resound with the cooing, chirping and twittering of birdsong; the flutter of wings is heard everywhere, and vivacity and harmony abound. Bold sparrows enter houses and peck from women's and children's hands; swallows nest over the café doors and under the arches of the bazaars; innumerable flocks of pigeons, maintained by legacies from Sultans and private individuals, form garlands of black and white along the cornices of the cupolas and around the terraces of the minarets; seagulls swoop around the caiques over the water, thousands of turtle doves coo amorously among the cypresses in the cemeteries; about the Castle of the Seven Towers crows caw and vultures wheel; halcyons come and go in long files between the Black Sea and the Sea of Marmara; and storks clatter their bills upon the cupolas of the solitary mausoleums. For the Turks, each one of these birds has some sweet significance or benign virtue: turtle doves are favourable to lovers, swallows ward off fire from the roofs where they build their nests, storks make yearly pilgrimages to Mecca, halcyons carry the souls of the faithful to paradise. So the people protect and feed them through a sentiment of gratitude and piety, and they enliven the house, the sea, and the sepulchre. Their noisy flocks circle and wheel and skim over every quarter of Stamboul, bringing a sense of the pleasures of country life to the city, and continually refreshing the soul with a reminder of the natural world.

# Memories

In no other city in Europe do places and legendary or historical monuments excite the imagination as in Stamboul, for in no other city do they record events so recent and yet so fantastic. Anywhere else, in order to find the poetry of the past, one must go back in thought some centuries, but in Stamboul a few years will suffice. Legend, or that which has the nature and the effect of legend, is of yesterday. It is but a few years since the fabled massacre of the janissaries was carried out in the Atmeydanı; only a few years since the twenty sacks containing the bodies of Mustafa's courtesans were thrown up by the Sea of Marmara on the shores of the Imperial gardens; since the family of Brancovan* were put to death in the Castle of the Seven Towers; since two *kapıcı başıs* led European ambassadors by both arms into the presence of the *Grand Signor*, only half of whose face could be seen, lit by a mysterious light; and since the strange life of the Seraglio ceased, that mingling of love, horror and madness which makes it seem centuries distant. Wandering about Stamboul with these thoughts, one is conscious of a feeling of astonishment at seeing the city so tranquil and cheerful with all its colour and verdure. "Ah! Traitress!" you exclaim, "What have you done with those mountains of severed heads, and those lakes of blood? Is it possible it is all so well hidden, swept and washed away, that no trace of it remains?" On the Bosphorus, opposite the tower of Leander that rises from the water like a monument to love, under the walls of the Seraglio gardens, you can still see the slope down which faithless concubines were rolled into the sea; in the midst of the Atmeydanı the serpentine column still bears the mark of the famous sabre-stroke of Mehmet the Conqueror; on the bridge of Mahmut the spot is still shown where the fiery Sultan struck dead with one blow of his sword the audacious dervish who hurled an anathema in his face; in the cistern of the ancient church of Balıklı the miraculous fish which predicted the fall of the city of the Paleologi still dart about; under the trees of the Sweet Waters of Asia the shady groves can be shown where a dissolute sultana demanded from the men her favour had momentarily lit upon a love that would end in their death. Every door, every tower, every mosque, every square recalls some prodigy, or some carnage, some love or mystery, a Padishah's prowess or Sultana's whim, every place has its legend; and every near at hand object and every distant view, the air and the silence, carry the visitor's imagination steeped in these memories away from the present and the city of today and from himself, and conjure up the past, until the idea of going back to one's hotel seems incongruous and strange. "What?" you think, "Is there such a thing as a hotel?"

\* \* \*

## *Resemblances*

During my first few days in the city, fresh as I was from my preparatory reading, I saw the famous personages of history and of legend everywhere around me, and the figures that recalled them resembled sometimes so closely my images of them that I had to stop and stare at them. How many times have I seized my friend by the arm, and pointing to a person passing by, exclaimed: "But just look at him! Don't you recognize him?" In the square of the Sultana Valide, I frequently saw the gigantic Turk who threw boulders down from the walls of Nicaea on the heads of Bouillon's soldiers;* in front of the mosque I came face to face with Umm Jamil, the old hag from Mecca who sowed brambles and nettles in front of Mohammad's house; in the book market I came across Jalal al-Din,* the eminent scholar from Bursa, who knew the whole of the Arabic dictionary by heart, carrying a volume under his arm; I passed quite close to Aishah, the favourite wife of the Prophet, who fixed her eyes on me, brilliant and gleaming "like the reflection of a star in a well'; in the Atmeydanı I recognized the celebrated beauty of that poor Greek woman, killed by a cannon ball from one of Urban's cannon* at the foot of the serpentine column; in Fener I encountered Kara Abdurrahman, the handsomest young Turk from the time of Orhan; I saw al-Qaswa, the she-camel of the Prophet, and Karabulut, Selim's black steed; I met the poor poet Fighani,* who was condemned to go about Stamboul tied to an ass, for penning a satirical couplet on Ibrahim's Grand Vizier; I sat in the same café with Süleyman the Fat, the monstrously corpulent admiral, who needed four strong slaves just to lift him from his divan; Ali, the Grand Vizier, who could not find in the whole of Arabia a horse capable of carrying him; Mahmut Pasha, the ferocious strongman who strangled the son of Süleyman; and the idiot Ahmet II, who continually repeated "*Koç! Koç!*" ("Very good! Very good!"), as he crouched in front of the door of the scriveners' market in Beyazit square. All the characters in the *Arabian Nights*, the Aladdins, the Zobeides, the Sinbads, the Gulnares, the old Jewish merchants, owners of magic carpets and miraculous lamps, passed before me like a procession of phantoms.

\* \* \*

## *Clothing*

Now is the best time to see the Muslim population of Constantinople – in the last century they were too uniform, and in the next they'll probably be the same. Today we catch them in the process of transformation, and thus they present an extraordinary variety. The progress of the reformers, the resistance of the old Turks, and the uncertainties and hesitations of the great mass of people who oscillate between the two extremes – all the phases, in short, of the struggle between the old and the new Turkey – are faithfully represented in the variety of costume. The inflexible old Turk still wears the turban, the kaftan and the traditional slippers of yellow morocco leather; and the more obstinate the man, the bigger his turban. The reformed Turk wears a long black frock coat buttoned to the chin, dark trousers with spats, and nothing Turkish but the fez. The more youthful among them, however, have already discarded the black frock coat, and wear open waistcoats, light-coloured trousers, elegant cravats, watch chains, a flower in the buttonhole, and carry a walking stick. Between these and the others, the kaftans and the frock coats, there is an abyss; they have nothing in common but the name of Turk; they are two entirely different peoples. The turbaned Turk still believes firmly in the bridge of Sirat over the infernal regions, finer than a hair and sharper than a scimitar; he performs his ablutions at the proper hours, and goes home at sunset. The Turk in the black frock coat laughs at the Prophet, likes to be photographed, speaks French, and spends his evenings at the theatre. Between them there is the waverer, who still wears the turban, but a very small one, so it would hardly be noticed if he changed it for a fez; some still wear the kaftan, but have already started to wear a fez; others dress in the old style, but without sash, slippers, or bright colours; and little by little they will get rid of the rest. The women keep only the veil and mantle that conceal their bodies; but the veil has become transparent and sometimes lets you catch a glimpse of a plumed hat underneath, and the mantle often covers a gown cut after a Parisian model. Every year sees the fall of thousands of kaftans, and the rise of thousands of frock coats; every day an old Turk dies, and a reformed Turk is born. Newspapers replace *tesbih*s, cigars rather than chibouks are smoked, wine is drunk instead of sugared water; the coach displaces the araba; French not Arabic grammar is studied; pianos take the place of timbrels and houses are built of stone rather than wood. Everything is changing, everything is being transformed. Perhaps in less than a century from now we will have to search out what remains of old Turkey in the furthest reaches of the more distant provinces of Asia Minor, just as we now find old Spain only in the most remote villages of Andalusia.

## The Future of Constantinople

This thought often came to me as I contemplated Constantinople from the bridge of the Sultana Valide. What will this city have become in one or two centuries' time, even if the Turks are not driven out of Europe? Alas! The great sacrifice of beauty to modern civilization will already have been accomplished. I see her, the Constantinople of the future, that London of the East, rising up in gloomy, oppressive majesty upon the ruins of the loveliest city on earth. The hills will be levelled, the groves cut down, the brightly painted houses demolished; the horizon will be closed on every side by long, rigid lines of apartment blocks, workers' housing and workshops, interspersed with a thousand factory chimneys and clock towers with pyramid-shaped roofs. Long, straight, regular avenues will divide Stamboul, gridlike, into ten thousand enormous districts; telegraph wires will criss-cross over the roofs of the noisy city like a vast spider's web; a black torrent of top hats and caps will flow all day long over the bridge of the Sultana Valide; the mysterious hill of the Seraglio will be a zoological park; the Castle of the Seven Towers a prison, the Hebdomon a museum of natural history: the whole will be solid, geometrical, useful, grey and ugly, and a great dark ever-present cloud will cover the beautiful skies of Thrace, towards which neither the prayers of the pious, the tender gaze of lovers nor the songs of the poets will be raised. When this image comes before me, my heart grows heavy; but then a thought consoles me: who knows if in the twenty-first century, some Italian bride, on her honeymoon here, may not exclaim: "It's such a shame that Constantinople has changed so much. It's not at all like the place described in this old moth-eaten book I came across by chance in Grandmama's cupboard!"

\* \* \*

CONSTANTINOPLE

## *The Dogs*

And by then no doubt one of the city's most engaging peculiarities will also have disappeared: its dogs. This is a fascinating subject and one it's worth spending some time on. Constantinople is one vast dog kennel; everyone notices it as soon as he arrives. The dogs constitute a second population of the city, less numerous, but no less strange than its human one. Everyone knows how much the Turks love them and protect them. I couldn't find out whether this is because charitableness towards all creatures is enjoined in the Koran, or because, like certain birds, the dogs are thought to bring good fortune, or because the Prophet loved them, or because the sacred books speak of them, or because, as some claim, Mehmet the Conqueror brought in his train a numerous company of dogs, who entered the city in triumph along with him through the breach in the St Romanus gate. The fact is they are highly regarded: many Turks leave large sums in their wills for their support, and when Sultan Abdülmecit had them all removed to an island in the Sea of Marmara, the people protested and held a huge celebration when they were brought back. In order to avoid provoking such discontent again, the government has left them in peace ever since. However, according to the Koran, the dog is also an unclean animal, and every Turk believes he would contaminate his house by sheltering one under his roof, so it follows that not one of the innumerable dogs of Constantinople has a master. They form a great free and vagabond republic, collarless and nameless, without tasks to perform, without a home to go to, without rules to obey. They pass their lives in the streets: here they dig small dens, sleep, eat, are born, suckle their young, and die; and no one, at least in Stamboul, ever thinks of disturbing their occupations or their repose. They are the masters of the public highways. In our cities the dogs make way for the horseman or pedestrian; there it is the people, the horses, the camels, the donkeys, who make way for the dogs. In the busiest parts of Stamboul four or five dogs, curled up asleep in the middle of the road, will cause the entire population of the area to go out of their way for half a day. It is the same in Galata and Pera, although here they are left in peace, not so much out of respect, but because otherwise you would spend the entire working day chasing them away.

They are with difficulty disturbed even when in the crowded streets a four-horse carriage is seen approaching like the wind, too fast to swerve and avoid them. Then, but not before the very last moment, when the horses' hooves are nearly coming down on their heads, do they get up and lope a couple of yards out of the way – just enough and no more to save their lives. Laziness is the distinctive trait of the dogs of Constantinople. They lie down in the middle of the road, five, six, ten in a row, or in a ring, curled up so that they look more like a heap of dung than living creatures, and there they sleep the whole day through, among throngs of people coming and going, surrounded by a deafening hubbub, and neither cold nor heat, rain nor shine can get them to budge. When it snows they stay under the snow; when it rains they lie in the mud up to their ears, so that when at length they get up they look like clay models of dogs, with no visible eyes or ears or muzzles.

In Pera and Galata, however, they are less indolent because it is not so easy to find food there. In Stamboul they are on full board, but in Pera and Galata they have to eat *à la carte*. They are the scavengers, the living brooms of the street. What the swine reject is a choice dish for them. Except for stones, they eat everything, and when they've eaten enough to keep starvation at bay, they curl up and go to sleep again until the pangs of hunger wake them. They almost always sleep in the same spots. Just like the human population, the canine inhabitants of Constantinople are divided into districts. Every quarter, every street is inhabited, or rather owned by a certain number of dogs, their relatives and friends, who never leave it, and never allow strangers to enter. They exercise a sort of police patrol. They have their guards, their advance posts, their sentinels; they do the rounds and reconnoitre. Woe to any dog from another quarter who, driven by hunger, dares to enter his neighbours' precincts! A pack of enraged curs fall upon him at once, and if they catch him, it is all over with him; if they cannot get him, they chase him furiously as far as the frontier of their territory – but no further: the enemy's country is always feared and respected. It is impossible to describe the fury of the tussles and fights that take place over a bone, an attractive bitch, or a territorial violation. At every moment a confused scrum of dogs can be seen, half invisible in a cloud of dust; their barks and yelps and howls would wake the dead; then they disperse – and through the dust appear the victims stretched out over the field of battle. Love, jealousy, duels, blood, broken legs and torn ears are everyday incidents. Sometimes larger groups of them form and make such a disturbance in front of some shop that the shopkeeper and his assistants have to arm themselves with sticks and stools and make a military sortie to clear the street: you can hear the crack of heads and spines, and the dogs' howling fills the air.

In Pera and Galata especially, the poor beasts are so ill treated and so used to getting a blow whenever they see a stick that the mere tap of an umbrella or cane puts them on the alert; and even when they seem to be asleep, they keep one eye half open, the pupil like a pinprick, to follow attentively and from far off the slightest movements of anything which appears to be a stick. So little accustomed are they to kindly human attention that it is enough to stroke one in passing, and ten others will run and jump about you, wagging their tails and whining, and follow you to the end of the street, their eyes shining with joy and gratitude. It is enough to say that the condition of a dog in Pera and Galata is worse than that of a spider in Holland, which is the most persecuted creature in the animal kingdom. When you see them, you have to believe they will be compensated in the afterlife. And they too, like everything else in Constantinople, called up a historical memory for me, but a bitterly ironical one: the famous hunting dogs of Sultan Beyazit that coursed through the imperial forests on Olympus in crimson coats and jewelled collars. What a difference in social status! Their unhappy fate depends also in part upon their ugliness. They are almost all mastiffs or German shepherds. There is something of the wolf and the fox in their appearance. They are the horrible products of fortuitous couplings, spotted with strange colours, about the size of so-called butchers' dogs, and so lean you can count their ribs twenty yards off. Besides being thin as rakes, most of them have been reduced by repeated scuffles to such a physical state that if you didn't see them move you would think they were carcasses. Broken tails, torn ears, mangy fur and scarred necks, one-eyed, lame, covered with galls and devoured by flies: reduced to the worst state a living dog can be in, they are relics of war and hunger and sexual disease. Tails can be said to be a great luxury: it is rare for a Constantinople dog to have its entire tail for more than two months of public life. Poor beasts! A heart of stone would be moved with pity. Yet there are some among them, so bizarrely lopped and gnawed, with such an odd languid waddle or grotesque totter, that it is impossible not to laugh at them. And hunger and fights and beatings are not their worst afflictions. A cruel usage has lately become common in Galata and Pera. The tranquil residents are often woken in the night by a diabolical racket; looking out of the window they see in the street below a terrifying crowd of dogs leaping up high in the air, whirling round and round, and beating their heads furiously against the walls. In the morning the ground is strewn with their corpses. The young doctor of the neighbourhood and the local apothecary have been studying at night: to stop the dogs disturbing their studies, they have managed to ensure a week of quiet by distributing poisoned meatballs. This and other measures mean that the number of dogs in Pera and Galata is in continual decline, but what is the point? In Stamboul they increase and multiply, until they run out of food and emigrate to the other shore and so replace with their innumerable progeny all the gaps made in their ranks by battle, famine and poison.

## The Eunuchs

But there are other beings in Constantinople who excite more compassion than the dogs: the eunuchs, who still survive as they were first introduced among the Turks, despite the explicit precepts of the Koran, which condemns this infamous degradation of nature, and notwithstanding the recent laws which prohibit the trade in them, since the monetary greed which motivates the crime and the ruthless egotism which avails itself of it are stronger than the law. These unfortunates are to be met with everywhere in the city, just as they are found on every page of the history books. In the background of every event in Turkish history stands one of these sinister figures weaving an intricate plot; covered with gold or running with blood, victim or favourite or executioner, openly or covertly powerful, looming like a spectre in the shadow of the throne, or crouching at the keyhole of a mysterious door. So today in Constantinople, in the midst of the busy crowd, in the bazaars, among the holidaymakers at the Sweet Waters, between the columns of the mosques, beside carriages, on steamers and caiques, at all the festivals, in every crowd, you can see this shadow of a man, this doleful figure, whose presence is a lugubrious stain upon all the pleasant amenities of oriental life. Their political influence has diminished along with the power of the court, just as their importance in private houses has also much declined with the relaxation in the strict code of oriental decorum. Thus the benefits of their condition are disappearing: it is much more difficult for them now to find a compensation for their misfortune in the acquisition of wealth and power. No Gazanfer Aga* could now be found to consent to mutilation in order to become chief of the white eunuchs. Today they are all certainly mere victims, and victims without hope of redress; bought or abducted as children in Abyssinia or in Syria, one in three survives the infamous knife and is sold in defiance of the law, with a hypocritical secrecy more hateful than any open market would be. They do not need to be pointed out as they are easily recognized from their appearance. Almost all are tall, fat and flabby, with beardless, withered faces, short in the body, with very long legs and arms. They wear a fez, a long dark frock coat and European-style trousers, and they carry a whip of hippopotamus hide, which is their insignia of office. They walk with long lazy strides like lanky children. They accompany the ladies on foot or on horseback, either preceding or following their carriages, singly or in pairs, and keep a vigilant eye about them; the slightest irreverent look or gesture from a passer-by receives a ferocious and frightening glare. Except when this happens, their faces remain completely impassive or express only infinite weariness. I do not recall ever having seen one smile. There are some very youthful eunuchs who look as if they were fifty and some elderly ones who seem like adolescents who've grown old in a day. Many are so plump and round, pudgy and white they look like fattened pigs; all are dressed in fine clothes, groomed and perfumed like vain young dandies. Some heartless men can see these unfortunate beings and laugh. Perhaps they think that since they've been like this from childhood they are oblivious to their own wretchedness. On the contrary, we know that they do understand and feel it; and even if we didn't, how could it be doubted? They belong to no sex, they merely seem like men; they live among the rest of us and see themselves separated by an abyss; they feel life beating around them like a sea and they must stand there, motionless and solitary as a rock; their intimate thoughts and feelings are strangled by an iron circlet that no human force can ever break; they have perpetually before them an image of happiness, towards which all things tend, around which all things move, by which all things are coloured and illuminated, and they feel themselves immeasurably remote, in darkness, in a great, cold void, like creatures accursed of God. They are in fact the custodians of that felicity, the barriers which jealous husbands plant between their pleasures and the world, bolts on the door, rags which conceal the treasure wrapped inside; they have to live among perfumes and seductions, youth, beauty, and merrymaking, with shame on their faces, rage in their souls, scorned and sneered at, without a name, without a family, without a mother, without sweet memories, segregated from humanity and nature. It must be a torment inconceivable to the human mind, like living with a dagger fixed in the heart.

And this infamy is still allowed; these unhappy wretches walk about the streets of a European city, live in the midst of men, and do not howl, or bite, or kill, or spit in the faces of that cowardly humanity that can look upon them without blushing or weeping, and that forms international associations for the protection of cats and dogs! Their lives are one continual torture. When their mistresses do not find them helpful in their intrigues they hate them as spies and jailors, and torment them with cruel coquetries that drive them mad with fury, like the poor black eunuch in the *Persian Letters* as he puts his mistress into the bath.* Sarcasm dogs them; they are named after flowers and perfumes, in allusion to the ladies whose custodians they are: "possessors of the hyacinths, guardians of the lilies, custodians of the roses and the violets". Sometimes the miserable wretches fall in love! – since only the effects but not the causes of passion have been eradicated in them. They are jealous and weep tears of blood; and when they see someone paying court to their mistress who welcomes their attentions they often lose their reason altogether and lash out. At the time of the Crimean war, a eunuch struck a French officer across the face with his whip; the officer then split the eunuch's head open with his sabre. Who can say what pangs they feel at the sight of beauty, a smile, an ingratiating gesture, or how often at the sound of a kiss they finger the hilts of their daggers? It is small wonder that in the immense void of their hearts there is only room for the cold passions of hatred, revenge and ambition; that they grow up bitter, sharp-tongued, cowardly, ferocious; that they are either stupidly loyal or cunningly treacherous, and that when they are powerful they seek to avenge upon men the wrong that has been done to them. But however sad they become, their need for the companionship of women remains strong, and since they may not take them as lovers, they seek them as friends; they marry, choosing a pregnant woman, like Sünbül, the chief eunuch of Ibrahim I, in order to have a child they can love. They have a harem of virgins, like the chief eunuch of Ahmet II, so that they are surrounded by beauty and grace, affectionate embraces, an illusion of love; they adopt a daughter in order to have a woman's breast on which to rest their heads when old, so as not to die without one caress, and to hear in their final years a kind and loving voice, after having heard throughout their lives nothing but the sarcastic laugh of contempt; and there are those among them, who, after they have become rich at court or in great private houses, where they are often both chief eunuch and major-domo, purchase a pretty villa on the Bosphorus in their old age, and there try to forget, to deaden the remembrance of their own wretchedness in the gaiety of parties and guests. Among the many stories that were told me about these unhappy beings, one has remained vivid in my memory: it was recounted by a young doctor in Pera and it confutes the arguments of those who insist that eunuchs do not suffer: "One evening," he said, "I was coming out of a wealthy Muslim's house, where I had gone for the third time to visit one of his four wives, who was ill with heart disease. At my departure, as at my arrival, I was accompanied by a eunuch, calling out in the customary way: "Women, withdraw," in order to warn the ladies of the house and their slaves that a stranger was in the harem and that they must not be seen. In the courtyard the eunuch left me to find my own way to the gate. Just as I was about to open it, I felt a touch upon my arm, and turning, saw before me in the twilight another eunuch, a pleasant-looking young man of eighteen or twenty years of age, who stared at me with eyes brimming with tears. I asked him what he wanted. He hesitated a moment before replying, and then seizing my hand in both of his, and pressing it convulsively, said in a trembling voice, full of despairing grief: "Doctor! You who know the remedy for every ill, do you know of one for mine?" I cannot tell you how those simple words affected me; I tried to answer, but my voice failed me, and not knowing what to say or do, I quickly opened the door and fled. But for the rest of that evening, and for many days after, I seemed to see that young man and hear his words, and I almost wept with pity."

O philanthropists, public men, ministers, ambassadors, and you, deputies to the Parliament of Stamboul, and senators of the Crescent, raise your voices in the name of God against this ignominy, this horrid blot upon the honour of humanity, so that in the twentieth century it may become, like the massacres in Bulgaria,* merely a painful memory.

\* \* \*

# The Army

Although I knew before going to Constantinople that all traces of the splendid army of olden times had long gone, I was still eager to see its soldiers, since military matters always interest me, as soon as I arrived. But I found the reality much worse than I had anticipated. In place of the loose-fitting, picturesque and warlike costume of former times, I found tight black uniforms, red trousers, narrow jackets, ushers' stripes, schoolboys' belts, and on every head, from the Sultan down to the private, the deplorable fez, which, besides looking mean and silly, especially on top of the heads of corpulent Muslims, is the cause of endless eye-strain and headaches. The Turkish army has lost its former handsomeness and has not yet acquired that of a European army; the soldiers looked sad, unkempt and dirty; they may be brave, but they do not inspire sympathy. As for their breeding, the following incidents will show what this amounts to: I have seen both officers and soldiers in the street blowing their noses into their hands; a soldier on guard duty on the bridge, where smoking is prohibited, snatching the cigar out of a vice-consul's mouth; and another soldier in the Mosque of the Whirling Dervishes in Pera who wanted to make three Europeans understand they had to remove their hats and so knocked all three off their heads with one blow. And I learned that if you complain about such behaviour, you are seized like a sack of potatoes and carted off to the guardhouse. For which reason, all the time I was in Constantinople, I treated soldiers with scrupulous respect. But I also ceased to wonder at their ways when I saw what manner of men they were before they joined the army. One day I came across about a hundred recruits, probably from the interior of Asia Minor, passing through the streets of Stamboul, and was filled with pity and disgust. I seemed to be looking at the frightful bandit troops of Hassan the Mad, who marched through Constantinople at the end of the sixteenth century, on their way to die under Austrian grapeshot in the plains of Pest. I can still see those sinister faces, those long tangled tresses of hair, those half-naked and tattooed bodies, the savage ornaments they wore, and can smell the odour which they left in their wake, like a zoo of wild beasts. When the first news of the massacres in Bulgaria arrived, I thought of them at once. It must have been done by my friends in Scutari, I said to myself. However, they are the sole picturesque image that remains to me of Muslim soldiers. The splendid armies led by Beyazit, Süleyman and Mehmet – would that I might see them just once, arrayed upon the plain of Davutpaşa! Every time I passed in front of the triumphal Adrianople gate, those armies came before my mind's eye like a luminous vision, and I would stop to look up at the edifice, as if at any moment the pasha quartermaster, herald of the imperial staff, might appear.

For it was the pasha quartermaster who marched at the head of the army, with two horsetails, the insignia of his office. Behind him in the distance a vivid gleam could be seen, produced by eight thousand copper spoons stuck in the janissaries' turbans, in the midst of which the waving heron plumes and glittering armour of the colonels were visible, followed by a crowd of servants loaded with weapons and provisions. Behind the janissaries came a small army of irregular soldiers and pages, in silken vests, chainmail armour, and gleaming helmets, accompanied by bands of musicians; after these, the cannoneers, dragging their cannon all attached with iron chains, then another small army of agas, pages, chamberlains and vassals, mounted upon mailed and plumed steeds. And this was merely the vanguard. Above the serried ranks fluttered standards of every colour, horsetails waved, lances, swords, bows, quivers and muskets clashed: among them the sunburnt faces of the soldiers from the wars in Candia and Persia could scarcely be made out; and the discordant sounds of drums, flutes, trumpets and timbrels, the voices of the singers who accompanied the janissaries, the clash of armour, the jingling of chains, the shouts of "Allah!" were all mingled in one festive and warlike noise that resounded from the camp of Davutpaşa to the opposite shore of the Golden Horn.

Ah! Painters and poets who have lovingly depicted that beautiful oriental world, now vanished forever, help me to conjure out from the old walls of Stamboul the legendary army of Mehmet III.

The vanguard has gone by; another dazzling throng advances. Is it the Sultan? No, the god has not yet perhaps left the temple. It is only the entourage of the favourite vizier. There are forty agas dressed in sables, upon forty horses caparisoned in velvet and with silver reins, behind which comes a crowd of pages and magnificent grooms leading another forty steeds covered with gold, and loaded with shields, maces and scimitars. Another cortège advances. It is not yet the Sultan. They are the members of the Council of State, the high dignitaries of the Seraglio, and the Grand Treasurer, accompanied by musicians and a swarm of irregular troops in crimson caps ornamented with birds' wings, and dressed in furs, flesh-coloured silk, leopard skins, and Hungarian *kalpaks*,* and armed with long lances wound round with silk, and garlanded with flowers.

Another glittering swarm of cavalry sweeps through the gate of Adrianople. It is not yet the Sultan. It is the cortège of the Grand Vizier. First comes a crowd of harquebusiers on horseback, of quartermasters and agas favoured by the *Grand Signor*, and then come a further forty agas of the Grand Vizier surrounded by a forest of twelve hundred bamboo lances carried by as many pages, and another forty pages of the Grand Vizier dressed in orange and armed with bows and quivers embroidered with gold, and another two hundred young boys divided into six bands of six different colours, among which ride provincial governors and the Prime Minister and their families, followed by a throng of grooms, armourers, clerks, servants, pages, agas in golden vests and banner-bearers with silken flags; last of all comes the Kiaya, or Minister of the Interior, surrounded by twelve *çavuş*, or state executioners, followed by the Grand Vizier's band.

Another throng issues from the gate. It is not yet the Sultan. It is a crowd of *çavuş* and quartermasters and other officials, dressed in splendid livery, who escort the judges, mullahs and the *müderris*; behind them comes the chief keeper of the falcons, vultures, sparrowhawks and kites, with a train of horsemen carrying on their saddles leopards trained for the hunt, and a procession of falconers, grooms, quarterers, ferret-keepers, trumpeters, and packs of caparisoned and bejewelled hunting dogs.

Another company appears. The closely packed spectators prostrate themselves; it is the Sultan! No – not yet; it is not the head, but the heart of the army; the sacred ark, the fire of courage and pious zeal, the Muslim caroche, around which corpses will pile up and torrents of blood will flow, the green standard of the Prophet, the ensign of ensigns, taken from the Mosque of Sultan Ahmet, fluttering over a ferocious crowd of dervishes, covered with lion skins and bear skins, encircled by a band of enraptured preaching sheikhs, wrapped in camel-hair cloaks, between two ranks of emirs, descendants of the Prophet, wearing green turbans; and all together they raise a threatening and sinister clamour of hurrahs and roars, shouts and prayers and sacred songs.

Yet another wave of men and horses. It is not yet the Sultan. It is a troop of *çavuş*, brandishing their silver batons to make way for the

Judge of Constantinople, and the Grand Judge of Europe and of Asia, whose enormous turbans tower above the crowd; then the favourite vizier, and the vizier kaimakam, in turbans starred and striped with silver and gold; then all the viziers of the Divan in front of whom henna-dyed horsetails wave from the tips of red and blue spears; and finally the military judges followed by an interminable line of servants in leopard skins carrying poles, together with pages and armourers and *vivandiers*.

Another great mass of glittering colour and splendour: this at last must be the Sultan. But it is not yet the Sultan. It is the Grand Vizier, dressed in a purple kaftan lined with sable, mounted upon a horse covered with steel and gold, followed by a swarm of servants dressed in red velvet, and surrounded by a throng of high dignitaries and lieutenant generals of the janissary troops, among whom the muftis can be seen like white swans in the middle of peacocks. Behind these, between two ranks of lancers in gilded *justaucorps* and a double file of archers with crescent crests, come the resplendent Seraglio grooms, leading a troop of Arab, Turkoman, Persian and Karamanian horses, with velvet saddles, braided silver ribbons, golden bridles, damascened stirrups, and carrying bucklers and weapons sparkling with precious gems; last of all, two sacred camels, one of which carries the Koran and the other a relic of the Kaaba.

Once the cortège of the Grand Vizier has passed by, there is a great crash of loud music from drums and trumpets, the spectators hastily draw back, the cannon booms, a troop of outriders bursts through the gate, whirling their scimitars round their heads, and here at last, in the midst of a dense forest of spears, plumes and swords, surrounded by a dazzling glitter of gold and silver helmets, under a vast canopy of silken banners, is the Sultan of Sultans, the King of Kings, the distributor of crowns to the princes of the world, the shadow of God on earth, the Emperor and Sovereign Lord of the White Sea and the Black Sea, of Rumelia and Anatolia, of the province of Dulkadir, of Diyarbakir, of Kurdistan, Azerbaijan, Ajem, Shaam, Aleppo, Egypt, Mecca, Medina, Jerusalem, and all the regions of Arabia and of Yemen, together with all the other provinces conquered by his own glorious predecessors and august ancestors, or subjected to his glorious majesty by his own flame-like victorious sword.* The solemn and awe-inspiring cortège passes slowly by, and every now and then a glimpse may be caught of the three jewelled feathers in the turban of the god, his pale and serious face, his breastplate flashing with diamonds; then the circle closes in, the cavalcade passes on, the menacing scimitars are lowered, the terrified spectators lift their eyes, the vision has disappeared.

The imperial entourage is followed by a throng of court officials, one of whom carries on his head the Sultan's footstool, another his sabre, another his turban, another his mantle, a fifth the silver coffee pot, and a sixth the golden coffee pot; other groups of pages pass; a troop of white eunuchs, three hundred chamberlains on horseback, dressed in white kaftans; then come the hundred carriages of the harem with silver wheels, drawn by oxen garlanded with flowers, or by horses with velvet trappings, and flanked by a legion of black eunuchs; then three hundred mules laden with the baggage and treasury of the court, a thousand camels carrying water, a thousand dromedaries carrying provisions; troops of armourers, engineers and workmen, accompanied by bands of jesters and jugglers, and finally the bulk of the fighting army: the hordes, the janissaries, yellow *silahtars*, purple azabs, spahis with red ensigns, foreign horsemen with white standards, cannon that can spew forth lumps of marble and lead, vassals from three continents, savage volunteer troops from the remote provinces of the empire; clouds of banners, forests of plumes, torrents of turbans, avalanches of iron that go to overrun Europe like some malediction from God and leave in their wake a desert strewn with smoking ruins and heaps of human skulls.

## Idleness

Although at some times of the day Constantinople appears to be very busy, in reality it is perhaps the most indolent city in Europe. In this the Turkish and European inhabitants are alike. Everyone gets up as late as possible. Even in summer, at an hour when all our cities are awake, Constantinople is still sleeping. The sun is high before it's possible to find a shop open or get a cup of coffee. Hotels, offices, bazaars and banks are all snoring merrily away, and not even a cannon would wake them. Then there are the holidays: Friday for Turks, Saturday for Jews, Sunday for Christians, the innumerable saints' days of the Greek and Armenian calendars, all faithfully observed; and even though these holidays only involve part of the population, they nevertheless oblige the other inhabitants to take time off as well. All this will give an idea of how much work is done in Constantinople over the entire week – there are some offices that are only open for twenty-four hours in the course of one. Every day one or other of the five peoples of the great city goes lounging about the streets, in holiday dress, with no other thought than to kill time. The Turks are masters of this art. They are capable of making a cheap cup of coffee last for half a day, and of sitting without stirring for five hours at the foot of a cypress tree in a cemetery. Their idleness is absolute idleness, brother to death, like sleep, a profound repose of all the faculties, a suspension of all cares, a mode of existence quite unknown to Europeans. They do not wish even to think of walking. In Stamboul there are no public promenades, and if there were, Turks would not frequent them, because going to a place where you are supposed to walk about would seem to them like hard work. The Turk enters the first cemetery, or the first street he turns into, and follows wherever his legs carry him, wherever the twists and turns of the road or the flow of the crowd take him. Rarely does he go to a place in order to see that place. There are Turks in Stamboul who have never been beyond Kasımpaşa, and Turkish gentlemen who have never gone beyond the Princes' Islands, where they have friends, or their villa on the Bosphorus. For them the height of beatitude consists in total inertia of mind and body. Therefore they are content to leave to restless Christians all the great enterprises which demand constant attention, bustle and travel; and confine themselves to small business matters which can be dealt with while seated, and more by looking than thinking. Work with us dominates and regulates all the other occupations of life, but in Constantinople it takes second place to pleasure and comfort. With us, rest is only an interruption of labour; for them, work is merely a suspension of repose. The main thing at all costs is to slumber, dream, smoke so many hours of the day away; and then in the time that is left, do something or other to earn a living. Time, among the Turks, has a quite different meaning from the one it has for us: the currency of days and months and years possesses only a hundredth part of the value it has in Europe. The shortest time that an official of a Turkish ministry requires to give a response to the simplest matter is two weeks. Diligence in finishing business merely for the pleasure of seeing it done is unknown to them. From the porters upwards not one Turk is ever seen hurrying in the streets of Stamboul. They all walk at the same leisurely pace, as if they all took their time from the beat of one drum. For us life is a rapid torrent, for them it is a standing pool.

## The Night

Constantinople is by day the brightest and by night the darkest city in Europe. Street lamps are few and far between and scarcely break the obscurity of the main thoroughfares; the others are as black as caverns, and no one risks entering them at night without a lantern. At nightfall the city is deserted; a few watchmen, packs of dogs, some furtive prostitutes, gangs of young men bursting noisily out of the beer cellars, and mysterious lanterns, which appear and disappear like will-o'-the-wisps here and there in the alleys and graveyards, are all that can be seen. This is a good time of day to go and see Stamboul from the heights of Pera and Galata. The innumerable lighted windows, the ships' lamps and their reflections in the water, and the stars above form a vast expanse of quivering points of fire in which the port, the city and the sky seem like one great firmament. And when the sky is clouded and the moon shines through a rift in the clouds, above the darkness of Stamboul, above the black masses of groves and gardens, the imperial mosques shine white, like enormous marble tombs, and the city resembles the necropolis of some giant race. But it is even more beautiful and solemn in the starless and moonless nights at the hour when all lights are extinguished. Then there is one vast black mass from Seraglio Point to Eyüp, a measureless form in which the hills seem like mountains, and the innumerable points that crown them take on the fantastic appearance of forests, or armies, ruins, castles and rocks, that carry the mind off into the realm of dreams. On such dark nights it is beautiful to contemplate Stamboul from some high terrace and give free rein to one's fantasy; to penetrate in thought the great shadowy city, to uncover the myriads of harems lit by faint lamps, to see the favourites who celebrate their triumph and the overlooked ones who weep, and the trembling eunuchs listening at doors; to follow nocturnal lovers through the labyrinths of steep alleys; to wander in the silent galleries of the Grand Bazaar, and in the vast deserted cemeteries; to lose oneself in the midst of the innumerable columns of the great underground cisterns; to imagine oneself shut up alone in the great Mosque of Süleyman, making the dark spaces echo with cries of fear and horror, tearing your hair and invoking the mercy of God; and then all at once to exclaim: "What a lot of nonsense! Here I am, on my friend Santoro's terrace, while in the room below a sybaritic supper is waiting for me in the company of the most agreeable people in Pera."

## Life in Constantinople

Every evening there was a gathering of Italians in the house of my
good friend Santoro: lawyers, artists, doctors, merchants, in whose
company I spent some delightful hours. What a convivial get-together!
If our talk could have been taken down in writing, each evening a most
entertaining book would have been the result! The doctor who had
been called to a harem, an artist who'd been commissioned to paint
a pasha's portrait in a villa along the Bosphorus, the lawyer who had
to defend a case before the tribunal, some fop who'd had an amorous
escapade with a Turkish woman – each had his story to tell, and every
tale was a charming sketch of oriental manners. There was a new one
every minute. A guest arrived: "Do you know what happened this
morning? The Sultan threw an inkstand at the Minister of Finance."
And then another: "Have you heard the news? The government, after
three months' delay, has finally paid the salaries of its employees, and
all Galata is flooded with a torrent of cash." A third guest comes in
and tells how a Turkish judge, irritated by the faulty reasoning of a
bad French lawyer defending a pointless case, paid him this pretty
compliment in front of the assembled court: "My dear advocate,
you're wasting your breath trying to make this case seem worthwhile.
The" – and here he pronounced Cambronne's word* plain and clear
– "however you stir it, is still" – and again he pronounced the word
for all to hear.

The conversation, naturally, took in parts of the world which were
quite unknown to me. In the same way as we speak of people and events
in Paris, Vienna, or Genoa, so various cities of the Orient came up in
talk: one had a friend in Tbilisi, another had just been to Trabzon, a
third was about to leave for Damascus. I felt at the centre of another
world, with new horizons all around me, and sometimes I thought
regretfully of the day when I would have to go back to the narrow
circle of my everyday existence. How can I, I wondered to myself, ever
adapt again to the usual talk and the usual events? All Europeans in
Constantinople must feel this; for to those who have witnessed the life
led there, all others will appear uniform and drab. One leads a lighter,
easier, more youthful kind of existence there than in any other city in
Europe. Living as though encamped in a foreign land, in the midst of
a constant succession of strange and unforeseen events, one acquires
a certain sense of the futility and instability of all worldly business,

which closely resembles Muslim fatalism, and which produces in one a kind of nonchalant adventurousness and equanimity of mind. The nature of a people which lives, as the poet says, in a sort of familiar intimacy with death, looking on human existence as a mere pilgrimage, so brief that there's neither time nor any need to lay down plans which require commitment and effort, enters little by little into the European visitor, and he too begins to take each day as it comes, not examining himself too much, and adopting – so far as he can – the simple and restful role of a spectator of the world's affairs. To have to do with people who are so different, and to think and talk a little as they do, lends a kind of lightness to the spirit which can make it soar above many of the sentiments and ideas to which we try to make our own world conform, exhausting ourselves in the impossible effort to achieve this. Besides, the presence of the Muslim population is a constant source of curiosity and observation, a daily spectacle which diverts the mind from many thoughts and cares. The form of the city too helps in this: in our cities the eyes and mind are almost always imprisoned in a narrow circle of streets and houses, while there, at every step, they can wander off into immense distances and pleasant prospects. And finally, there is an unconfined freedom of life, the result of the great variety of customs and manners; everything is possible, nothing astonishes; in that immense moral anarchy the most remarkable events are forgotten as soon as they occur. Europeans live there as if in a confederation of republics; they enjoy the same freedom that they might enjoy in their own cities at the moment of some great political upheaval; it is like an unending party or perpetual carnival. Because of this, even more than because of its beauty, Constantinople is a city where no one can live for any length of time without subsequently recalling it with an emotion akin to yearning; and consequently Europeans develop an ardent love for the place and tend to take root there. It is in this sense that the Turks call the city "the enchantress with a thousand lovers", or, as their proverb has it, "the man who drinks the waters of Tophane is in love for life – there is no cure".


## The Italians

The Italian colony is one of the largest in Constantinople but not one of the most prosperous. There are only a few rich men and many very poor ones, especially labourers from Southern Italy who cannot find work, and it is also the worst served of any of the colonies as far as newspapers are concerned, because they never last long. While I was there, they were expecting the appearance of the *Levantino*; a specimen issue had already been published which listed the academic qualifications and special merits of the editor: seventy-seven in all, not including modesty. Taking a walk on Sunday morning in the main street of Pera, one can see all the Italian families going to mass, and hear all the dialects of Italy spoken. Sometimes I enjoyed this, but not always. On occasion I felt almost sorry for so many of my expatriate fellow citizens, many of whom had no doubt been uprooted there by who knows what strange or painful set of circumstances; I was grieved at the sight of those old people who would perhaps never see Italy again; those children, for whom its name could only produce a vague and fleeting image of a dear and distant country; those young girls, many of whom would marry men of another nationality, and bring up families where nothing of Italy would remain apart from the mother's name and her memories. I saw beautiful Genoese women who might have come that moment from the gardens of the Acquasola park, pretty Neapolitan faces, saucy little heads that seemed as familiar to me as if I had met them a hundred times under the porticoes along the Po, or in the Galleria in Milan. I should have liked to tie them all together, in pairs, with pink ribbons, and send them back to Italy in a ship sailing at a brisk fifteen knots an hour. As a curiosity I should also have liked to take back to Italy a specimen of the Italian language as I heard it spoken in Pera, by the Italians born there, more especially those of the third and fourth generations. An academician from the Crusca* would no doubt take to his bed with apoplexy if he heard them. The language that might result if you mixed together the dialect of a Piedmontese porter, a Lombard cab driver, and a Romagnol carter would, I think, be less unpleasant to the ear than that which is spoken on the shores of the Golden Horn. It is a mongrel Italian mingled with four or five other tongues in the same condition. And the most curious thing about it is that in the midst of innumerable barbarisms, you hear, every now and then – in the conversation of those who have some cultivation – some choice word or polished expression, like "*puote*" or "*imperocché*", "*a ogni piè sospinto*", or "*havvi*" or "*puossi*",* remembered from the literary anthologies which many of our worthy compatriots in the city read in their spare time in order to keep alive in their own speech the "divine Tuscan tongue".* But compared to the rest these individuals can claim to be eloquent speakers of Italian. There are some who can scarcely make themselves understood. One day I was accompanied somewhere by a lad of sixteen or seventeen, the friend of a friend of mine, born in Pera. On the way I tried to engage him in conversation, but he seemed reluctant to talk. He answered monosyllabically, with his head held low, and blushing. It was obvious he was uncomfortable.

"What's the matter?" I asked.

"It's that I speak Italian so badly!" he sighed. In fact as he went on to talk he did come out with the oddest Italian, full of invented and incomprehensible words, closely resembling the so-called lingua franca, which, according to some French humourist, consists of a certain number of words and phrases in Italian, Spanish, French and Greek, which tumble out rapidly one after the other until one at length emerges that can be understood. It is not necessary, however, to resort to this in Pera, where almost everyone, Turks included, understands a little Italian. But the language, if it can be called a language, is only used in conversation, if it can be called conversation. French is most commonly used for writing. There is no Italian literature. I only recall one day reading, in a busy café in Galata, crowded with businessmen, at the bottom of a page of a minor commercial newspaper, under "News of the Stock Exchange", eight melancholy little verses, written partly in Italian and partly in French, which spoke of zephyrs, stars, and sighs. Poor poet! I pictured him buried under a pile of merchandise, exhaling his last breath in those verses.

## The Theatres

At Constantinople, anyone with a strong stomach may pass the evening at the theatre and take his choice from a host of fleapits of every kind, many of which have gardens and sell beer. In some you can find the Italian *commedia dell'arte*, or rather a crew of Italian actors whose performances would be most appropriately rewarded with ripe tomatoes. The Turks, however, prefer to frequent the places where certain French actresses, painted, half naked and impudent, perform popular songs to the accompaniment of a tinpot orchestra. One of these theatres was the Alhambra, in the main street of Pera; one long room which was always full with a sea of red fezzes from the stage to the door. It is impossible to describe the kind of songs they sang and the gestures which accompanied them as these intrepid ladies strove to make their Turkish audience understand the innuendoes. Only those who have been at the Capellanes Theatre in Madrid will have seen or heard anything like it. At every obscene gesture or provocative joke, the audience of fat Turks, seated in long rows, shook with laughter, and as their habitual mask of dignity fell from their faces, the depths of their real nature and the secrets of their grossly sensual lives became apparent. And yet there is nothing that the Turk hides so carefully as the sensuality of his nature and his existence. In the streets he never accompanies a woman; rarely looks at one; still more rarely speaks to one; he takes it almost as an offence if anyone asks after the health of his wife; to judge by appearances, they seem the chastest and most austere people in the world. But these are mere appearances. That same Turk who blushes to his ears when asked about his wife, will send his children, both boys and girls, to listen to the filthy obscenities of Karagöz, which corrupts their imaginations before their senses are fully awakened; and he himself will often neglect the delights of his harem for the perverse pleasures which were first notoriously pursued by Beyazit the Thunderbolt and more recently by Mehmet the Reformer. Karagöz alone is enough to give an idea and a proof of the profound corruption which is concealed under the mask of Muslim austerity. He is a grotesque figure representing a caricature of the middle-class Turk, a kind of shadow-puppet that moves its head and limbs behind a semi-transparent screen, and is almost always the protagonist in certain outrageously farcical comedies, which usually have a love intrigue as their plot. He is a sort of depraved version of Punch, foolish, cunning and cynical, as foul-mouthed as a fishwife and lustful as a satyr, and he excites yells of laughter and shouts of enthusiasm in his audience with every kind of extravagant joke or pun or gesture, which are either explicitly obscene or have an indecent innuendo. And it is easy to imagine what kind of obscenities they are if I tell the reader that while Karagöz in his character is similar to Punch, in his physical form he resembles Priapus. Before censorship imposed some limits on his freedom, the resemblance was frequently and openly displayed: indeed, the noble member in question was often the pivot of the whole drama.

* * *

# Turkish Cooking

Wishing to make a study of Turkish cuisine, I asked my good friends in Pera to take me to a restaurant, any particular one, where we would find oriental dishes, from the most exquisite delicacy of the Seraglio down to camel meat prepared in the Arab fashion and horseflesh *à la* Turkoman. My friend Santoro ordered a strictly Turkish meal, from first course to last, and I, calling to mind all the famous men who have given their lives for science, tried a bit of everything, without a word of protest. About twenty dishes were served. The Turks, like other Eastern peoples, are rather like children, who prefer to eat a small amount of many things than sate themselves on a few dishes; since they have become urban folk, they seem to disdain their recent rural past and consider simplicity of diet a sign of ill-bred stinginess. I cannot give an exact account of all the dishes, since I have only retained a dim and sinister recollection of most of them. I remember the kebab made of very small pieces of mutton roasted in the fire, heavily seasoned with pepper and cloves, and served between two soft greasy patties; this is a dish which might be suitable as a punishment for petty criminals. I can also recall the flavour of the pilau, composed of rice and mutton, which is the sine qua non of all meals and may be called the sacramental dish of the Turks, as macaroni is for the Neapolitans, couscous for the Arabs, and puchero for the Spanish. I remember, and it is the only thing that I should care to taste again, the *hoşaf* which is sipped with a spoon at the end of dinner; made of raisins, apples, plums, cherries and other fruits, stewed in water with a great deal of sugar, and flavoured with musk, rose water and limes. There were also numerous small dishes of lamb and mutton, shredded and boiled until it was almost tasteless; fish swimming in oil; balls of rice rolled in vine leaves, marrows reduced to a syrup, mixed salads, compotes and conserves of various kinds, sauces seasoned with every sort of aromatic herb – so many dishes you could assign one to every article in the penal code as a punishment for repeat offenders. Finally, a great dish of pastries, the crowning work of some Arab pastry-cook, among which there was a small steamboat, a chimera-like lion, and a little house with grated windows all made of sugar.

It seemed to me that I had swallowed the contents of a portable pharmacy, or had eaten one of those toy meals that are prepared by children in their play, when the dishes are made from powdered brick, pounded grass and mashed fruit, which, at a distance, look very appetizing. The dishes at a Turkish meal are served rapidly, three or four at a time, and the Turks help themselves with their fingers, since only spoons and knives are used; only one drinking glass is used for all the company, which a servant keeps constantly filled with sugared water. Such, however, were not the ways of the Turks who were dining next to us. They clearly liked to be comfortable, for they kept their slippered feet upon the table; each one had his own plate, and they could handle forks skilfully. They were also openly drinking alcohol, despite the Prophet's prohibition. I observed too that they did not kiss their bread as good Muslims should before beginning to eat, and that they openly cast many greedy glances at our bottles, although according to the law laid down by the muftis, it is a sin even to look at a bottle of wine. However, this "father of abominations", of which a Muslim only needs to drink one drop to call down upon his head "the anathema of all the angels in heaven and earth", is every day gaining converts among the Turks, and it is perhaps only some remaining sense of decorum which prevents them from rendering public homage to it. I believe that if one day a thick black cloud descended over Constantinople, and, after an hour had gone by, the sun unexpectedly shone out again, fifty thousand Turks would be found with a bottle at their lips. In this as in many other Ottoman transgressions, the sultans laid the foundation stone; and it is curious that among all the European royal families it has been the dynasty which reigns over a people for whom it is a sin against God to drink wine that has given history the greatest number of drunkards: so sweet is forbidden fruit even for the lips of the shadow of God upon earth. It was, they say, Beyazit I who began the interminable series of imperial drunken revels, and as with original sin, it was a woman who made the first move: it was the wife of this same Beyazit, daughter of a king of Serbia, who offered her husband his first glass of Tokay. Then the second Beyazit got tipsy on Cyprus and Shiraz wine. Then Süleyman I, who set fire to all the ships in the port with cargoes of wine and poured molten lead down the throats of drinkers, died in a state of intoxication, pierced by the arrow of one of his archers. Then came Selim I, known as *Mest*, or "the sot", who indulged in drinking bouts which lasted for three days, and during whose reign both lawyers and clerics were known to drink openly. In vain Mehmet III thundered against the "abomination of the demon"; in vain Ahmet I closed down all the taverns and all the wine presses in Stamboul; Murat IV went about the city accompanied by an executioner and promptly sheared off the heads of those whose breath smelt of wine. He himself, the brutal old hypocrite, staggered about the halls of the Seraglio like any tavern-crawling commoner; and after his reign, the bottle, like a small black cheerful imp, broke into the Seraglio, hid itself in the bazaar, peeped from under the soldier's bed, poked its silvered or purple head from the cushions and divans of the harem, violated the precincts of the mosques, and spouted its sacrilegious foam over the yellowed pages of the Koran itself.

## Mohammad

In connection with religion, I could not get this question out of my head as I walked about Constantinople: if the voices of the muezzins were not heard, how would a Christian know that this people's religion was not the same as his own? The Byzantine architecture of the mosques can make them seem like Christian churches; there is no exterior sign of the rites of Islam; Turkish soldiers escort the viaticum through the streets: an ignorant Christian might live a whole year in Constantinople without coming to realize that Mohammad rather than Christ reigns over the greater part of the population. And this thought always brought me back to the small but substantial differences, the blade of grass – as the Abyssinian Christians said to the first followers of Mohammad – which divides the two religions; and to the small reason why the Arab world converted to Islam rather than Christianity – or if not to Christianity, then to a religion so closely related to it that whether it eventually merged with it or continued to exist separately the event would have completely altered the destinies of the Orient. And that small reason was the sensual nature of a handsome young Arab, tall and fair-skinned, with black eyes, a deep voice and an ardent soul, who lacked the strength to subdue his own sensuality, and so when he should have eradicated the dominant vice of his people contented himself with pruning it. Instead of proclaiming conjugal union as he proclaimed the unity of God, he merely circumscribed men's wantonness and egotism in a narrower circle, consecrated by religion. Certainly he would have had to overcome very strong opposition, but it does not seem improbable that he could have achieved it, since, in order to establish the worship of one

God among an idolatrous people, he destroyed a vast and centuries-old web of interconnecting traditions, superstitions, privileges and interests of every kind, and introduced among the dogmas of his religion a paradise for which millions of believers would subsequently lay down their lives, but which when it was first announced provoked a storm of indignation and scorn among the people. But the handsome Arab boy came to a compromise with his sensual needs, and half the world changed its face, for polygamy was in truth the principal vice of his system of law, and the primary cause of the decadence of all the peoples who embraced his faith. Without this degradation of one sex in favour of the other, without the sanction of this monstrous injustice, which disturbs the whole order of human duties, corrupting the rich, oppressing the poor, encouraging sloth, weakening family ties, generating confusion over birthrights within ruling dynasties and so disrupting kingdoms and states, and raising itself as an insuperable barrier to the union of Muslim populations with those of other faiths in the Orient; if, to return to the initial reason, the handsome Arab boy had had the misfortune to be born a little less robust, or the courage to live a little more chastely, who knows! Perhaps there would now be a well-ordered and civilized Orient, and the prospect of universal civilization would be one century nearer.

## Ramadan

Finding myself in Constantinople in the month of Ramadan, which is the ninth month of the Turkish year, and the Muslim equivalent of Lent, I witnessed every evening a comedy which is worth describing. During the whole of this period it is prohibited for the Turks to eat, drink, or smoke, from sunrise to sunset. Almost everyone, as a consequence, spends the night eating and drinking, but as long as the sun is above the horizon, almost all of them respect the religious interdict, and no one dares to transgress it publicly. One morning my friend and I went to visit an acquaintance, one of the Sultan's aides-de-camp, a young officer of a freethinking turn of mind, and we found him in a room on the ground floor of the imperial palace, with a cup of coffee in his hand. "What!" exclaimed Junck, "Do you dare to drink coffee after sunrise?" The officer shrugged his shoulders and replied that Ramadan and fasting were a joke as far as he was concerned, but just at that moment a door suddenly opened and he made so rapid a movement to hide his cup that it overturned and spilt the coffee on his boots. This incident goes to show how rigorously all those who are all day long under the eyes of others have to obey the rule of abstinence; the boatmen, for instance. It is amusing to watch them from the bridge of the Sultana Valide a few minutes before the sun goes down. About a thousand boatmen may be seen at this point, near and far, coming and going, or sitting still. Each of them has been fasting since dawn, they are frantic with hunger, and have their little supper ready in the caique; their eyes continually move from the food to the sun, from the sun to the food, while there is a general agitation and restlessness among them, as in a zoo when the animals are about to be fed. The setting of the sun is announced by a cannon. Before that longed-for moment no one puts a crumb of bread or a drop of water into his mouth. Sometimes, along the Golden Horn, we tried to encourage our boatmen to eat before the lawful moment, but they always answered; "*Yok! Yok! Yok!*" ("No! No! No!"), pointing to the sun with a fearful gesture. When the sun is half hidden behind the hills, they begin to handle their bread, to touch it and smell it; when there is nothing but a thin luminous sliver of sun left visible, then all those who are resting oars and those who are rowing, those who are crossing the Golden Horn and those who are skimming over the Bosphorus, those who are sailing in the Sea of Marmara and those who are resting in the most solitary bays of the Asian shore, all turn towards the west and stand fixed with their eyes on the sun, mouths open, bread in hand, and an expression of joyful anticipation. When nothing is visible but one small fiery point, the bread is poised at their lips; at last the fiery point vanishes, the cannon thunders, and in that very instant thirty-two thousand teeth bite off enormous morsels from a thousand pieces of bread – but what am I saying? A thousand! In every house, in every café, in every tavern the same thing is happening at the same moment; and for a few minutes the Turkish city is nothing but a monster with a hundred thousand mouths, eating and drinking.

## Old Constantinople

But what must this city have been like in the great days of Ottoman glory! I could not get that thought out of my head. Then, over the Bosphorus, white with sails, no black smoke rose to stain the azure of the sky and sea. In the port and the bays of the Sea of Marmara, among the old warships, with their high carved prows, silver crescents, crimson standards, and golden lanterns, floated the shattered and blood-stained hulks of Genoese, Venetian and Spanish galleys. There were no bridges over the Golden Horn, but from one shore to the other a myriad of splendid boats perpetually darted back and forth, among which stood out the white cutters of the Seraglio, with scarlet canopies fringed with gold, rowed by boatmen in silken robes. Scutari was still a village; beyond Galata there were only a few scattered houses; no great palace had yet reared its head upon the hill of Pera; the appearance of the city was less grandiose than it is now, but it was more obviously oriental. The colours of the houses indicated the religion of their owners, since the law which prescribed this was still in force. Stamboul was all yellow and red, apart from the sacred and public edifices, which were as white as snow; the Armenian quarters were ash-grey, the Greek district dark grey, the Jewish purple. The passion for flowers was universal, as in Holland, and the gardens were great masses of hyacinths, tulips and roses. The luxuriant vegetation of the hills had not yet been cleared to make way for new suburbs, and Constantinople was like a city concealed in the middle of a forest. Inside the city there were only narrow alleyways, but they were full of a wonderfully picturesque crowd.

All the male population wore enormous turbans which gave them stature and magnificence. All the women, except the mother of the Sultan, went completely veiled, leaving nothing but the eyes visible, and formed an anonymous and enigmatic population apart, lending a gentle air of mystery to the city. A strict law determined the way everyone dressed: social classes, offices, ranks and ages could all be distinguished by the form of the turban, or the colour of the kaftan, as if Constantinople were one great court. The horse was still "man's only coach", and the streets were filled with horsemen; long trains of camels and dromedaries belonging to the army traversed the city in all directions, giving it the primitive and grandiose air of an ancient Asian metropolis. Gilded arabas drawn by oxen intersected the carriages of the ulemas draped in green and of the *kadıaskers* draped in red, or the light *talikas* with satin curtains and sedan chairs painted with fantastic scenes. Slaves from every country, from Poland to Ethiopia, hurried by, rattling the chains that had been fixed on them on the battlefield. The crossroads and squares and mosque courtyards were filled with groups of soldiers clothed only in venerable rags, who showed their lopped limbs and scars still fresh from the battles of Vienna, Belgrade, Rhodes, Damascus. Hundreds of storytellers, with booming voices and excited gestures, recounted to proud Muslims the glorious deeds of the army that was fighting three months' march away from Stamboul. Pashas, beys, agas, musellims, an endless crowd of dignitaries and great noblemen, dressed with theatrical splendour and accompanied by a throng of servants, pushed their way through the press of people that gave way before them like a field of ripe grain before the wind; ambassadors from European states passed by with princely entourages, coming to treat for peace or conclude alliances; and caravans bringing gifts from African and Asian monarchs went in long procession. Swarms of richly apparelled and insolent *silahtars* and spahis trailed their huge sabres stained with the blood of twenty peoples along the street, and the handsome Greek and Hungarian pages of the Seraglio, dressed like princes, walked haughtily among the obsequious masses, who respected in them the unnatural desires of their sovereign. Over some of the doorways a trophy of gnarled sticks was hung: it was a corps of janissary guards, who at that time were the city's police force. Jews carrying the bodies of executed criminals to the Bosphorus were to be seen. Every morning in the Balık Pazarı, a corpse could be found stretched on the ground, with the severed head placed under the right arm, the written sentence, held down by a stone, upon the chest; in the streets, the bodies of noblemen hung from the first hook or beam that the hurried executioner had come across; in the night a passer-by would trip over the body of some poor wretch thrown into the street from some torture chamber where his hands and feet had been smashed with a club; and under the noonday sun, merchants who had been caught cheating were nailed by one ear to the doors of their shops. There was as yet no law which restricted freedom of burial, so graves were dug and the dead were buried at any hour of the day, in gardens, in alleyways, in squares, in front of the doors of houses. In the courtyards the bleating of lambs and sheep sacrificed to Allah on the occasion of a birth or a circumcision could be heard. From time to time a troop of eunuchs galloped by, shouting out a warning: the streets would empty, doors and windows would shut, the whole area seemed dead. Then a line of glittering carriages containing the beauties from the Sultan's harem passed by, filling the air with their laughter and perfumes. Sometimes a personage of the

court, making his way through the crowded street, would suddenly
turn pale at the sight of six mean-looking men entering a shop: those
six men, dressed like commoners, were the Sultan, with four officials
and an executioner, going from shop to shop to verify weights and
measures. All the streets of Constantinople hummed with a feverish
excess of activity. The treasury overflowed with jewels, the arsenals
with arms, the barracks with soldiers, the caravanserais with travellers;
the slave markets swarmed with beauties, merchants and great lords;
learned men crowded the great archives of the mosques; indefatigable
viziers prepared for future generations the interminable annals of the
Empire; poets, with an official pension from the Seraglio, gathered at
the baths to sing of imperial wars and loves; armies of Bulgarian and
Armenian labourers toiled to build mosques with blocks of Egyptian
granite or marble from Páros, while columns from the temples of
the Greek islands were arriving by sea, and by land spoils from the
churches of Pest and Ofen. In the port they were preparing the three-
hundred-strong fleet which would spread terror to the shores of the
Mediterranean; in the open country between Stamboul and Adrianople
cavalcades of seven thousand falconers and seven thousand huntsmen
spread out, and in the intervals between soldiers' mutinies, foreign
wars, conflagrations that could destroy twenty thousand houses in
a single night, wedding feasts were celebrated with plenipotentiaries
from all the countries of Africa, Europe and Asia, lasting for thirty
days. Then Muslim enthusiasm turned wild. In the presence of the
Sultan and his court – in the midst of huge palm trees, filled with
birds, fruits and mirrors, to make way for which, as they were brought
to the palace, entire houses and walls had had to be demolished,
among rows of lions and sirens sculpted in sugar, carried by horses
caparisoned in silver damask, surrounded by mountains of regal gifts
gathered from all parts of the Empire and from all the courts in the
world – alternated the mock battles of the janissaries, the furious
dances of the dervishes, the bloodthirsty fights of Christian prisoners,
and the street banquets in which ten thousand dishes of couscous were
served; elephants and giraffes danced in the hippodrome; bears were
unleashed among the crowd, and foxes with rockets tied to their tails;
allegorical pantomimes were followed by lascivious ballets, grotesque
masques, fantastic processions, races, symbolic floats, games and
plays and round dances; as the sun went down the feast gradually
degenerated into a mad tumult, while five hundred mosques glittering

with lamps gave off an immense fiery glow over the city that proclaimed the orgies of the new Babylon to shepherds in the mountains of Asia and sailors on the Propontis sea. Such was Stamboul, a powerful, pleasure-loving and unrestrained sultana, compared to which the city of today is nothing but a hypochondriac old dowager.

## The Armenians

Occupied as I was in general with the Turks, I didn't have the time, as my reader will understand, to study much the three nations – Armenian, Greek and Jewish – that form the rest of the rayah population. This would in any case require a lot of time and attention, since, though each of these peoples has more or less preserved its own characteristics, the exterior life of all three has become overlaid with a Muslim colouring, which is now being merged in its turn into a shading of European culture; as a result they are as difficult to observe as a painting which moves and changes all the time might be.

The Armenians in particular, "Christians in faith and spirit, and Asiatic Muslims by birth and blood", are not only difficult to study closely, but also difficult to distinguish at first sight from the Turks, because those among them who have not yet adopted European costume still wear Turkish dress with only very slight modifications; and the old felt cap that with certain special colours used to mark them out as a race is now scarcely ever seen. Nor do they differ much in appearance from the Turks. In general they are tall of stature, robust, corpulent, light-skinned, grave and dignified in movement and manner. Their faces reveal the two qualities which are particular to their nature; an open, quick, industrious and pertinacious spirit, with which they are wonderfully well suited to commerce, and that placidity – which some call pliant servility – by means of which they succeed in insinuating themselves everywhere, from Hungary to China, and in rendering themselves acceptable, particularly to the Turk, whose trust and good will they have gained as docile subjects and obsequious friends. They have neither in character nor appearance any trace of warlike or heroic qualities. Perhaps they were not so formerly in the Asian region from which they came, and indeed their brethren who remain there are said to be quite different, but the transplanted ones are truly a mild and prudent race, modest in their lives, with no ambitions beyond their business, and more sincerely pious, it is said, than any other people in Constantinople. The Turks call them "the camels of the empire", and the Europeans say that every Armenian is born shrewd: these two sayings are largely justified by the facts; for thanks to their physical strength, and their agile mental acuity, they not only furnish Constantinople with a large number of architects, engineers, doctors and ingenious and patient artisans of many kinds, but also most of the porters and bankers: porters who carry extraordinary weights and bankers who amass fabulous treasures. At first sight, however, no one would notice there was an Armenian population in Constantinople, so completely has the plant adapted itself to the soil. Their women, because of whom Armenian private houses are as off limits to strangers as any Muslim home, dress like their Turkish counterparts, and only an experienced observer can distinguish them from their Muslim neighbours. They are for the most part fair and plump, and have the aquiline profile and the large, long-lashed eyes of Orientals; very tall in stature, and matronly in form, when crowned with a turban they look like elegant sheikhs. Their appearance is both dignified and modest, only lacking, if anything, the bright intelligence that shines in the faces of Greek women.

## The Greeks

It is as easy to recognize a Greek at first sight as it is difficult to distinguish an Armenian, even setting aside the diversities of dress, so different is he in nature and appearance from the other subjects of the empire, and especially from the Turk. To become aware of this diversity, or rather of this contrast, it is enough to observe a Turk and a Greek seated side by side in a café or on a steamboat. They may be of the same age and class, and both dressed in European fashion, and even alike in feature, but it is not possible to mistake one for the other. The Turk is motionless, and all his lineaments repose in a kind of unthinking calm, like that of a well-fed animal; if his face does reveal a thought, it must be as motionless as his body. He looks at no one, and gives no sign of being conscious of the observation of others; his attitude displays a profound indifference towards everyone and everything around him; his face expresses something of the resigned sadness of a slave as well as the proud coldness of a despot;

something hard, closed and stubborn which would drive anyone trying to persuade or urge him to a decision to desperation. He has, in short, the look of those men made all of one piece, with whom one can live only as master, or as slave; with whom, however long you live with them, the relationship can never become entirely easy. The Greek on the other hand, is very mobile, and reveals in a thousand changing expressions of eye and mouth everything that is passing through his mind; he tosses his head with the movement of a spirited horse; his face expresses a kind of youthful, sometimes almost childish haughtiness; if he is not observed, he puts himself forward; if he sees he is being watched, he attitudinizes; he seems to be always seeking or fancying something; his whole person betrays self-consciousness and ambition; and yet he is likeable, even if he looks like a rogue, and you would shake hands with him even if you were reluctant to entrust him with your wallet. You only need to see these two men, the Turk and the Greek, side by side, in order to understand that the former must appear to the latter a barbarian, a proud, brutal, overbearing creature; and on the other hand, the Turk must judge his neighbour to be frivolous, false, malignant and restless; and that they must scorn and detest each other reciprocally with all the strength of their souls and never succeed in living amicably together. The same difference can be noted between Greek and the other Levantine women. In the midst of handsome and florid Turkish and Armenian women, who touch the senses rather than the soul, we see, with a feeling of grateful wonder, the pure and elegant faces of Greek women, lit up by thoughtful eyes, whose every glance inspires or ought to inspire an ode; and the beautiful figures, at once slight and majestic, make one want to clasp them in one's arms, but only in order to place them upon a pedestal rather than carry them off to a harem. There are some who still wear their hair in the old-fashioned way, falling in long, wavy tresses, with one thick braid wound round the head like a diadem; so beautiful, so noble, so classical, that they might be taken for statues by Praxiteles or Lysippus,* or for young immortals discovered after two thousand years in some unknown valley of Laconia, or on some forgotten island in the Aegean. This sovereign beauty is rare however, even among the Greeks, and nowadays almost the only examples of it are to be found among the old aristocracy of the empire, in the silent and melancholy quarter of Fener, where the soul of old Byzantium has taken refuge. Occasionally you can still come across one of these superb women leaning on the balustrade of a balcony, or looking through the gratings of some high window, with her eyes fixed upon the empty street, like some captive queen; and when the lackeys of the descendants of the Paleologi and the Comneni do not happen to be lounging in front of the main door, one may stop and contemplate her for a moment, and believe that a vision of an Olympian goddess has been revealed through a rift in a passing cloud.

## The Jews

With regard to Jewish women, I can affirm, after having been in Morocco, that those in Constantinople bear no resemblance at all to those in North Africa, in whom learned observers believe the purity of the original oriental type of Jewish beauty may be found. In the hope of seeing this beauty I took my courage in both hands and wandered for a long time through the vast ghetto of Balat, which winds like some dirty snake along the shore of the Golden Horn. I pushed on into even the most wretched alleys, between mildewed houses like the walls in one of Dante's circles of hell, over crossroads which I wouldn't cross again without stilts or stopping my nose. Through windows hung with sickeningly filthy rags, I looked in on dark and damp-infested rooms; I paused before the entrances into courtyards, and gagged at the fetid odours which met me. I pushed a path through groups of children sick with scrofula and ringworm, brushed against horrible old men, who looked like resuscitated plague victims, skirted round scabby dogs and puddles of mud, avoided great heaps of rotting rubbish, and ducked hanging lines of dirty linen, but my perseverance went unrewarded. Among the many women I encountered, muffled in the national *kalpak*, a sort of long turban that covers the hair and ears, I did see here and there a face in which I recognized that delicate regularity of feature, and that soft air of resignation, which are considered to be the distinctive traits of the Jewish women of Constantinople; some vague profile like Rebecca or Rachel, with almond-shaped eyes, full of grace and sweetness, some elegant form in Raphaelesque pose standing in a doorway with her hand resting upon a child's curly head. But in general I saw nothing but signs of racial degradation. What a difference between these stunted figures, and those opulent forms robed in splendid colours and with a fiery expression in the

eyes, that I admired afterwards in the mellahs* of Tangiers and Fez!
It was the same with the men, who were insignificant, sallow, flabby:
what vitality remained in them seemed to be all in their eyes, gleaming
with avarice and cunning, restlessly shifting from side to side, as if
they heard everywhere the chink of coin. And now I expect to hear
from my worthy Israelite critics, who have already rapped me over the
knuckles apropos of my opinion of their co-religionists in Morocco,
the same old song, attributing the degradation and decay of the Jews
of Constantinople to the oppressions and injustices of their Turkish
rulers. But let them remember that all the other non-Muslim subjects
of the Porte live in precisely the same political and civil conditions as
the Jews; even if this were not the case, it would still be very difficult
to prove that the disgusting lack of hygiene, early marriages and
abstention from all hard-working trades, which are all considered to
be the immediate causes of this decadence, are a logical consequence
of their lack of freedom and independence. And if instead my critics
tell me that it is not the political oppression of the Turks which is the
cause of this degradation, but the lesser persecution and contempt
they meet with from everyone, let them first ask themselves whether
the contrary is not in fact the case: that is, whether the primary reason
is not rather to be sought in the Jews of Constantinople's own customs
and way of life; and if, instead of trying to cover up the sore, they
wouldn't do better to cauterize it themselves.

## The Bath

After a tour of Balat, one might do worse than visit a Turkish bath. The
bathhouses can be recognized by their exterior: they are windowless
edifices in the form of small mosques, surmounted by a cupola, and
some tall conical chimneys, which are always smoking. But before
entering, it is well to think twice, and ask oneself "*quid valeant
humeri*",* because not everyone can endure the harsh treatment which
is meted out to a man within those health-giving rooms. I confess
that after all I had heard I entered with some trepidation, and the
reader will see that, as it turned out, I was much to be pitied. Even
now when I recall the episode, two large drops of sweat appear on my
forehead and hang there before running down my cheeks when I am in
the middle of my tale. Here is what befell your poor author: entering

timidly, I found myself in a large room that might have been either a theatre or a hospital. In the middle a fountain, surrounded by flowers, was gushing, and around the walls ran a wooden gallery in which a number of Turks, stretched out upon mattresses and wrapped from head to foot in white towels, were fast asleep or smoking peacefully. While I looked about in search of an attendant, two brawny and half-naked mulattos suddenly emerged from nowhere like two spectral visions, and both in cavernous voices asked: *"Hamam?"* (Bath?) – *"Evet!"* ("Yes!") I replied, faintly. They beckoned me to follow them, and led me up a wooden stairway into a room full of mats and cushions, where they made me understand that I was to undress. Then they wound round my loins a blue and white cloth, tied a muslin scarf on my head, made me slip my feet into a pair of huge wooden pattens, took me under the arms like a tipsy man, and led or rather carried me into another room, warm and dimly lit, where they laid me down upon a carpet and waited, arms akimbo, until my skin was softened up. All these preparations, which rather resembled those in a torture chamber, filled me with anxiety, which changed to an even less honourable sentiment when my two tormentors touched me on the forehead and exchanged a meaningful look, which just signified: "He's ready," but seemed to me to mean: "On the rack with him!" They took me by the arms and accompanied me as before into a third room. Here I experienced a very strange sensation. I felt as though I were in an underwater temple. I could dimly make out, through a white veil of vapour, high marble walls, columns and arches, the vault of a dome with windows through which filtered red, blue and green beams of light, white phantoms that sidled along the walls, and in the centre of the room, half-naked men extended like corpses on the floor, over whom other half-naked men were bending in the posture of doctors engaged in an autopsy. The temperature of this room was so high that on entering perspiration broke out all over me: I thought I would leave the place changed into a stream, like Arethusa's lover.*

The two mulattos carry my body into the middle of the hall and stretch it out upon a kind of anatomy table, which is an immense slab of white marble, raised above the floor under which the stoves are burning. The slab scorches me and I see stars, but now I'm tied to the stake and must endure. The two mulattos begin the vivisection, chanting a funeral song. They pinch my arms and legs, they squeeze my muscles, they crack my joints, they pummel and stretch and knead me; they turn me on my face and begin again; they turn me back and go on as before; they pull and flatten me like a piece of pastry which they are trying unsuccessfully to shape. They get angry and take a short rest; and then the pinchings, squeezings and stretchings begin again, until I think that my final hour has come. At last, when my whole body is running with water like a squeezed sponge, when they can see the blood circulating under my skin, when they recognize that I can bear it no more, they lift my remains from that bed of torture, and carry them into a corner, where in a small niche there are two copper pipes pouring hot and cold water into a marble basin. But, alas! Here begins another kind of torment, and I ask myself in all seriousness whether I shouldn't start to lash out with a punch or a slap and defend myself as best I can. One of my two tormentors slips on a camel-hair glove and begins to rub my spine, chest, arms and legs with all the grace and delicacy with which he would curry-comb a horse, and the curry-combing goes on for five whole minutes. This done, they deluge me with a torrent of tepid water, and take breath once more. I also breathe again, and thank Heaven that it is over. But it is not over! The ferocious mulatto takes off his glove and begins again with his bare hand; I finally lose patience and make signs to him to stop, but he shows me his hand and proves, to my great amazement, that I am still in need of being rubbed. When he has done rubbing, there is another deluge of water and then another operation begins. They each take a great bunch of tow, sopping wet with soap from Candia, and cover me from head to foot with a lather of suds. After this soaping, another drenching with perfumed water and another rubbing, this time with dry tow. Once I'm dry they again tie the scarf round my head, put on my loincloth, wrap me in a sheet, and lead me back to the second room, and, after a short pause there, again into the first. Here I find a warm mattress on which I stretch out languidly, while the two executioners of justice give me a few last pinches in order to equalize the circulation of the blood in all my limbs. This done, they place an embroidered cushion under my head, a white blanket over me, put a pipe in my mouth, a glass of lemonade beside me, and leave me there, fresh, light and perfumed, with a serene mind and a contented heart, and with such a pure and youthful sense of life that I feel as though I had just risen, like Venus, from the sea-foam, and can hear the flutter of cherubs' wings about my head.

## The Tower of the Seraskerat

Feeling oneself thus "pure and ready to see again the stars",* nothing can be better than to climb up to the head of that stone Titan known as the tower of the Seraskerat. If Satan should ever wish again to tempt anyone with the offer of all the kingdoms of the earth, he'd be sure of success were he to bring his victim up here. The tower, built in the reign of Mehmet II, is on the highest of the hills of Stamboul, in the centre of the vast courtyard of the War Ministry, at the point the Turks call the city's navel. A regular sixteen-sided polygon, it is largely constructed of white marble from Marmara, and it rises bold and slender as a column, surpassing in height even the immensely tall minarets of the neighbouring Süleymaniye Mosque. You climb up a spiral staircase, lit by small square windows, through which you catch glimpses of Galata, Stamboul and the suburbs along the Golden Horn, and you already seem to be in the clouds when you are only halfway up.

Every now and then during the ascent, you hear a slight noise above your head, and almost at the same moment a shape passes you and disappears, more like an object falling than a man going down: it is one of the watchmen who spend day and night on the lookout at the top of the tower, who has probably seen at some distant point on the horizon a suspicious cloud of smoke, and goes to raise the alarm at the office of the Seraskerat. There are about two hundred steps, which lead to a kind of circular terrace, roofed and enclosed all round with glass, where a watchman is always on duty, who offers coffee to visitors. When you first venture out into that transparent cage, which seems suspended between heaven and earth, at the sight of the great azure emptiness all around, and at the sound of the wind that buffets and rattles the glass panes and makes the whole construction creak, you are seized with vertigo and are almost tempted to forgo the view. But courage returns when you see the ladder leading up to the roof window; you climb up with a beating heart and exclaim with astonishment. It is a sublime moment. You are thunderstruck: the whole of Constantinople lies spread out before you, all the hills and all the valleys of Stamboul, from the Castle of the Seven Towers to the cemeteries of Eyüp; all Galata and all Pera, as if they were directly below you; all Scutari; towns, woods, groves and fleets of ships, stretching as far as the eye can see along three enchanting shores, with other villages and gardens winding and disappearing into the distance. The whole of the Golden Horn lies still and crystalline, dotted with innumerable caiques that look like waterflies; the whole of the Bosphorus, which here and there is closed off by some of the larger promontories and looks like a series of lakes, each with a town beside it and, behind the town, gardens; beyond the Bosphorus the Black Sea, whose blue waters merge into the sky. On the other side, the Sea of Marmara, the Bay of Nicomedia, the Princes' Islands, the European and Asian shores, white with villages; further in the distance the Dardanelles, gleaming like a narrow silver ribbon, and beyond them, a vague whiteness, which is the Aegean Sea, and a dark curve, which is the shore of the Troad. Beyond Scutari, Bithynia and Olympus; beyond Stamboul the tawny undulating emptiness of Thrace; two bays, two straits, two continents, three seas, twenty towns, a myriad of silver domes and golden pinnacles, a glory of colour and of light: is this really a view on our own planet or on some other star more favoured by God?

## Constantinople

On the towers of the Seraskerat and of Galata, on the old bridge and in Scutari, I asked myself over and over again: "How could you fall in love with Holland?" Not only that country, but Paris, Madrid, Seville, all now seemed to me dark and melancholy places where I couldn't have lasted a month. Then I thought of my poor attempts to describe them and said to myself bitterly: "You wretch! How many times have you wasted the words 'beautiful', 'immense', 'splendid'. And now what will you say about this spectacle?" It already seemed to me that I would be incapable of writing even a single page about Constantinople. My friend Rossasco said to me: "But why not try?" And I answered: "But I've got nothing to say!" Sometimes – who would believe it? – that spectacle, for a few seconds, at certain times of day, under a certain light, appeared poor and mean, and I exclaimed, almost with dismay: "Where has my Constantinople gone?" At other times I was seized by a feeling of sadness at the thought that while I was there in the presence of all that grandeur and loveliness, my mother was in a small room from which she could see nothing but a gloomy courtyard and a narrow strip of sky; and it seemed my fault, and I would have given my right arm to have the good old lady walking by my side on the way to

Outdoor kitchens

Mosque of Süleyman

Inside Hagia Sophia

show her Hagia Sophia. The days, however, flew by, light and joyous as an hour of intoxication. And on the rare occasions when a black mood settled on us my friend and I knew a way to get free of it. We went down to Galata in two two-oared caiques, the most gaily painted and brightly gilded to be found, and calling out "Eyüp!" we were at once in the middle of the Golden Horn. Our rowers were named Mahmut, Beyazit, Ibrahim, Murat; they were each about twenty years old, and with their strong arms they rowed along in a race, egging each other on with cries and boyish laughter. The sky was serene, and the water clear; we threw our heads back and breathed in deep draughts of the fragrant air, while we dipped our hands in the water; the two caiques flew along, and on either side kiosks and palaces, gardens and mosques sped past us; we seemed to be flying on the wind through a realm of enchantment; we felt an inexpressible joy in being young and in Stamboul. Junck sang and I recited Victor Hugo's *Oriental Poems*,* and saw, now to the right, now to the left, now near, now far, floating in the air, a beloved face, crowned with silver hair and radiant with a gentle smile, which said: "Be happy, my son! I bless you and I am with you!"

## Hagia Sophia

And now – if a mere travel writer is allowed to invoke a muse – I invoke her with my hands joined in prayer, because my mind falters "before the noble subject",* and the grand outlines of the Byzantine basilica tremble before me like an image reflected in rippling water. May the muse inspire me, Hagia Sophia enlighten me, and the Emperor Justinian pardon me!

One fine morning in October, accompanied by a Turkish kavass from the Italian consulate and a Greek dragoman, we at last went to visit the "earthly paradise, the second firmament, the chariot of the cherubim, the throne of God's glory, the marvel of the earth, the largest temple in the world after Saint Peter's". Which last sentence – my friends in Burgos, Cologne, Milan, Florence, please note – is not my own, and I should not dare to claim it is, but I have cited it together with other quotations, because it was one of the many devoutly enthusiastic claims which our Greek interpreter kept repeating as we walked round. We had deliberately chosen an old Greek dragoman and an elderly Turkish kavass to accompany us, in the hope, which turned out to be fulfilled, of hearing in their explanations and in their legends, the clash between two religions, two histories, two peoples: that while one would exalt the church, the other would glorify the mosque, and so between them show us Hagia Sophia in the way she should be seen, with one Turkish and one Christian eye.

My expectations were high and my curiosity keen, yet, as I went along, I thought, as I still think, that the pleasure, however vivid and intense, of seeing a monument, however famous and worthy of its fame, never equals the pleasure of anticipation in going to see it. If I were to live over again any hour of those that I have spent in seeing some renowned work or place, I should choose the one between the moment when I said "Let's go!" and the moment when I hear "We've arrived." The happiest hours in travelling are those. While on the way, your soul expands in the effort to contain the feeling of wonder which is about to enter it; you remember your youthful desires that were then only dreams; you see again your old geography teacher, who after pointing out Constantinople on the map of Europe, traced in the air, with a pinch of snuff in his fingers, the outlines of the great basilica; you see the room and the hearth-side where, next winter, you will describe the monument to a wondering and intent circle of friends; the name of Hagia Sophia seems to resound in your head, in your heart, in your ears, like the name of some living person who is waiting for you and beckons you on in order to reveal to you some great secret. Above you the arches and columns of a prodigious edifice that seems to lose itself in the clouds rise up. So near the goal, you feel an inexpressible pleasure in stopping and dawdling for a moment – to look at a cobblestone, to watch a lizard, to tell a funny story – in order to delay that event in your life which you have longed for over the past twenty years and which you will remember for ever. So that very little remains of the celebrated pleasure of admiration if the anticipation that precedes and the memory that follows it are taken away. It is almost always an illusion, followed by a slight disappointment from which we, obstinate as we are, manage to hatch further illusions.

The Mosque of Hagia Sophia stands opposite the principal entrance of the Old Seraglio. The first thing, however, which attracts the eye upon arriving in the square is not the mosque, but the famous fountain of Sultan Ahmet III.

It is one of the richest and most original monuments of Turkish art. But, more than a monument, it is a marble jewel which a gallant sultan placed on the forehead of his beloved Stamboul. I believe that only a woman could describe it well. My pen is not fine enough to trace its image. At first sight it does not look like a fountain. It is in the form of a small square temple, with a Chinese-style roof with undulating slopes which project a long way, giving it a somewhat pagoda-like appearance. At each of the four corners there is a small round tower, with little grated windows, or rather four charming little kiosks, which are matched above the roof with four slender little cupolas, each one surmounted by a graceful pinnacle, and all encircling a larger cupola in the middle. On each of the four sides there are two elegant niches flanking a pointed arch, and under each arch a jet of water falls into a small basin. An inscription runs all round the edifice which says: "This fountain speaks to you in the verses of Sultan Ahmet; turn the key of this pure and tranquil spring and invoke the name of God; drink of this inexhaustible and limpid water and pray for the Sultan." The little edifice is all of white marble, which is scarcely visible under all the decorative ornament which covers the wall surfaces; there are little arches and niches and columns, rosettes and polygons, ribbons and lace carved in marble, gilding on blue ground, fringes around the cupolas, inlays under the roof, many-coloured mosaics and arabesques of many forms, which draw the eye in and almost irritate one's sense of wonder. There is hardly an inch of surface which is not carved and gilded and fretted. It is a miracle of grace, richness and patient craft, which should be kept under glass; it's as if it's not made only for the eyes but must have a flavour – one would like to suck a piece of it; or it's a jewel case that one would like to open, and find inside a goddess in the form of a doll, or a gigantic pearl, or a magic ring. Time has in part dimmed the gilding, blurred the colours, and blackened the marble. What must this enormous jewel have been like when it was first unveiled, glittering and new, a hundred and sixty years ago? But old and blackened as it is, it is still supreme among all the smaller marvels of Constantinople; and it is besides so utterly Turkish that it takes its place among the small number of images which spring immediately to mind whenever the name Stamboul is heard, and form the background to our enduring memories of the Orient.

From the fountain can be seen the Mosque of Hagia Sophia, occupying one whole side of the square.

The exterior has nothing worthy of note. The only features to attract the eye are the four tall white minarets that rise at the corners of the edifice on pedestals as large as houses. The famous dome looks small. It does not seem to be the same dome that swells into the blue air, like the head of a Titan, when seen from Pera, from the Bosphorus, from the Sea of Marmara, and from the hills of Asia. It is flattened, flanked by two half-domes, covered in lead, with a circle of windows, and supported upon four walls painted in wide bands of pink and white, which are supported in turn by enormous buttresses at the foot of which there is a huddle of several small, mean-looking buildings, baths, schools, mausoleums, hospitals, soup kitchens, which conceal the original architectural form of the basilica. You see nothing but a heavy, irregular mass, dull in colour, stark as a fortress, and apparently not at all large: anyone who did not already know would find it difficult to believe it contained the vast nave within. Of the ancient basilica nothing is really visible except for the dome, but even this has lost the silvery splendour that once made it visible, according to the Greeks, from the summit of Olympus. All the rest is Muslim. One minaret was built by Mehmet the Conqueror, one by Selim II, the other two by Murat III. Murat also had the buttresses added at the end of the sixteenth century to support the walls which had been shaken by an earthquake, and the enormous bronze crescent planted upon the top of the dome, of which the gilding alone cost fifty thousand ducats. The ancient atrium has disappeared; the baptistery was converted into a mausoleum for Mustafa and Ibrahim I; almost all the smaller edifices annexed to the Greek church were either destroyed or are hidden by later walls, or so transformed as not to be recognizable. On every side the mosque confines, oppresses and hides the church, of which only the head is free, though even over that the four imperial minarets keep watch like four enormous sentinels. On the eastern side there is a door flanked by six porphyry and marble columns; on the south there is another door by which you enter a courtyard, surrounded by low, irregular buildings, in the middle of which there is a fountain for ritual ablutions, covered by an arched roof on eight small columns. Looked at from the outside, Hagia Sophia can scarcely be distinguished from the other great mosques of Stamboul, apart from its being shabbier and heavier; much less would you think it the "greatest temple in the world after St Peter's".

Our guides led us through a narrow passage that ran along the northern side of the edifice to a bronze door which turned slowly on its hinges and through which we entered the vestibule. This vestibule is a very long and lofty hall, lined with marble and with some of the ancient mosaics still glittering here and there, and gives access to the nave from the eastern side by nine doors – and on the opposite side another five doors once opened on to another vestibule, which, with a further thirteen doors, communicated with the atrium. As soon as we had crossed the threshold, we showed our entrance firman to a turbaned sacristan, put on slippers, and at a sign from the guide, advanced hesitantly to the central door on the eastern side that stood open to receive us. As soon as we were inside, we were transfixed: the first impression is truly grand and unexpected. The gaze takes in an enormous void, a bold architecture of half-domes that seem suspended in air, of immense pillars, gigantic arches, colossal columns, galleries, tribunes and porticoes, on which a flood of light descends from a thousand large windows; there is something theatrical and princely rather than sacred; a display of grandeur and power, an air of worldly elegance, a confusion of the classical and the barbarian, capricious, overbearing and magnificent; a grand harmony, in which the powerful, thundering notes of cyclopean arches and pillars, which call to mind the cathedrals of northern Europe, mingle with the sweet subdued strain of oriental chants, the clamorous music of the banquets held by Justinian and Heraclius, echoes of pagan songs, faint voices of an unmanly and exhausted race, and the distant cries of Goths, Avars and Vandals. There is a disfigured majesty, a sinister bareness, a profound peace; it is like St Peter's on a smaller scale, and made more austere, or a larger and emptier version of St Mark's; a unique mixture of temple, church and mosque, of severity and frivolity, of things ancient and modern, of ill-assorted colours, and unfamiliar bizarre furnishings; a spectacle, in short, which inspires astonishment and chagrin, and leaves the mind for a moment uncertain, seeking the right words to express and assert what it really thinks.

The edifice is constructed upon an almost square plan, over the centre of which rises the principal dome on four great arches supported by four very tall columns, which are the fundamental frame of the building. The two arches which face you as you enter support two large half-domes covering the whole of the nave, and each of these opens out into two other smaller half-domes, which thus form four small round temples within the great one. Between two of these, directly opposite the entrance, there is the apse, also covered by a quarter-sphere vault. There are thus seven half-domes which surround the principal dome, two beneath it, and five below those two, without any apparent support, so that they present an appearance of extraordinary lightness, and seem indeed, as a Greek poet once wrote, to be suspended by seven threads from the vault of heaven.* All these domes are lit by large arched symmetrical windows. Between the four massive pillars which form a square in the middle of the basilica, rise, on either side, eight marvellous columns of green breccia from which spring the most graceful arches, carved with foliage, forming an elegant portico on either side of the nave, which support two immense high galleries, with two more ranges of columns and sculptured arches. A third gallery, which communicates with the first two, runs right along the side where you enter, and opens on to the nave with three great arches, supported by twin columns. Other minor galleries, supported by porphyry columns, cross the four temples placed at either end of the nave, with more columns supporting tribunes. This is the basilica. The mosque is, so to speak, distributed within this space and attached to its walls. The mihrab, or niche indicating the direction of Mecca, is carved out of one of the pillars in the apse. To the right of it, high up, is hung one of the four carpets which Mohammad used for his prayers. On the corner of the apse nearest the mihrab, at the top of a very steep and narrow staircase with two exquisitely carved marble balustrades, under a curious conical roof and between two of Mehmet II's triumphal standards, is the pulpit where the ratib* climbs up to read the Koran, holding an unsheathed scimitar in his hand as a sign that Hagia Sophia is a mosque acquired by conquest. Opposite the pulpit is the Sultan's tribune, closed with a gilded lattice. Other pulpits or platforms, with balustrades in openwork carving and resting on small marble columns and arabesqued arches, are placed at various points along the walls, or project towards the middle of the nave. To the right and left of the entrance are two enormous alabaster urns, found among the ruins of Pergamum and brought to Constantinople by Murat III. At a great height on the pillars huge green disks with inscriptions from the Koran in letters of gold are suspended. Below, large porphyry cartouches are attached to the walls, inscribed with the names of Allah, Mohammad and the first four Caliphs. In the angles formed by the four arches which support the dome the enormous wings of four mosaic cherubim are still visible, but their faces have been covered by gilded rosettes.

From the vaults of the domes innumerable thick silk cords hang down, measuring almost the entire height of the basilica, to which ostrich eggs, carved bronze lamps and crystal globes are attached. Here and there are lecterns in the form of an X, inlaid with mother-of-pearl and copper, with manuscript Korans upon them. The paving is covered with carpets and mats. The walls are bare, whitish, yellowish, or dark grey, with a few faded vestiges of their original mosaic decoration. The overall appearance is melancholy.

The chief marvel of the mosque is the great dome. Looked at from the centre of the nave below, it seems indeed, as Madame de Staël said of the Dome of St Peter's, like an abyss suspended over one's head.* It is immensely high, has an enormous circumference, and its depth is only one-sixth of its diameter which makes it appear still larger. A narrow gallery runs round the base and above this gallery there is a circle of forty arched windows. At the top of the dome is written the sentence pronounced by Mehmet II, as he sat on his horse in front of the high altar on the day Constantinople was captured: "Allah is the light of heaven and of earth"; and some of the letters, which are white upon a black ground, are nine metres tall. As every one knows, this aerial miracle could never have been constructed with ordinary materials: its vaults were built of pumice stone that floats on water and with bricks from the island of Rhodes, five of which weigh only slightly more than a single normal one. Each brick was inscribed with David's sentence: *"Deus in medio eius non commovebitur; adiuvabit eam Deus vultu suo."** At every twelfth course of bricks, the relics of saints were enclosed. While the workmen laboured, the priests chanted, Justinian in a linen tunic watched, and an immense crowd gaped in wonderment. And such a reaction need not astonish us when we think that the construction of this "second firmament", so marvellous even in our own day, was in the sixth century an undertaking without precedent. The vulgar crowd believed it was suspended in the air by magic, and, for a long time after the Conquest, when the Turks were praying in the mosque, they had to force themselves to keep their faces towards the east and not turn them upwards to "the stone sky". The dome, in fact, covers almost half the nave, so that it dominates and lights the whole edifice, and a part of it may be seen from every side; whichever way you turn, you always find yourself beneath it, and your gaze and your thoughts repeatedly return to rise and float within its circle with an intensely pleasurable sensation, like that of flying.

But the nave and the dome are only the beginning of a visit to Hagia Sophia. Anyone with an ounce of historical curiosity could spend an entire hour just studying the columns, for example. Here are the spoils from all the temples in the world. The columns of green breccia which support the two great galleries were given to Justinian by the magistrates of Ephesus, and came from the temple of Diana that was burnt down by Herostratus. The eight porphyry columns that stand in pairs between the pillars belonged to the Temple of the Sun built by Aurelian at Baalbek. Other columns in an infinite variety of sizes and colours come from the Temple of Jove at Cyzicus, from the temple of Helios of Palmyra, from the temples of Thebes, Athens, Rome, the Troad, the Cyclades, and from Alexandria… Among the columns, the balustrades, the pedestals and the panels which survive from the ancient lining of the walls, you can see marbles from all the quarries of the Archipelago, from Asia Minor, from Africa and from Gaul. The white marble of the Bosphorus, spotted with black, contrasts with black Celtic marble veined with white; the green marble of Laconia is reflected in the blue marble of Libya; the speckled porphyry of Egypt, the starred granite of Thessaly, the red-and-white-streaked stone of Mount Jassy with the purple, pink, gold and snow-white marbles from Phrygia, Synada, Mauritania and Páros. Together with this profusion of colours there is the indescribable variety of the forms of friezes, cornices, rosettes, balustrades, and bizarre Corinthian capitals – in which animals, leaves, crosses and chimeras are all woven together – and others which belong to no order, fantastic in design and differing in size, paired at random; and shafts of columns and pedestals decorated with inventive carvings, worn by time and chipped by scimitars. The whole presents a bizarre appearance of magnificent and barbarous disorder: good taste might shudder with disdain, but you cannot take your eyes off it.

Standing in the nave, however, one cannot appreciate the immense size of the mosque. The nave is, in fact, only a small part of the whole. The two porticoes that carry the lateral galleries are two large edifices in themselves, out of which two temples might be made. Each is divided into three parts, separated by very high arches. Here too the columns, architraves, pillars and vaults are all enormous. Walking under these lofty arcades, the great nave can just be glimpsed between the columns from the Temple of Ephesus, and you almost think you are in another basilica. The same effect can be experienced from the galleries, to which you climb on a gently sloping spiral staircase – or rather, since there are no steps, not a staircase, but a road, by which a man on horseback could ascend without difficulty. The galleries were the *gynaeceum*, or the part of the church reserved for women; the penitents remained in the vestibule, and the common crowd of the faithful in the nave. Each gallery could hold the entire population of one of Constantinople's neighbourhoods. You do not feel as if you were in a church, but rather as though you were strolling in some titanic theatre, where at any moment a chorus of a hundred thousand voices might burst forth. To see the mosque, you need to look over the balustrade: then you see it in all its grandeur. The arches, vaults, pillars, all seem gigantic. The green disks, which from below looked as if you could span them with your arms, seen from up here would cover a house. The windows are like palace gateways; the wings of the cherubim are ships' sails; the tribunals are public squares; the dome makes your head swim. Looking down, you experience another wondrous effect. You weren't aware you had climbed up so high. The floor of the nave is the bottom of an abyss, and the pulpits, the urns from Pergamum, the mats, the lamps, have all shrunken and grown tiny. A curious feature of the Mosque of Hagia Sophia can also be observed more clearly from this viewpoint: because the nave does not lie precisely in the direction of Mecca, towards which Muslims must turn in prayer, all the prayer rugs are arranged aslant the lines of the building, and offend the eye like an elementary error in perspective. From above, all the life of the mosque can be seen and contemplated. There are Turks on their knees, with their foreheads touching the floor; others standing like statues with their hands turned upwards in front of them, as though they were reading their palms; some seated cross-legged at the foot of columns, as if they were resting under the shade of a tree; some veiled women on their knees in solitary corners; old men seated before the lecterns, reading the Koran; an imam listening to a group of boys reciting sacred verses; and, here and there, under the distant arcades and in the galleries, imams, ratibs, muezzins, servants of the mosque in peculiar costumes, coming and going silently as if they were sliding along the floor. The vague harmony of the low, monotonous voices of those reading or praying, the thousand strange lamps, the clear and equal light, that deserted apse, those vast silent galleries, that immensity, those memories, that peace, instil an impression of mystery and grandeur in the soul which words cannot express, nor the passage of time efface.

But ultimately, as I have said, the impression is one of sadness and confirms the great poet who likened the Mosque of Hagia Sophia to a "colossal sepulchre",* because on every side the traces of horrible devastation can be seen, exciting more regret for what was than admiration for what remains. Once the first feeling of amazement has died down, the mind turns irresistibly to the past. And even now, three years after visiting it, I cannot recall the image of the great mosque without trying at the same time to see the church instead. I pull down the Muslim pulpits, get rid of the lamps and urns, remove the disks and the porphyry cartouches, open the walled-up windows and doors, scrape off the whitewash from walls and ceilings, and see the basilica new and entire, as it was thirteen centuries ago, when Justinian exclaimed: "Glory to God, who has judged me worthy to complete this work! Solomon, I have outdone you!" Everywhere the eye turns, the building shines, sparkles, gleams like a palace in a fairy tale. The great walls, lined with precious marbles, send back reflections of gold, of ivory, of steel, of coral, of mother-of-pearl; the innumerable veins and specks in the marble resemble crowns and garlands of flowers; when a ray of sun falls upon them, the endless expanses of crystal mosaic make the walls shine like silver set with diamonds. The capitals, the cornices, the doors, the friezes of the arches are all of gilded bronze. The vaults of portico and gallery are painted with the giant figures of saints and angels foreshortened on a gold background. In front of the pillars, in the chapels, beside the doors, among the columns, stand statues of marble and bronze, enormous candelabra of massy gold, huge figures of the evangelists bending over lecterns resplendent as royal thrones, tall ivory crosses, vases glimmering with pearls. At the bottom of the nave there is a confused lustre as of many candles burning. It is the balustrade of the choir, in gilded bronze; the pulpit, encrusted with forty thousand pounds of silver, which cost one entire year's tribute money from Egypt; the seats of the seven priests, the thrones of the Patriarch and of the Emperor, gilded, carved, inlaid, set with pearls, so that when the light strikes full upon them, the eyes are blinded by the dazzle. Beyond all this splendour, there is yet greater magnificence in the apse. It is the altar, of which the table, supported on four golden columns, is made of gold and silver, pewter and pearls together, while the pyx is formed of four columns of solid silver, covered by a golden dome which is surmounted by a globe and cross of gold weighing two hundred and sixty pounds. Behind the altar rises the immense figure of the Divine Wisdom, whose feet touch the floor and whose head reaches to the vault of the apse. Soaring aloft over all these treasures are the seven half-domes covered with gold and crystal mosaics, and the great central dome on which are depicted the towering forms of apostles and evangelists, the Virgin and the Cross, all glittering with gold and coloured like jewels and flowers. And everything – domes and columns and statues and candelabra – is mirrored in the vast floor of undulating marble flagstones, the surface of which, seen from the four main entrances, looks like four great rivers ruffled by the wind. Such was the interior of the basilica. But we must also imagine the great atrium, surrounded by columns and walls lined with mosaic and decorated with marble fountains and equestrian statues; the tower, from which thirty-two bells made their resounding chimes echo to the seven hills; the hundred bronze doors decorated with bas-reliefs and inscriptions in silver; the halls of the synods, the rooms of the Emperor, the dungeons of the priests, the baptistery, the vast sacristies brimming with treasures, and a labyrinth of vestibules and triclinia, of corridors, of hidden staircases that wind about in the thickness of the walls and lead to galleries and secret oratories. And now we can imagine the spectacle such a basilica presented on the grand occasions of imperial weddings, councils, coronations, when from the great Palace of the Caesars, along a route lined with columns and strewn with myrtle and flowers, perfumed with myrrh and incense, between houses displaying precious vases and silk tapestries, amid the chants of poets and the shouts of heralds hurrahing in all the languages of the empire, the emperor advanced, wearing the tiara surmounted by a cross, bejewelled like an idol, seated upon a golden car with purple curtains drawn by two white mules, and surrounded by a court worthy of a Persian monarch. Then the clergy of the basilica in all their pomp come out to meet him in the atrium, while into the church lit by six thousand candles through twenty-seven doors the throng pours: courtiers, equerries, logothetes, protospathaires, admirals, high constables, chief eunuchs, thieving governors, bribed magistrates, brazen-faced patricians, craven senators, slaves, buffoons, casuists, mercenaries of every nation – the whole resplendent rabble, one gilded mass of corruption. Along the balustrades of the choir, under the porticoes and in the galleries there was an excited coming and going of elaborately coiffed hairstyles and purple caps, a dazzle of gem-encrusted berets and gold necklaces and silver breastplates, courtly exchanges of greetings and bows and smiles, an ostentatious rustle of trailing silk cymars and the clank of ceremonial swords, while languid perfumes filled the air and the vast congregation of the profane and the debased made the vaults echo with their shouts and their applause. After making several silent perambulations about the mosque, we turned to our guides, who began by showing us the chapels placed beneath the galleries, despoiled of all their contents like every other part of the basilica. Some of them now serve as treasuries, like the opisthodomos in the Parthenon in Athens, in which Turks who are departing on a long journey, or who are in fear of robbers, deposit their money and their precious belongings, often leaving them there for years under God's protection; others, enclosed by a wall, have been converted into infirmaries, in which the insane or incurably ill await cure or death, and from where from time to time laments and high-pitched laughs echo through the mosque. They now lead us back into the centre of the nave and the Greek dragoman begins to recount the marvels of the basilica. The design, it is true, was drawn up by the architects Anthemius of Tralles and Isidore of Miletus,* but it was an angel who inspired the original conception. It was another angel who suggested to Justinian opening three windows in the apse to represent the three persons of the Trinity. Thus the one hundred and seven columns of the church also represent the one hundred and seven columns which support the House of Wisdom.* It took seven years to gather together all the materials needed for the construction. A hundred master-builders supervised the project, and ten thousand labourers worked under them, five thousand on one side, and five thousand on the other. The walls were only a few palms high when already more than four hundred and fifty quintals of gold had been spent. The total cost of the building alone amounted to twenty-five million lira. The church was consecrated by the Patriarch, five years, eleven months and ten days after the first stone was laid, and on that occasion Justinian ordered sacrifices, feasts, distributions of alms and food, which lasted for two weeks.

Here the Turkish kavass struck in, and pointed out the pillar on which Mehmet II, when he entered as a conqueror into Hagia Sophia, left the bloody imprint of his right hand as if to seal his victory. Then he showed us, near the mihrab, the so-called "cold window", from which a draught of fresh air is always blowing, inspiring the greatest preachers of Islam with the most moving sermons. He pointed out, at another window, the famous "shining stone", a slab of transparent marble which glows like a piece of crystal whenever the sunlight falls on it. On the left of the entrance on the north side he made us touch the "sweating column": a column sheathed with a bronze covering, through a small aperture in which can be seen the marble which is always moist. And finally he showed us a hollowed-out block of marble, brought from Bethlehem, in which, it is said, was laid, as soon as he was born, Sidi Issa, "the son of Mary, the apostle of God, the spirit that proceeds from Him, and merits honour in this world and the next". But it seemed to me that neither the Turk nor the Greek believed much in any of this. The dragoman now took up the tale, passing before a walled-up door in the gallery, to relate the celebrated legend of the bishop, and this time he spoke with conviction, which if it wasn't genuine was well simulated. At the moment when the Turks broke into the church of Hagia Sophia, a Greek bishop was saying mass before the high altar. At the sight of the invaders he abandoned the altar, climbed up into the gallery, and disappeared through this little door before the eyes of the pursuing soldiers, who instantly found themselves stopped by a stone wall. They began to pound furiously upon it, but only succeeded in denting it with their weapons. Masons were called, but after labouring away for a whole day with pick and mattock they were obliged to give up; all the masons in Constantinople tried their hands at it, and all failed to open a breach in the miraculous wall. Yet that wall will open: it will open on the day when the profaned basilica is restored to Christian worship, and then the Greek bishop will emerge, dressed in his pontifical robes, with the chalice in his hand, and a radiant countenance, and, mounting the steps of the high altar, he will resume the mass at the exact point where he left off; and on that day the dawn of a new age for the city will shine resplendent.

As we were going out, the Turkish sacristan, who had followed us about shuffling and yawning, gave me a handful of mosaic pieces which he had just prised out from the wall, and the dragoman, stopping in the doorway, began the recital, which I immediately cut short, of the profanation of the basilica. But I should not wish my reader to be similarly deprived of it now that the description of the basilica has revived the details of the scene in my mind's eye.

Hardly had the news spread, towards seven in the morning, that the Turks had passed over the walls, when an immense crowd fled for refuge to Hagia Sophia. There were about a hundred thousand of them: deserting soldiers, monks, priests, senators, thousands of virgins fleeing from the convents, patrician families carrying their treasures, great state dignitaries and princes of the imperial house, running through the galleries and the nave, hiding in all the recesses of the edifice. Together with them came all the dregs of society, slaves and criminals spewed out of the prisons and the galleys. The whole church resounded with their shrieks of terror, as in a crowded theatre when a fire breaks out. When the nave, the galleries and the vestibules were all packed full, the doors were closed and barred, and the horrible din was followed by an eerie silence. Many still believed that the conquerors would not dare to profane the church of Hagia Sophia; others with an unquestioning confidence awaited the apparition of the angel, announced by the prophets, who would destroy the Muslim army before the advance guard reached the pillar of Constantine; others who had climbed up into the inner gallery of the dome, watched from the windows the approaching danger and made signs to the hundred thousand pallid faces that looked up at them from the galleries and nave below. From their vantage point they could see an immense white cloud covering the walls from the Blachernae to the Golden Gate; and inside the walls four glittering lines advancing among the houses like four torrents of lava, widening and roaring in the midst of smoke and flame. They were the four assault columns of the Turkish army, driving before them the disordered remnants of the Greek troops and converging on Hagia Sophia, the Hippodrome and the Imperial Palace, pillaging and burning as they came. When the vanguard arrived on the second hill, the blare of trumpets was suddenly heard, and the terrified crowd in the church fell to their knees. But even then many continued to believe that the angel would appear, while others hoped that a feeling of reverence and awe would deter the invaders and stop them in their tracks in front of the majestic edifice consecrated to God. But this last delusion soon vanished. The trumpets sounded nearer, a confused noise of weapons and shouting burst into the church through its thousand windows, and in a moment the first blows of Muslim axes were heard upon the bronze doors of the vestibules. Then that great throng felt the chill of death upon them, and commended themselves to God. The doors were smashed in or torn off their hinges and gave way, and a savage horde of janissaries, spahis, timariots, dervishes, çavuş – covered with dirt and blood, transformed by the fury of battle, by plunder and rape

– appeared on the threshold. At the first sight of the great nave and all its splendid treasures, they let out a great shout of wonder and delight; and then the dreadful torrent rolled on its furious course. One part fell upon the women, upon the nobles, precious slaves who, paralysed with terror, let themselves be tied and chained; the rest rushed for the treasures of the church. The tabernacles were pillaged, the statues overthrown, the ivory crucifixes smashed to smithereens; the mosaics were thought to be gems and were gouged out by the scimitars, falling in sparkling showers into the kaftans and cloaks held out to catch them; the pearls of the sacred vessels, prised out with the points of daggers, rolled about the pavements, pursued like living things and fought over with bites and sword-blows; the high altar was shattered into a thousand fragments of gold and silver; the seats, the thrones, the pulpits, the balustrades of the choir vanished as if pulverized by an avalanche of stone. And meanwhile the Asiatic hordes continued to pour in in bloodthirsty waves. Soon nothing could be seen but a whirling throng of drunken robbers, many wrapped in sacerdotal robes and wearing tiaras on their heads, waving chalices and sacred vessels in the air, dragging along rows of slaves bound together with pontifical girdles, surrounded by camels and horses laden with booty which slipped upon the paving stones strewn with the shards of broken statues, torn leaves from the Gospel, and the scattered relics of saints: a wild and sacrilegious orgy, accompanied by a horrible noise of triumphant shouts, threats, horses neighing, laughter, the shrieking of women and girls, and the blare of trumpets; until suddenly all fell silent, and upon the threshold of the great portal there appeared the figure of Mehmet II on horseback, surrounded by a group of princes, viziers and generals, proud and aloof like the living image of God's vengeance. Rising in his stirrups, with a resounding voice he fills the devastated basilica with the first and fundamental invocation of the new religion: "Allah is the light of heaven and of earth!"

## Dolmabahçe

Every Friday the Sultan goes to pray in one of the mosques of Constantinople. We saw him one day as he was going to the Mosque of Abdülmecit, on the European shore of the Bosphorus, near the imperial palace of Dolmabahçe.

To get to Dolmabahçe from Galata, you pass through the densely populated district of Tophane, between a huge arsenal and a great cannon-foundry, and then cross the Muslim quarter of Fındıklı, which occupies the site of the ancient Aianteion, after which you come out onto a spacious square, open towards the sea, beyond which, by the shore of the Bosphorus, is the famous residence of the Sultans. It is the largest marble edifice reflected in the waters of the strait from Seraglio Point to the entrance into the Black Sea, and it is only possible to get a view of the whole of it from a boat. The façade, which is nearly half an Italian mile in length, faces Asia, and can be seen from a great distance, shining white between the blue of the sea and the dark green of the hill behind. It cannot really be described as a palace because the building was not conceived as a whole; the different parts are unconnected, and different styles – Arabic, Greek, Gothic, Turkish, Roman and Renaissance – are mingled outlandishly together; it has the majestic appearance of European royal palaces, as well as the almost feminine graces of the Moorish buildings in Seville and Granada. Rather than "Palace", it might more appropriately be called "the Imperial City", as in China; and its form rather than its size would suggest that it is the residence not of a single sovereign, but of ten, brothers or friends, who pass their time there in idleness and pleasure. From the Bosphorus the building presents a sequence of temple or theatre façades, decorated so profusely that, as a Turkish poet puts it, a madman seems to have been at work on the design; they remind one of those fabled Indian pagodas, which tire the eye as soon as you look at them and seem to symbolize the sensual and luxurious existence of the licentious princes who dwell within their walls.

There are rows of Doric and Ionic columns, slender as spear-shafts; windows framed in festooned cornices with small fluted columns; arches full of leaves and flowers that curve above doors worked in delicate tracery; charming terraces with openwork parapets; trophies, rosettes and tendrils; intertwined and knotted garlands; marble ornamentation vying for space on the cornices, over the windows and around the reliefs; a network of arabesques extending from the doors to the pediments, a sumptuousness and delicacy of architectural ornament that gives to each of the smaller palaces – which go to make up the great composite edifice – the appearance of having been miraculously carved and chased by the engraver's hand. It seems impossible that a sober Armenian architect designed

it; rather some enamoured sultan must have seen it in a dream while
sleeping in the arms of his most ambitious mistress. In front there is
a row of marble columns linked by gilded wrought-iron railings, in
which flowers and branches are shown interlacing, and which, seen
from a distance, looks like lace curtains that the wind might blow
away. Long flights of marble steps descend from the gates to the water
and disappear into the sea. Everything is white, fresh and clean as
if the finishing touches to the palace had been done the day before.
An artist's eye might pick out a thousand flaws of harmony or taste,
but the overall effect is rich and splendid, and one's first sight of that
array of regal residences – white as snow, enamelled like jewels, with
the green hill behind reflected in the water – leaves an impression of
power, mystery and beauty which almost puts the memory of the Old
Seraglio in the shade. Those who have had the good fortune to enter
the palace say that the interior matches the façade: there are long
suites of rooms frescoed with fanciful subjects and glowing colours;
doors of carved and gilded cedar and mahogany which open upon
endless corridors illuminated by a soft light, by which you pass into
other rooms lit up with a glowing red from small domes of crimson
glass, and bathrooms which seem carved from a single block of Parian
marble; and from these you move on to airy terraces suspended above
mysterious gardens and groves of cypresses and roses, from where you
glimpse the blue sea at the end of long rows of Moorish porticoes;
windows, terraces, balconies, kiosks are all resplendent with flowers,
and everywhere water glints and splashes in misty veils over verdure or
marble, and from every side there are divine views of the Bosphorus,
off which lively breezes blow, wafting a delicious marine freshness
through all the rooms of the palace.

On the side facing Fındıklı there is a monumental and highly
ornamented gate through which the Sultan was to come out of the
palace and cross the square. There is no other monarch on earth who
has such a beautiful square on which to make a solemn progress from
his palace. Standing at the foot of the hill, the gate of the palace can
be seen on one side, looking like a triumphal arch built for a queen;
on the other side is the graceful Mosque of Abdülmecit, flanked by
two pretty minarets; opposite is the Bosphorus; beyond, the hills of
Asia, green and dotted with a multitude of brightly coloured kiosks,
palaces, mosques and villas, which look like a large town decked out
for a festival; further in the distance, you can see majestic Scutari with

her dark crown of cypresses; and between the two shores there is a continual coming and going of sailing ships, war vessels with their pennants fluttering, small crowded ferry steamers looking as though they were filled with flowers, Asian boats in strange and antique shapes, cutters from the Seraglio, private boats and flocks of birds skimming the water; a scene so full of beauty and vivacity and joy that the stranger who stands waiting for the appearance of the imperial entourage can't help imagining a sultan as handsome as an angel and as blithe as a child.

For half an hour already, two companies of soldiers dressed in Zouave uniform, whose duty it was to keep the way open for the passage of the Sultan, had been stationed in the square, along with a thousand or so curious spectators. Nothing is odder than the variety of people who gather on such occasions. Here and there were some splendid closed carriages belonging to noble Turkish ladies, guarded by giant eunuchs on horseback, stationed motionless by the doors; a few English ladies in hired open carriages; several groups of travellers, with binoculars slung on straps over their shoulders, among whom I recognized the conquering count from the Hotel Byzantium, who had perhaps come to transfix with one triumphant stare his powerful and unhappy rival. Walking among the crowd were a few long-haired characters with albums under their arms, who I guessed might be artists wanting to make a furtive sketch of the imperial likeness. Seated right at the front, near the band, was a handsome French woman, dressed rather oddly, somewhat forward in appearance and in manner, whom I took to be a cosmopolitan adventuress, come there to catch the Sultan's eye, for I could read in her face "the trembling joy of a great purpose".* There were a few of those old Turks, suspicious and fanatical subjects, who never miss seeing their Sultan when he makes a public appearance, because they wish to be assured with their own eyes, for the sake of the glory and prosperity of the universe, that he is alive and well – indeed the Sultan appears punctually every Friday precisely in order to give his people proof of his existence, since several times in the past a sultan's natural or violent death has been kept secret by some court conspiracy. There were beggars, Turkish dandies, eunuchs at a loose end, and dervishes. Among the latter I noticed an old man, tall and emaciated, standing quite still, who kept his terrible gaze fixed upon the palace gate with a sinister expression. The thought crossed my mind that he might be waiting for the Sultan so that he could block

his path and yell in his face – as the dervish in the *Oriental Poems* does
to Ali Pasha of Tepelenë – "You are nothing but a cursed dog!"* But
there has been no new example of such sublime audacity since the
famous sabre stroke of Mahmut. There were also sundry groups of
Turkish women standing apart, looking like carnival masqueraders,
and all the usual assemblage of stage extras that make up a crowd
in Constantinople. Their heads were all silhouetted against the blue
waters of the Bosphorus and probably they were all saying the same
things.

At the time of which I write, rumours of the eccentricities of
Abdülaziz had begun to circulate. His insatiable greed for money
had long been known and talked about. People said: "Mahmut liked
bloodshed, Abdülmecit was keen on women, Abdülaziz is mad about
gold." All the hopes that had been placed in him when he was still
a prince and had struck an ox down with his fist, declaring: "Thus
will I end barbarity", had long since vanished. The leanings towards
a simple and austere way of life which had characterized the early
years of his reign, when he had kept only one wife and curtailed the
enormous expenses of the Seraglio, were now only distant memories.
It was possibly years since he had given up his studies of law, military
science and European literature, which had created such a stir, as if
people's hopes for the renewal of the empire had all rested in him. For
a long time now his only thought was for himself. Every day rumours
abounded of some angry outburst against the Minister of Finance,
who would not or could not give him all the money he wanted. When
the minister started to remonstrate, Abdülaziz would throw the first
object that came to hand at the head of his unfortunate Excellency,
reciting with what strength of voice was left to him the venerable
imperial oath: "By the God that created the heavens and the earth,
by the Prophet Mohammad, by the seven variations of the Koran, by
the hundred and twenty-four thousand prophets of God, by the soul
of my grandfather and by the soul of my father, by my sons and by
my sword, give me the money or I'll stick your head on the top of the
highest minaret in Stamboul." And by one means or another he got
what he wanted, and the money he managed to extort in this way he
would sometimes hoard and gloat over like some common miser, or else
squander entirely on puerile whims – one day he wanted some lions,
another day tigers, and would send messengers off to procure them in
India and Africa; then, for a month on end, five hundred parrots all

squawking the same word filled the imperial gardens with cacophony; then came a passion for carriages, and pianos, which he wanted to play with the instrument supported on the backs of four slaves; then a mania for cockfights, which he watched with enthusiasm, hanging with his own hands a medal round the neck of the victorious bird while sending the vanquished fowl into exile beyond the Bosphorus; then a craze for gambling, for kiosks, for paintings: the court seemed to have returned to the days of Ibrahim I. Yet the poor prince found no peace, and merely passed from one anxiety and trouble to another; he was troubled and gloomy and seemed to foresee the unhappy end that awaited him. Sometimes he got it into his head that he would die of poisoning and for a time, suspicious of everyone, would eat nothing but hard-boiled eggs; on other occasions, seized with a terror of fire breaking out, he would have all the wooden objects in his rooms removed, even the mirror frames. It was said that, because of his dread of fire, he read every night by the light of a candle floating in a bucket of water. And despite these follies, the main reason for which – so it was said – needed no explanation, he preserved all the strength of his imperious will, and knew how to make himself obeyed, and to make the boldest of men quail before him. The only person who had any influence over him was his mother, a woman of a vain and haughty disposition, who in the early years of his reign used to have the streets leading to the mosque where her son went to pray carpeted with brocade, the next day giving all these carpets away to the slaves whose duty it was to remove them. In all the disorder of his troubled existence, and in the intervals of his major obsessions, other more trivial whimsies affected Abdülaziz, such as wanting to have a still life frescoed on a certain door, but only with particular flowers and with certain fruits in one special arrangement, and once the painter had been given his instructions down to the smallest details, he would stand and watch every brush stroke, as if he had no other care in the world. The whole city gossiped about these eccentricities, greatly embellished no doubt by the thousand wagging tongues in the Seraglio palace, and perhaps the first stirrings of the conspiracy which toppled him from his throne two years later date from this period. His fall, as the Muslims say, was written down as his destiny, and with it the judgement that was pronounced on him and on his reign – which is not so very different from the judgement which might be passed on almost all the Sultans of more recent times. Imperial princes, encouraged to adopt European manners with a superficial yet varied and liberal education, and in the fervour of their youthful eagerness for novelty and glory, dream of carrying out reform and renewal when they ascend to the throne, and vow to dedicate austere and industrious lives to that end. But after they have reigned for a few years and discover all their efforts to be futile, surrounded by a thousand obstacles, blocked by habit and tradition, opposed by men and circumstances, they become terrified by the unforeseen difficulties of the undertaking and give up in despair. They seek in pleasure what they cannot obtain by glorious achievement and little by little are lost in an entirely sensual life, in which the memory of their early ambitions and even the awareness of their present degradation vanishes. Thus it always happens that at the accession of each new Sultan, hopes are raised, not without reason, which are always followed by complete disillusion.

Abdülaziz did not make us wait. At the appointed time, a trumpet sounded, the band burst into a military march, the soldiers presented arms, a company of lancers suddenly emerged from the palace gate, and the Sultan appeared, advancing slowly on horseback, followed by his entourage. He passed very close to me and I had plenty of time to examine him attentively. I was oddly disappointed. The King of Kings, the prodigal, violent, capricious, imperious Sultan, who was then about forty-four years of age, had the air of a good-natured Turk, who seemed to be masquerading as Sultan without being aware of it. He was a stout, thickset man, with a handsome face, large calm eyes, and a short thick beard, slightly grizzled; he had an open, mild countenance, and his bearing was easy, almost casual; his gaze was steady and slow, and betrayed not the slightest awareness of the thousands of eyes then staring upon him. He rode a beautiful grey horse with gold housings, led by two splendidly apparelled grooms. His entourage followed him at a great distance, and it was only this which made you realize he was the Sultan. His dress was very plain. He wore a simple fez, a long dark frock coat buttoned to the chin, light-coloured trousers and leather boots. He advanced very slowly, looking about him with an expression of mingled benevolence and weariness, as if he were saying to himself: "Ah! If only you knew how bored I am!" The Muslims made deep bows; many Europeans raised their hats; but he acknowledged no one. Passing near to us, he gave a glance at a tall officer who saluted with his sabre, another at the Bosphorus, and then a rather longer look at two young English ladies who were gazing at him from a carriage, and who blushed as red as beetroot under his stare. I observed that his hand was white and well-shaped, the same right hand that two years later was to cut open his wrist in his bath. Behind him came a throng of pashas, courtiers and dignitaries on horseback; almost all large men, with big black beards, dressed simply, silent, grave, composed, as if following a funeral cortège; then came a number of grooms leading some magnificent horses; then a crowd of officials on foot with their chests covered with gold braid; after these had gone by, the soldiers lowered their weapons, the onlookers dispersed about the square, and I remained standing, with my eyes fixed upon the summit of Mount Bulgurlu, reflecting upon the strange conditions in which the Sultan of Stamboul finds himself.

He is a Muslim monarch, I thought, and he has his palace at the foot of a Christian city, Pera, which towers above him on its hill. He is the absolute sovereign of one of the largest empires in the world, yet only a short distance away in his own capital, in grand palaces that look down upon his Seraglio, a handful of ceremoniously mannered foreigners play the master in his house, and when they treat with him, conceal under their respectful language a perpetual menace which makes him tremble. He has measureless power over the lives and fortunes of millions of subjects, and possesses the means of satisfying his wildest desires, but he cannot choose what headgear to wear. He is surrounded by an army of courtiers and guards, ready to kiss his footprints, yet he lives in perpetual fear for his own life and for that of his children. He possesses a thousand of the most beautiful women in the world, and he alone, among all the Muslims of his Empire, cannot give his hand in marriage to a free woman. His children can only be born of slaves and he himself is called "Son of a slave" by the same people who call him the "shadow of God". His name evokes reverence and fear from Tartary to the Maghrib, while in his own city there is a large and ever-growing number of people who deride his person, his authority, and his religion, and over whom he has no control. Over the face of his immense empire, among the most wretched tribes in the remotest provinces, in mosques and solitary monasteries in savage lands, ardent prayers are said for his life and for his glory; and he cannot take a step in his own states without finding himself among enemies, who hate him and call down the vengeance of Heaven upon his head. For all that part of the world which lies in front of his palace, he is one of the most august and formidable monarchs in the universe;

for the part which lies behind, he is the weakest, most pusillanimous and most wretched man to wear a crown. A vast current of ideas, of will, of forces contrary to the nature and to the traditions of his power, swirls round and over him, busily transforming – in spite of him and without his knowledge – laws, customs, manners, usages, beliefs, men, all things. And he is there, between Europe and Asia, in his great palace washed by the sea, as in a ship ready to spread her sails, in the midst of an infinite confusion of ideas and events, surrounded by fabulous pomp and the deepest poverty, neither one thing nor the other, no longer a true Muslim but not yet a real European, reigning over a people already partly transformed, barbarian by blood, civilized in appearance, two-faced like Janus, worshipped like a god, watched like a slave, adored, undermined, deceived: every day that passes extinguishes a ray of his halo and detaches a stone from his pedestal. Were I in his shoes, tired of such a condition, sated with pleasures, sick of adulation, worn out with constant suspicion, indignant at that insecure and futile sovereignty over nameless disorder, I would at times, when the vast Seraglio is plunged in sleep, want to dive into the Bosphorus like a fugitive galley slave to go and spend the night at a tavern in Galata surrounded by a crowd of sailors, with a glass of beer and a clay pipe, singing the "Marseillaise".

After half an hour the Sultan passed again on his return, this time rapidly, in a closed carriage, followed by a number of officers on foot, and the spectacle was over. What made the deepest impression upon me was the sight of those officers in full ceremonial uniform running along like a crowd of lackeys behind the imperial coach. Never had I seen military dignity so debased.

As the reader can see, the spectacle of the Sultan's procession has today become a rather drab affair. The sultans of olden times issued forth in great pomp, preceded and followed by swarms of horsemen, slaves, guards, gardeners, eunuchs and chamberlains, who, seen from a distance, so enthusiastic chroniclers tell us, looked like a sea of tulips. The sultans of today on the contrary seem to shun pomp and circumstance as though it were a mere theatrical display of lost grandeur. What would one of those early sultans say were he to rise up from his tomb at Bursa or turbeh in Stamboul and see one of his nineteenth-century descendants passing by, dressed in a black frock coat, without a turban, without a sword, unadorned with jewels, surrounded by a crowd of insolent foreigners? I suspect he would blush with rage and shame and, as a sign of his supreme displeasure, cut off the beard of his unworthy representative, as Süleyman I did to Hassan, with one sweep of his scimitar – the deadliest insult which can be offered to an Ottoman. It is true that there is the same difference between the Sultans of the past, whose names alone were enough to strike terror in Europe between the twelfth and sixteenth centuries, and those of today as there is between the Ottoman Empire as it is now and that of earlier centuries. Those former Sultans summed up all the youth and beauty and vigour of their race; they were not only a living image of their own people, a beautiful emblem, a precious pearl upon the sword of Islam, but in their very selves were one of its great strengths: it is impossible not to see in their personal qualities one of the main reasons why Ottoman power grew in such an extraordinary way. The most glorious period of Ottoman history lies in the dynasty's first youth which lasted 193 years from Osman to Mehmet II, a remarkable succession of powerful princes. With one exception, and taking due account of the times and conditions of the race, they were austere and wise and loved by their subjects. They were often fierce but rarely unjust, and frequently even generous and benevolent towards their enemies. All of them were princes befitting their race, handsome and imposing in appearance, true lions, as their mothers called them, "whose roar made the earth tremble". The Abdülmecits, the Abdülazizes, the Murats, the Abdülhamits, are mere shadows of Padishahs in comparison with those formidable young men, born to girls of fifteen and youths of eighteen, bred from the finest Tartar stock, and from the flower of Greek, Persian and Caucasian beauty. At fourteen years of age they were commanding armies and governing provinces, and their mothers were rewarding them with slave-girls as beautiful and ardent as themselves. At sixteen they were already fathers and were still capable of procreating at seventy as well. But the act of love in them did not undermine and weaken their natural vigour of mind and body. Their minds were made of iron, as the poets sang, and their bodies of steel. They all had certain features that have been lost in their degenerate descendants, the high forehead, the arched eyebrows meeting like those of the Persians, the blue eyes of the sons of the steppe, the nose curving above the full red lips "like the beak of a parrot over a cherry", and the full black beard, for which the Seraglio poets were forever racking their brains in the effort to find gracious or striking similes.

They had "the glance of a Taurus eagle and the strength of the king of the desert; necks like a bull, broad shoulders, and wide chests, that could contain all the warlike fury of their people", long arms, large joints, short bowed legs, that could make the strongest Turkoman horses neigh with pain, and large hairy hands that could wield with ease the bronze maces and huge bows carried by their soldiers. And their epithets were worthy of them: the Wrestler, the Champion, the Thunderbolt, the Bonecrusher, the Shedder of Blood. After Allah, war was their first thought, and death their last. They may not have possessed the strategic genius of great generals, but all were endowed with that resolution and promptness of action that often takes the place of genius, and with that fierce obstinacy which often obtains the same results. They flew, like winged furies, over the field of battle: the long heron plumes of their white turbans and their wide kaftans of gold and purple were visible from afar; their blood-curdling yells drove the troops back to face Serbian and German gunfire when the oxhide whips wielded by a thousand enraged *çavuş* no longer sufficed. They plunged on horseback into the rivers, whirling their scimitars dripping with blood over their heads; they seized slothful or cowardly pashas by the throat and tore them from the saddle as they rode by; they sprang down from their horses in the rout and planted their daggers glittering with rubies in the backs of fleeing soldiers; and, struck down with a fatal blow, they held the wound together and rode up onto a prominent part of the battlefield to show their janissaries their pale but still imperious and menacing countenance, before they fell, groaning with rage, but not with pain. What can those young Circassian or Persian girls, hardly out of childhood, have felt when there appeared before them for the first time, on the evening of the day of battle, in the dim light of a crimson tent, one of those terrifying proud sultans, drunk with victory and bloodshed? But they would become kind and loving; they would clasp those little hands in their own enormous grip, still shaking from the sword, and search for images with which to praise the beauty of their trembling slaves – flowers in their gardens, pearls in their daggers, the most beautiful birds in their forests, the most richly coloured dawns over Anatolia or Mesopotamia – until the girls grew excited and replied in their own passionate and extravagant style: "Crown of my head! Glory of my life! Sweetest, most terrifying of Lords! May your face always shine bright over the two worlds of Asia and Europe! May victory follow you wherever your horse takes you! May your shadow cover the whole earth! I wish I were a fragrant rose in your turban or a butterfly beating its wings on your brow!" Afterwards, in a low voice, as their satisfied lovers doze on their breasts, they tell them childish tales about palaces of emeralds and mountains of gold, while all round the tent, across the dark blood-soaked battlefield, the fierce army is at rest. But the sultans shed their softness on the threshold of the harem and left after their love-making even more ferocious and brave. They were gentle in the harem, fierce on the battlefield, humble in the mosque, proud upon the throne. Seated there they spoke a language full of dazzling hyperbole and sudden menace; every sentence was an irrevocable pronouncement, which declared war, or raised one man to the height of fortune, or sent the head of another rolling down its steps, or unleashed a storm of fire and steel on a rebellious province. Thus raging like a whirlwind from Persia to the Danube and from Arabia to Macedonia, amid battles, triumphs, hunting expeditions and love trysts, they passed from the flower of their youth to a manhood which was even more turbulent and audacious, and then to an old age undetected, unfelt by the lovers they embraced, the horses they rode, the sword-hilt they grasped. Sometimes – and not only in old age, but also when they were younger – oppressed by the weight of their monstrous power, suddenly overwhelmed, in the heat of victory and triumph, by the consciousness of a more-than-human responsibility, and seized by a kind of terror in the solitude of their own greatness, they turned with all their soul to God, and passed days and nights in the shadowed bowers of their gardens, composing religious poems, or they went down to the seashore to meditate upon the Koran, or they joined the frantic dances of the dervishes, or mortified the flesh with fasts and haircloth shirts in the cavern of some aged hermit. And as in life so in death almost all of them were regarded by their subjects with veneration and awe, whether they died in saintly serenity like the head of the dynasty, or weighed down by years of glory and sadness like Orhan, or by a traitor's dagger like Murat I, or in the despair of exile like Beyazit, or in placid conversation among a circle of wise men and poets, like Mehmet I, or in the pain of defeat like Murat II. We can be sure that their threatening phantoms are all that will remain of grandeur and poetry in the blood-soaked annals of Ottoman history.

## *Turkish Women*

It is a great surprise for those arriving for the first time in Constantinople, after having heard so much about the state of slavery in which Turkish women are kept, to see them everywhere and at all hours of the day going about as in any European city. It seems as if all those imprisoned swallows have been let loose for the first time on that particular day, and that a new era of liberty for the Muslim fair sex has begun. The first impression is very curious. The foreigner wonders whether all those white-veiled figures in gaudily coloured cloaks are guests off to a masked ball, or nuns, or madwomen; and as not one of them is ever seen in the company of a man, they seem to belong to no one, and to be all young girls or widows, or members of a large company of those who have "made unfortunate marriages". At first it is hard to believe that all those men and women who see and brush against each other every day in the streets without any sign of reciprocal acknowledgement or of being in company can have anything actually in common. At every moment these strange figures and even stranger customs bring you up short. So these are the women, you think, whom the poets have described as "conquerors of the heart", "fountains of pleasure", "little rose leaves", "early ripening grapes", "dews of the morning", "auroras", "refreshments" and "full moons". These are the *hanums* and the mysterious concubines which peopled our dreams when we were twenty, and used to read Victor Hugo's ballads in the garden shadows: we imagined a single embrace from one of these creatures would leave all our youthful prowess exhausted. These are the oppressed beauties, imprisoned behind gratings, watched over by eunuchs, segregated from the world, who live their lives on earth like ghosts, with a cry of pleasure and a shriek of pain? Let us see if there's still any truth in all this poetry.

\* \* \*

First of all, the Turkish woman's face is no longer a mystery, and thus a great part of the poetry that surrounded her has vanished. That jealous veil which, according to the Koran, was intended to be a sign of her virtue and to put a stop to the world's chatter is now worn only for appearance's sake. Everyone knows what a yashmak is. There are two large white veils, one of which, bound tightly round the head like a bandage, covers the forehead down to the eyebrows, and is tied behind,

135

just above the nape of the neck, letting two long ends fall down the back as far as the girdle; the other covers the whole of the lower part of the face up to the eyes, and is knotted to the first so that the two seem to be a single piece of cloth. But these veils, which should be made of muslin and arranged in such a way as to leave only the eyes and the cheekbones exposed, are in fact of transparent tulle, and so loose that not only the face, but the ears, neck and hair are visible. Often, on the "reformed" ladies, you can see a European hat as well, trimmed with flowers and feathers. In this way the very opposite of what once obtained is now the case, for the older women, who were allowed to uncover their faces a little, are now the most closely veiled, in order to deceive the world, while the younger, and more especially the beautiful ones, who were always rigorously hidden, now put themselves on show. Thus many charming surprises and lovely mysteries, treasured by poets and novelists, are no longer possible; one myth, among others, is the belief that husbands behold the faces of their brides for the first time on their wedding night. But apart from the face, every thing else – breasts, waist, arms and hips – is carefully hidden by the feredgi, a kind of long tunic, with a shoulder cape and long sleeves, broad and shapeless, falling like a large cloak from shoulders to feet, made of cloth in winter and silk in summer, and almost always of one brilliant colour – bright red or orange or green – which changes each year according to the dictates of fashion, although the form of the garment itself remains the same. But even though they are wrapped up in this manner they can adjust the yashmak so artfully that those who are beautiful seem even lovelier and the plain-faced become attractive. It is impossible to describe what they contrive to do with those two veils, with what grace they arrange them in coronets or turbans, with what ample, noble folds they twist and pleat them, with what lightness and elegant nonchalance they loosen them and let them fall, using them to display, conceal, promise, puzzle, or unexpectedly reveal some small marvel. Some seem to be wearing a white diaphanous cloud around their heads that might vanish with a puff of wind; others look as if they were crowned with garlands of lilies and jasmine flowers; all seem to have very white complexions, and the veil adds new charms of whiteness and softness and freshness. It is a costume at once severe and welcoming, that has something both virginal and priestly about it. You would suppose that under the veil only gentle thoughts and innocent fancies are to be found... Instead, there is a little of everything...

\* \* \*

It is difficult to define the beauty of Turkish women. Whenever I think of them, I see a fair complexion, two black eyes, a crimson mouth and a sweet expression. Almost all of them, however, use cosmetics. They whiten their faces with almond and jasmine paste, they lengthen and darken their eyebrows with Indian ink, they tint their eyelids and powder their necks, they outline their eyes in black and wear beauty spots on their cheeks. But all this is done with taste, not like the beauties of Fez, who paint their faces as though they were whitewashing them. Most of them have fine oval faces, slightly arched noses, full lips and round chins with dimples; many have dimples also in their cheeks; a beautiful neck, long and pliant; and small hands, which are almost always hidden, unfortunately, by the long sleeves of their mantles. Almost all are plump, and many are above average height; the beanpole-thin and pancake-flat types, which you find in our countries, are few and far between. If they have a fault it is that they walk with a stoop, and somewhat clumsily, like children who are gauche or sleepy; it is said this gait comes from a weakness in the legs caused by spending too much time at the baths, and also because they wear the wrong kinds of shoes. In fact it is common to see very elegant ladies, who must have small, delicate feet, wearing men's slippers, or tall thick leather boots, which a rag-picker back in Europe would reject. But even in this ugly manner of walking they have a kind of childish grace, which when one has learnt to discern it, is not displeasing. The kind of strutting figures so frequently seen in European cities – who dress like fashion plates, take mincing, puppet-like steps, and look as if they were hopping over the squares of a chessboard – are not to be found. They have not yet lost the heavy, negligent grace of the oriental way of moving, and if they were to lose it they might have a more dignified bearing, but they would certainly be less charming. There is a great variety of beauty among them, since there is a mingling of Turkish, Arabic, Circassian or Persian strains. There are thirty-year-old matrons, whose buxom forms the feredgi fails to conceal, very tall, with great dark eyes, full lips and dilated nostrils – *hanım* whose mere look would strike terror into a hundred slaves, and the very sight of whom makes one think that the idea Turkish men can manage to satisfy four wives is all so much braggadocio.

There are others who are small and plump and seem entirely spherical – face, eyes, nose and mouth – and with such a placid, kindly, childlike air, an appearance of such docile acceptance of their destined role as mere distractions or pastimes that when you encounter them you'd like to offer them a sweet to pop in their mouths. There are the slender forms of sixteen-year-old wives, ardent and lively, with eyes full of caprice and cunning, who make the onlooker pity the poor effendi who has to control them and the unfortunate eunuch who is obliged to keep an eye on them. The city makes a wonderful backdrop for their beauty and their way of dressing. Picture one of these white-veiled, purple-robed women sitting in a caique in the middle of the blue waters of the Bosphorus; or reclining on the grass under the green shade of the trees in the cemeteries; or even better, coming down a steep and lonely street in Stamboul, at the end of which there is a great plane tree, with the wind blowing, and her veil and feredgi billowing out, displaying neck and foot and ankle: at such moments, if Süleyman the Magnificent's indulgent law were still in force, which decreed you had to pay a fine for every kiss given to the wife or daughter of another man, Harpagon* himself would cast avarice aside. And when there's a strong wind Muslim women do not bother to hold down their feredgi, because their sense of modesty does not extend below the knees, and sometimes stops a good way above them.

* * *

One thing that initially takes you aback is their way of looking and laughing, which would seem to justify the boldest advances. It frequently happens that a young European man stares long and hard at a Turkish lady, even one of high rank, who returns his stare with a kindly expression or undisguised smile. It is not rare, either, for a handsome *hanım* in a carriage to give a gracious wave of her hand, behind the eunuch's back, to a young European gentleman whom she sees admiring her. Sometimes in a cemetery, or in a quiet street, a headstrong woman will even toss a flower as she passes by, or drop one with the obvious intention of letting the elegant *giaour* walking behind her pick it up. In this way a naive traveller may be led into making wildly mistaken assumptions: there are indeed some European men who, after a month in Constantinople, really believe that a hundred unhappy women are pining for them. These gestures are doubtless in part expressions of simple goodwill, but, more importantly, they arise from a spirit of rebellion common to all Turkish women: they chafe against the subjection in which they are held and they give vent to their irritation, when they can, with such foolish pranks, if only to spite their masters behind their backs. They do it more from childishness than flirtatiousness; their coquetry is of a singular kind, much resembling the behaviour of little girls when they first become aware they are the objects of attention. Laughing uncontrollably, or looking up, their mouths gaping with astonishment, pretending to have a headache or a twinge of pain in the foot, fidgeting petulantly with the uncomfortable folds of the feredgi – schoolgirlish tricks done more to amuse than to seduce. But you never see them affecting drawing-room airs or posing as if for a photograph. What little art they show is entirely rudimentary. One can see, as Tommaseo would say, that there are not many veils to lift; that they are not accustomed to being wooed for a long time, or "circled round silently", like Giusti's hieroglyphical women,* and that when they feel an attraction towards anyone, instead of standing there, sighing and simpering, they would – if they were allowed to say what they felt – go straight to the point: "Christian, you please me!" Not being able to say this, they show it by displaying two rows of pearly-white teeth, or by laughing in his face. Though they are beautiful and tame, they are still Tartars.

\* \* \*

And they are free; it is a truth which is obvious to the visitor almost as soon as he arrives. It is an exaggeration to say, like Lady Montagu, that they are freer than European women, but whoever has been in Constantinople will laugh when he hears them spoken of as "slaves". When they wish to go out, they order the eunuchs to prepare the carriage, ask no one's permission, and come back when they please, provided it is before nightfall. Formerly they could not go out without being accompanied by a eunuch, or by a female slave or friend, and the boldest were at least obliged to take one of their children with them, who would serve as a sign of respectability. If any woman appeared alone in a quiet street or square, some city watchman or austere old Turk would accost her and demand: "Where are you going? Where are you coming from? Why are you on your own? Is this the way you show respect to your husband? Go home at once!" But now hundreds of them go out alone and can be seen at all hours in the streets of the Muslim and European parts of town. They go to pay visits on their friends, they pass half the day at the baths, they take boat trips; on Thursdays they go to the Sweet Waters of Europe, on Sundays to those of Asia, on Fridays to the cemetery in Scutari, on other days to the Princes' Islands, to Therapia, to Büyükdere, to Kalender, to picnic with their slave-women, in groups of eight or nine. They go to pray at the tombs of the sultans and their wives, to see the dervishes in their monasteries, to visit public displays of wedding trousseaus, without a single man escorting or following them or even reprimanding them. To see a Turk in the streets of Constantinople in the company of a veiled woman – not arm in arm, but just walking by her side or stopping to talk to her – even if they carried placards round their necks declaring they were man and wife, would seem to everyone the most unheard-of thing, an act of unbelievable impudence, as we would react in our own countries if a man and a woman were to make love in public. In this sense, Turkish women enjoy greater freedom than their European counterparts, and their delight in their liberty is indescribable; they rush into noise, crowds, light, open air with wild excitement, while in their own homes they only ever see one man, and live behind grated windows and in cloistered gardens. They run about the city with the joy of a liberated prisoner. It is amusing to follow one of them from a distance to see how she manages to eke out and refine the pleasures of gadding about. She enters the nearest mosque to say a prayer, and then stays for a quarter of an hour under the portico chatting with a friend; then she's off to the bazaar to look in on a dozen shops and turn two or three upside down in search of some trifle; then she takes the tram, gets out at the fish market, crosses the bridge, stops to inspect all the braids and wigs in the hairdressers' windows in Pera, enters a cemetery to sit on a tomb and eat a cake, returns to the city, goes down to the Golden Horn, popping in and out everywhere, and glancing at everything out of the corner of her eye – shop windows, prints, advertisements, passers-by, carriages, signs, theatre entrances – buys a bunch of flowers, drinks a glass of lemonade, gives alms to a beggar, crosses the Golden Horn again in a caique, and starts zigzagging around Stamboul all over again; there she catches the tram a second time, and when she gets off at her own front door, is quite capable of turning back, just to have a stroll around the neighbourhood, just like children who are let out of home for the first time on their own and

Kadin

In the harem

Turkish ladies at the Sweet Waters

who try to make the most of their liberty and see a little of everything. Any poor stout effendi who tried to follow his wife to spy on her and see if she had a lover would be left behind panting and exhausted long before she'd finished.

\* \* \*

To see the Muslim fair sex, it is a good idea to go, on an important festival day, to the Sweet Waters of Europe at the end of the Golden Horn, or to those of Asia, near the village of Anadoluhisar. These are two great public parks, full of trees, cafés and fountains, with two narrow rivers running through them. There, over a wide grassy plain, under the green shady pavilions formed by groves of walnut trees, pines, plane trees and sycamores, thousands of Turkish women can be seen seated in groups and circles, surrounded by their female slaves, eunuchs and children, picnicking and frolicking for half the day in the midst of crowds of people strolling about. On entering you fall into a kind of dreamlike state. It seems like a festival in the paradise of Islam. All those white-veiled figures, in scarlet, yellow, green and grey feredgi, the endless groups of slaves in many-coloured garments, the romping about of children in fancy dress, the large Smyrna carpets spread out on the ground, the gold and silver beakers passing from hand to hand, the Muslim coffee-sellers in festive rig who run to and fro with fruits and ices, gypsies dancing, Bulgarian shepherds piping, horses with trappings of silk and gold tied to trees and pawing the ground, pashas, beys and young gentlemen galloping along the river banks, the movement of the crowds in the distance like a wind-rippled field of camellias and roses, gaily coloured caiques and splendid carriages arriving in quick succession to add yet more colour, and the confused sound of singing, flutes, bagpipes, castanets, children's voices – all bathed by green and shade, broken here and there with vivid glimpses of the sunlit landscapes beyond. It is so cheerful and unusual a spectacle you want to applaud and cry out "*Bravissimi!*" as in a theatre.

\* \* \*

Even here, despite the confusion, it is extremely rare to catch a Turkish couple exchanging amorous glances, or knowing smiles and gestures. Gallantry in public does not exist there as in our countries;

the lovesick sentinels pacing up and down under the windows of their beloved, or the pining rearguards who dog the footsteps of their goddess for three hours on end are not to be found. Love-making takes place within domestic walls. If you do happen in some empty street to come across a young Turk gazing up at a lattice, behind which a pair of black eyes gleam or a white hand waves, you may be quite certain that the couple are betrothed. Only the betrothed are allowed to indulge in the sweet childishness of official love-making, such as conversing at a distance by signs – sending a flower to each other, or a ribbon, or wearing a particular coloured dress or scarf. And in these matters Turkish women are experts. They have a thousand objects – flowers, fruits, leaves, feathers, stones – each one of which conveys an agreed meaning, an adjective or a verb or even a complete sentence, so that they can make a letter out of a bouquet of flowers, or say a hundred things with a box or purse full of various small objects that only seem to have been put together at random. Each object is associated with a line of verse, so lovers can compose a love poem in a few minutes. In translation, a clove, a strip of paper, a slice of pear, a bit of soap, a match, a snatch of gold thread and a pinch of cinnamon and pepper mean: "I have loved you for a long time. I burn, I languish, I die for love of you. Give me a little hope – do not reject me – send me one word of reply." They can say many other things besides; reprimand, advice, warning, news, everything can be communicated in this way. Young girls, when they feel the first pangs of love, find much to occupy them in learning this symbolical phrasebook and composing long letters addressed to the handsome and youthful sultans seen in their dreams. There is also the language of gesture, some of which is really charming: for instance the man who mimes stabbing his chest with a dagger, signifying: "I am torn by the furies of love"; to which the lady replies by letting both her arms fall to her sides, so that her mantle opens a little, which means: "I open my arms for you". But perhaps no European has ever witnessed such things, and they are in any case old-fashioned ways now falling into disuse. Nor will you learn about them from the Turks, though occasionally some good-natured *hanım* might confide in a Christian friend of her own sex.

\* \* \*

This is also the only way we can find out how Turkish women dress inside the harem, although we all have some idea of the beautiful, rich and inventive costume which bestows a princess-like dignity, as well as a childlike grace, on the women who wear it. We shall never see it, unless the fashion is adopted in our own country, for even if at some point in the future the feredgi should be thrown aside, by then Turkish women will be wearing European dress underneath as well. How galling for the painters, and what a disappointment for us all! Imagine a beautiful woman, "slender as a cypress" and blushing "with all the tints of the rose", wearing, cocked at a slight angle, a small round cap of crimson velvet or some silvery embroidered cloth; her black tresses tumble down her shoulders; her gown of white damask is embroidered with gold, with billowing sleeves and a long train, and parts in front to display pink silk trousers, which fall in many pleats over two small slippers with curling toes; a sash of green satin round her waist; with diamond necklaces, bracelets, brooches, clips in her hair, on the brim of her cap and her slippers, on the neck of her chemise and her belt, and encircling her forehead. Glittering from head to foot like a statue of the Madonna in a Spanish cathedral, she sprawls like a child on a broad divan, surrounded by her Circassian, Arab and Persian slave-women wrapped, like antique statues, in large flowing robes. Or imagine a bride, "white as the summit of Olympus", dressed in pale blue satin, and completely covered with a veil of woven gold, seated upon a pearl-embossed ottoman, in front of which, upon a carpet from Tehran, the bridegroom kneels, making his final prayer before uncovering his treasure. Or picture a favourite who is in love, who is waiting for her husband in the most private room in the harem, dressed only in a jacket and trousers, which show all the perfections of her supple body to best advantage, and give her the air of a handsome pageboy, slim and elegant. You have to admit that those ugly "reformed" Turks, with their shaven heads and black overcoats, have much more than they actually deserve. This wardrobe for wearing at home, however, is subject to changes in fashion. The women, having nothing else to do, pass their time in devising new adornments: they cover themselves with trinkets and frills, put feathers and ribbons in their hair, tie bands around their foreheads, and strips of fur about their necks and arms. They borrow something from every kind of oriental dress, but they mingle European fashions with their own as well: they wear wigs and hairpieces, and dye their own hair black or blonde or red, and adopt a hundred other outlandish fancies, competing among themselves just like the vainest women in European cities. If with the wave of a magic wand at the Sweet Waters all the feredgi and all the veils fell away, we should probably see Turkish women dressed like Asiatic queens and French milliners, noblewomen in ball gowns or merchants' wives dressed up to the nines, as *vivandières*, as circus riders, as Greeks or gypsies – in short, in as great and strange a variety of dress as can be seen among the men on the bridge of the Sultana Valide.

\* \* \*

The apartments in which these wealthy and beautiful Muslim women live correspond in a way to their seductive and bizarre attire. The rooms reserved for them are generally well situated, commanding marvellous views of country, sea and city. Below, there is a small garden, closed in by high walls covered with ivy and jasmine; above, a terrace; overlooking the street, small projecting rooms with large windows like the miradors seen in Spanish houses. The interior is exquisite. The rooms are almost always small; the floors covered with Chinese mats or carpets, the ceilings painted with flowers and fruit. Large divans line the walls, with a small marble fountain in the middle, vases of flowers in the window bays, and that dim, soft light, so characteristic of oriental houses, like a woodland grove or a cloister, or some sweet sacred spot, where you must tread quietly and speak low, and use gentle, mild words, discoursing only of love or of God. The suffused light, the fragrance wafting from the garden, the subdued splashing of water, the slave-girls gliding about like shadows, the deep silence, the blue peaks of the mountains on the Asian shore seen through the apertures in the lattice and the tendrils of honeysuckle which trail across the window – all these things affect the European women who visit a harem for the first time with an inexpressible feeling of sweetness and melancholy. Most harems are decorated in a simple, almost severe style, but there are some of great magnificence, with walls covered with white satin embroidered in gold, cedar-wood ceilings, gilded lattices and precious furniture. The furniture gives a clue to the way of life we find there. It consists of armchairs, ottomans both large and small, little carpets, stools and footrests, cushions of every description, and mattresses covered with shawls and brocades; everything is soft and delicate, inviting you to sit, stretch out, make love, fall asleep, dream. You find hand-mirrors and large ostrich-feather fans scattered about; carved chibouks are hung on the walls; there are birdcages in the windows, incense-burners and musical clocks on the tables, toys and knick-knacks of every kind which reveal all the whimsies of idle women with time on their hands. Nor is this luxury confined to the objects on display. There are houses in which the table service is of silver, the finger bowls of gold, the napkins are of satin with gold thread, gems glitter on the cutlery, coffee cups, urns, pipes, upholstery and fans. There are other houses – many more of course – in which almost nothing has changed since the days of the ancient Tartar tent, when all the household goods could be packed upon the back of a single mule, ready for a new journey across Asia; houses of strict religious austerity and observance, in which, when the hour for departure arrives, the only sound that can be heard is the master's calm voice saying: "*Olsun!*" ("Let it be!")

* * *

As everyone knows, the Turkish house is divided into two parts: the harem and the selamlik. The selamlik is the part reserved for men. Here they work, eat their meals, receive their friends, take their afternoon nap and sleep at night, when they do not feel the urge to make love. Women never enter it. Just as in the selamlik men are the masters, so the woman is mistress in the harem. There she governs and administers and can do anything she pleases, except receive men. When she does not choose to receive her husband, she can even decline his visit, and politely request him to come at another time. A single door and a small corridor divide the harem from the selamlik, but it's as if they were two houses at a great distance from each other. Men pay calls on the effendi and women visit the *hanım* but they never meet or exchange words – indeed they are often completely unacquainted with each other. There are different servants for each part, and almost invariably there are two kitchens. Rarely does the husband dine with his wife, especially when he has more than one. All they have in common is the bed on which they couple. The man never enters the harem as a husband – in the sense of a companion to his wife and a mentor to his children – but only as a lover. He leaves behind him on the threshold – if he can – all the concerns which might allay the pleasure he is seeking; all that part of himself which has nothing to do with the desire of the moment. He goes to the harem to forget all the

EDMONDO DE AMICIS

cares and troubles of the day, or at least to deaden his sense of them, not to ask his wife's calm advice or receive comfort from her kindness. Nor would she be capable of responding in this way. He does not even bother to appear intelligent or knowledgeable or powerful in order to increase her love for him: what would be the point? In this temple he is the god and her worship is his due. He doesn't have to earn it; the mere fact that he singles her out is enough for her to respond gratefully with the embrace he seeks and which can pass for love. In his mind, "woman" means "pleasure" – no more, no less. The very word "woman" is a synonym for pleasure and as such it seems to him indecorous to use it in speech: he avoids using it, and if he has to say, for example, that a baby girl has been born to him, he will refer to her as "a veiled one", "a hidden one", "a stranger". Thus husbands and wives can never have a relationship of real intimacy because a kind of screen of sensuality exists between them which conceals those parts of the soul which lie deep within us and only emerge clearly in the course of a tranquil and sustained relationship. Not only must the wife always be prepared for her master's visit, dressed and looking her best, continually on the alert to vanquish a rival or maintain a superiority which is constantly under threat; she must also be something of a courtesan, forcing herself to create a cheerful atmosphere for her husband even when her heart is sad, putting on the smiling mask of a happy and contented woman, so that he may not be annoyed and put off. Thus the husband is rarely familiar with his wife, just as he has never known her as a daughter, sister, friend or mother. And she allows the nobler qualities of her nature, which she cannot express and for which she is not prized, to wither slowly inside her; she does only what is asked of her, stifling the voices of her heart and spirit, to achieve, if not happiness, a kind of peace in a sort of sleepy animal-like life. She has, it is true, the comfort of her children, and her husband comes to visit them and caress them in her presence, but it is a comfort embittered by the thought that perhaps only an hour before he was caressing the children of another; that in an hour's time he may be caressing those of a third, and perhaps within a few years those of a fourth. The lover's passion, the father's affection, friendship, trust – everything is divided and subdivided, has its appointed hour, its forms and procedures and ceremonies; everything is cold and inadequate. There is besides something contemptuous and deeply offensive in the love of a husband which requires her to be supervised by a eunuch. It's

146

as if he were saying "I love you, you are 'my joy and glory' and 'the pearl of my house' – but if you had a real man to watch over you I'm certain you'd jump into bed with him at the first opportunity."

\* \* \*

The conditions of conjugal life vary greatly, however, according to the husband's income, even without taking into account the fact that the man who is not rich enough to maintain more than one woman is by necessity obliged to have only one wife. The wealthy man lives separately from his wife in his house and in his thoughts, because he can afford to keep an apartment or even a house for her sole use, and because, as he wishes to receive friends, clients, flatterers without his wives being seen or disturbed, he needs to have a separate residence. The middle-class Turk, for reasons of economy, lives at close quarters with his wife, sees her more frequently, and is on more familiar terms with her. Lastly, the poor Turk who has to live in a confined space and spend as little as possible, eats and sleeps and passes most of his free time in the close company of his wife and children. Wealth divides, poverty unites. In the poor man's house, there is not much difference between Turkish and Christian households. The woman who cannot keep a slave does her own housework, and work enhances her importance and authority. It is not unusual to see such a woman dragging her lazy husband from the café or the tavern, and driving him home with blows from her slipper. They treat each other as equals, passing the evening together at the door of their house; in the remoter suburbs, they often go out as a couple to do the family shopping; and husband and wife are often seen picnicking together in a cemetery near the tombstone of some deceased relative, with their children round about them, just like a working-class family in our own countries. The sight of such a family group is as moving as it is remarkable. On seeing one it is impossible not to believe that those bonds of body and soul, of unique affections, are necessary and right in some universal and eternal sense. The presence of another in that close-knit harmony would disrupt or destroy it. Whatever people say, the primal force, the essential element, the foundation stone of a just and well-ordered society lies in the family; other associations based on shared affections and interests lie outside the natural order of things. Only this can be called a family; the rest are like herds. Only these bonds constitute a home; all the others are brothels.

* * *

There are those who say that the women of the East are satisfied with polygamy, and do not understand the injustice of it. To believe this one must be ignorant not only of the East, but of the human soul itself. If it were true, why does almost every Turkish girl who accepts the hand of a man make it a condition that he shall not marry again during her lifetime? If it were true, there wouldn't be so many wives who return to their families because their husbands have fallen short of this promise, and the Turkish proverb would not exist which says: "a house with four women is like a ship in a storm." Even if she is adored by her husband, the oriental woman can only curse polygamy, which obliges her to live with the sword of Damocles over her head, her rival there day after day, not hidden or remote and furtive as the rivals of European wives have to be, but installed beside her, in her own house, bearing her title, claiming the same rights. She is condemned perhaps to see her own slave promoted to equality with herself, and giving birth to sons having the same rights as her own. It is impossible she should not feel the injustice of such a law. She knows that when the husband she loves introduces another woman into her home, he is but putting into practice the right given to him by the law of the Prophet. But in her heart of hearts she feels that there is a more ancient and more sacred law which condemns his act as treachery and an abuse of power; that the bond between them is undone, that her life is ruined and that she has the right to rebel and to curse. And even if she does not love her husband, she has a hundred reasons to detest the law: her children's interests are injured, her own self-respect is wounded, and she finds herself having to choose between complete abandonment or being sought out by her husband only because he pities her or wants to sleep with her. It may be said that Turkish women know that the same things happen to European women: true, but they also know that a European woman is not obliged by civil and religious law to respect and live in amity with the woman who poisons her life, and that she has at least the consolation of being regarded as a victim, as well as having many ways of vindicating and alleviating her position, without her husband being able to say, like the Turk: "I have the right to love a hundred women, but it is your duty to love me alone."

* * *

It is true that a Turkish woman has many legal guarantees, and many privileges conceded to her by custom. She is generally treated with courtly gallantry. No man would dare to lift his hand against a woman in the public street. No soldier, even in times of tumult and sedition, would run the risk of maltreating the most insolent woman of the people. The husband treats his wife with ceremonious courtesy. Mothers are the object of peculiar deference. No man would think for a moment of forcing his wife to work so he can live off her earnings. The husband at his marriage assigns a dowry to his bride; she brings nothing to his house but her wardrobe and a few female slaves. If he repudiates or divorces her, the man is obliged to give the woman enough to live on comfortably; and this obligation restrains him from maltreating her, for which she might seek and obtain a separation. The easiness of divorce remedies in part the sad consequences of marriages which are almost always entered into blindly since, in accordance with the characteristic arrangements of Turkish society, the sexes live entirely separate lives. Very little cause is needed for a woman to obtain a divorce: that the husband has ill-treated her once, that he has spoken ill of her to others, that he has neglected her for a certain time. She has only to present her written statement of grievances to the tribunal; or she can, when opportunity occurs, go in person before a vizier or the Grand Vizier himself, by whom she is received without delay and listened to kindly. If she cannot agree with the other wives, the husband is legally bound to give her a separate apartment; and even if she does get on with them, she has a right to one. The man cannot marry or take as his mistress any of the slave-women whom the wife has brought with her from her family home. A woman who has been seduced and abandoned can oblige her seducer to marry her if he does not already keep four wives; and if he does, he must take her in as a concubine and the child must be recognized – this is the reason why there are no illegitimate children among the Turks. Elderly bachelors are rare and spinsters even more uncommon; forced marriages are much less frequent than might be supposed, since the law punishes the father who is guilty of coercion. The state gives a pension to widows without relations and without means, and provides for orphans; many girls left without protection are taken in by wealthy ladies who pay for their education and arrange marriages for them; it is very unusual for a woman to remain in poverty. All this is true and is praiseworthy, but it still raises a smile when the Turks claim that the social condition of their women is better than that of ours, and that their society is free of the corruption which they find in Europe. What are these forms of respect worth when her very condition as a kind of supplementary wife is in itself so humiliating? What is the good of being able to divorce and remarry with ease if the man she marries again has the right to impose the same conditions on her which made her seek a divorce in the first place? What is the point of a man being obliged to acknowledge his illegitimate children if he hasn't got the means to support them? He can have fifty so-called legitimate children who may not have the status of illegitimacy, but suffer the effects of poverty and abandonment all the same. They tell us that infanticide is unknown among them, but what about voluntary abortions, for which they have special clinics, and which are frequent? They say that prostitution does not exist – but then what do you call the hundreds of Circassian concubines who are bought and sold every day? Ah, they reply, but there's no public prostitution. If that were true, what was Mustafa III doing when he ordered all the women of easy virtue in the city to be rounded up and sent off beyond the Bosphorus (and accounts tell us that the operation was an extensive one)? Then they want us to believe that it's easier for a man to have four faithful wives than a single one and that a Turk with four wives is less likely to indulge in sinful practices outside the home and against his religion. Finally what right have these men who are the most addicted on earth to the *nefanda voluptas** to preach to us of morality?

\* \* \*

From all this one may easily gather what kind of being the Turkish woman is likely to be. Most of them are merely pleasing and decorative feminine creatures. Most know how to read and write, but practise neither one nor the other, and those with only a smattering of knowledge are regarded as miraculously learned. Turkish men believe that women have "a lot of hair and little in the way of brains", and do not care to have them cultivate their minds, since they prefer them to remain in a position of inferiority. Thus, having no instruction from books, and receiving none from conversation, they are grossly ignorant. From the separation of the two sexes comes the absence of gentle manners in the one sex, and of dignity in the other; the men are coarse and the women vulgar. Having no society beyond their own small circle of women, they all retain even in old age something puerile and petty in their ideas and manners; they show a wild curiosity about everything, react with astonishment to the smallest matters, make a great fuss over trifles, are prone to schoolgirlish backbiting, spite and tantrums, scream with laughter for the slightest reason, are fond of childish games, such as chasing each other round the rooms or snatching sweets out of each other's mouths. It is true that they have, to turn the French saying round, the good qualities of their defects: their nature is transparent and plain, and they can be read like an open book; they are "real persons", in Madame de Sévigné's expression,* not puppets or caricatures or monkeys; open and all of a piece even in their sadness. And it's much to their merit that among them you'll find no humourless bluestockings or schoolmarms prating on about language and style, or refined poetesses who think they're too ethereal for real life. If it is true that no one takes their oaths seriously this only shows that they are not cunning enough to be deceitful. But it is also true that in that narrow existence, deprived of all mental or spiritual recreation, in which the instinctive desire of youth and beauty for praise and admiration remains forever ungratified, their souls become embittered, and, having no education to control and guide them, they rush into excess whenever some ugly passion moves them. Idleness stirs up in them a thousand meaningless whims, which they pursue obstinately, and will gratify at any price. Besides, in the sensual atmosphere of the harem, in the constant company of women inferior to themselves in birth and position, far from the man who could act as a restraining force, they acquire an extraordinary crudity of speech. They are ignorant of nuance and euphemism and describe things as they are; they have a predilection for words which might cause a blush, for scurrilous jokes or vulgar innuendo, and often come out with biting and insolent remarks. Europeans who understand the Turkish language may sometimes hear a *hanım* of distinguished appearance abusing some indiscreet or discourteous shopkeeper in language that in their own countries would only be heard among women of the lowest orders. As they become more familiar with European women and grow to find out more about our customs, their rebelliousness increases and their bitterness intensifies. If their husbands really love them, then they take their revenge on them mercilessly for the social injustice which oppresses them. Many have described Turkish women as all sweetness, softness and submission. But there are among

151

them some of a fierce and haughty spirit. In Turkey too, at times of popular unrest, women are to be seen in the front line; they take up weapons, gather together in the streets, block the carriages of the offending viziers, cover them with abuse, throw stones at them, and resist armed force. They are kind and gentle, like all women, when no passion gnaws or inflames them. They treat their slaves with kindliness, if they are not jealous of them; they show tenderness for their children, although they do not know how to – or do not care to – bring them up; they form the most tender friendships with one another – especially those who are separated from their husbands, or who share the same sorrows – friendships full of youthful enthusiasm, where they show their reciprocal affection by wearing the same colour, or the same fashion of garment, and using the same perfumes. And here I could add what has been written by more than one European female traveller, "that there are among them all the vices of Babylon"; but I am unwilling to say anything based solely on the evidence of others about so serious a matter.

\* \* \*

As is their nature, so are their manners. The majority of them are like those young girls of good family, but brought up in the country, who – no longer children but not yet women – are continually making a hundred amiable faux pas in company, causing their mammas to frown and shake their heads. To hear a European lady recount her experiences on a visit to a harem is truly comic. The *hanım*, for instance, who at first will be seated on the sofa in the same decorous attitude as her visitor, will suddenly throw her arms over her head and emit a loud yawn, or hug her knees. Accustomed to the liberty, not to say licence of the harem, to attitudes of sloth and ennui, and weakened by too many warm baths, she tires immediately of any rigid composure. She throws herself down on her divan, twisting and turning about and getting her long garments into a great tangle; she leans on her elbows, clasps her feet in her hands, puts a cushion on her lap and her elbows on the cushion, stretches and wriggles her limbs, arches her back like a cat, rolls off the divan onto the mattress, from the mattress onto the carpet, and from the carpet onto the marble floor, and sleeps wherever she feels sleepy, like a child. A French traveller has commented that there's something mollusc-like about their postures.

They're like rotund objects you could put your arms round and lift. Sitting with crossed legs is perhaps the most strenuous position they adopt, and this habit, acquired in infancy, is probably the reason why their legs are slightly bowed. But with what grace they sit! On their outings to cemeteries and gardens, they sink straight to the ground without using their hands to support them, and remain like statues, quite still, until they rise to their feet, again without support, in one fluid movement as if set on springs. But this is perhaps their only energetic motion. The gracefulness of Turkish women is all in repose, and in the art of displaying the soft lines and curves of their reclining forms, with the head thrown back, the hair tumbling loose, and the arms hanging limp – this is the art which extracts gold and jewellery from her husband and drives her eunuchs wild.

* * *

Studying how to perfect this art is not the least of the ways they contrive to alleviate the tedium which is so typical of life in the harem, a tedium which arises not so much from the lack of occupation and amusement as from their monotonous sameness, as with certain books which tell lively stories but are written in a boring uniformity of style. They'll do anything to escape boredom: their whole day is a continual battle against this stubborn and intrusive monster. Reclining on cushions or on carpets next to their slave-women, they sew borders on countless handkerchiefs as presents for their friends, they embroider nightcaps and tobacco pouches for their husbands and fathers and brothers; their fingers endlessly click the beads of their *tesbih*; they count up to the highest number they can manage; from the round windows of the upper-floor rooms they watch for hours on end the ships going to and fro on the Bosphorus and the Sea of Marmara; or they gaze at the spirals of blue smoke from their cigarettes and dream of wealth, love and liberty. When they're tired of cigarettes they'll smoke a chibouk filled with yellow Latakia tobacco; when they've done with smoking, they'll sip a cup of Syrian coffee, nibble at fruit and sweets, make an ice cream last for half an hour, and then have another smoke, this time with the narghile perfumed with rose water; after which they chew some mastic to take away the taste of smoking, then drink some lemonade to take away the taste of the mastic. They dress and undress, try on all the clothes in their wardrobes, try out all their cosmetics,

153

apply and remove beauty spots in the shape of stars or crescent moons, arrange all their mirrors in a dozen different ways to get a better view of themselves, until they get tired of all this. Then two slave-girls have to dance for them with castanets and tambourines, and a third will sing or recite for the hundredth time a ditty or tale which they all know by heart, or the usual two tomboys dressed like athletes will have the usual wrestling match which ends with one of them being pushed onto her back on the floor and some mirthless laughter. Sometimes a troupe of Egyptian dancers provides a novelty, which is the occasion for a small party; on other days a gypsy comes round and then the *hanım* will have her palm read, or buy a charm which will bring her eternal youth, or a potion which will give her sons or bring her love. They will sit for hours at the lattice watching people and dogs go by, or teaching a new word to their pet parrot, playing on the see-saw in the garden and then going back into the house to say their prayers or stretch out on the sofas for a game of cards, from which they'll jump up for the visit of a relative or friend, at which point the usual round of coffee, cigarettes, glasses of lemonade and titbits to eat, tired laughter and loud yawns begins again and goes on until the friend takes her leave and the eunuch appears on the threshold to announce the arrival of the effendi in a low voice: "And here he is at last, God be praised, even if he were the ugliest man in Stamboul."

\* \* \*

All this happens in the harem where harmony is the rule, but in others boredom is overcome by passion and daily life is very different. Those harems are tranquil where there is one woman who is loved by her husband, who in turn pays no attention to her slave-girls and doesn't have to carry on with women outside the home. And there is also peace, if not happiness, in harems where there are many wives who are all shallow or cold in temperament, and whom the husband treats with indifference since he has no preference for one in particular, so that each receives him in her turn without love or jealousy or wish for precedence. These good-natured wives try to squeeze as much money as they can from the effendi and live in the same house, get along together, call each other sister, and amuse themselves as best they can, and no more: the boat may be made by the devil but at least it floats. There is too a kind of peace in the harems where a wife finds herself subordinated to a new arrival but accepts the situation with resignation; while she might protest to her husband about the rations of love he gives her, she remains friends with him, stays in his house, takes comfort in her children, and lives in dignified retirement. But life is very different indeed in the harems where the women are proud and spirited and cannot submit to a rival or accept the shame of abandonment or seeing the children of another preferred to their own. These harems are hell on earth: they cry, they howl, they smash the porcelain and crystal, torment their slaves by sticking pins into them, lay plots and plan crimes, and on occasion take their own lives, by poisoning or stabbing themselves, or throwing acid in their own faces. Life here is only a succession of persecutions, implacable hatreds, fierce unrelenting wars. To sum up, the man with several wives either loves one in particular and has no peace, or loves them all in the same way in order to keep the peace but forfeits real love. In both cases, catastrophe is the result since if his wives are not jealous for love they are still driven by self-love, ambitious rivalry, competition to outshine the others. It is impossible for the husband to give his favourite wife some jewellery or a carriage or a villa on the Bosphorus without setting the whole lot of them at sixes and sevens, so that he is forced to do the same for each and every one of them and buy tranquillity with money. And what is true of the women is also true of their children: if they're the children of the woman who's been subordinated they too are full of hatred and if they're the sons of the favourite they are the object of others' resentment. It is all too easy to imagine the kind of upbringing they receive in such harems, surrounded by rancour and intrigue, slaves and eunuchs, without a father to guide them, without examples of hard work to inspire them, in such an atmosphere of pettiness and sensuality, especially the girls who from their earliest years learn to place all their hopes in their ability to seduce – not to dignify the term with any idea of love – and who learn these arts from their mother, her slave-girls, and even worse, from Karagöz.

* * *

There are two other kinds of harems in addition to the peaceful and the turbulent: the harem of the young freethinking Turk, who encourages his wife in her European tendencies, and that of the Turk who is conservative, either by conviction or because he is dominated

by his family, in particular by some elderly matriarch of inflexible
religious views, who dislikes anything newfangled and makes him rule
the house according to her laws. The two establishments could not
be more different. In the first there is a piano on which the wife takes
lessons from a Christian teacher; there are work-tables, straw chairs,
a mahogany bedstead and a writing desk; on the wall hangs a fine
pencil portrait sketch of the master of the house, done by an Italian
artist in Pera; in the corner there is a bookshelf with some books,
among them a small French and Turkish dictionary, and the latest
issue of *La Mode illustrée,** which the wife of the Spanish Consul
passes on when she has finished reading it. She is also keen on painting
watercolours of fruit and flowers. She assures her friends she never
gets bored. In the intervals between one occupation and another she
keeps a diary. At an appointed time she receives her French teacher
(elderly, hunchbacked, wheezing – as you might expect), with whom
she practises conversation. Sometimes a German photographer from
Galata comes to take her portrait. When she is ill, she is visited by
a European doctor, who may even be a handsome young man, since
her husband is not prone to fierce attacks of jealousy like some of
his more old-fashioned friends. And every once in a while a French
dressmaker will pay a visit to measure her for a costume modelled
on the very latest fashion design from *La Mode illustrée*, in which
she intends to surprise her husband on Thursday evening, a sacred
evening for Muslim couples, when the husband is expected to pay his
debts of gallantry towards his "rose-leaf". And the effendi, who has
contacts in high places, has promised her that the following winter she
shall have a glimpse through a door of the next grand ball to be given
by the English ambassador. In short, the *hanum* is a European lady
who happens to be a Muslim, and she tells her friends complacently
that she lives like a *kokona** – like a Christian. Indeed her friends and
relatives hold the same ideas even if they might not be able to live
their lives according to them, and when they meet, the talk is all of
the latest fashions and what's on at the theatre; they make fun of all
the superstitions and pedantries and bigotries of "old Turkey" and
end every conversation with the assertion that "really, it's time to start
living in a more reasonable way". But in the other harem all is strictly
Turkish, from the wife's attire down to the smallest household detail.
The Koran is the only book, *Stamboul* the only newspaper allowed. If
the *hanum* falls ill, the doctor isn't called out, but one of the numerous

female quacks who have a miraculous cure for every known malady. If her parents are Europeanizers they're only allowed to see their daughter once a week. All the openings in the house are well grated and bolted, and nothing European – apart from the air – can enter, unless the lady has had the misfortune to learn a little French in her childhood, in which case her sister-in-law is capable of lending her some bad French novel to read in order to tell her: "See the kind of society you'd like to ape! What fine goings-on! What truly admirable behaviour!"

\* \* \*

And yet Turkish women's lives are full of mishaps, intrigues and gossip, which at first sight you would not think possible in a society where the two sexes live so separately. In one harem, for instance, there is an old mother who wishes to drive one of the wives out to make room for a favourite of her own, so she tries in every way to keep him from the former's children and make sure their education is neglected so that he comes to prefer the children of the other woman. In another it is the wife who is jealous of a rival for her husband's affections; since she can't get him to love her alone she at least tries to vent her jealousy by distracting his attention and detaching him from the other woman, by putting a handsome slave-girl in his way who will catch his eye and with whom he will betray her hated rival... Another wife is a born matchmaker and racks her brains to bring about a marriage between some male relative and some young girl, thus circumventing her husband who has his eyes turned in the same direction. Here a number of ladies subscribe to a fund to buy an attractive slave, and present her to the Sultan or the Grand Vizier for some ulterior purpose; elsewhere, another group of high-born *hanım* are busy pulling all the strings they can to obtain what they want: to destroy some powerful enemy in government or get a friend promoted, obtain a divorce for one person and get another sent into a distant province. And although less social intercourse takes place than in our cities, there is just as much gossip about other people's affairs. The reputation of a woman known for her wit or her sharp tongue, for her fierce jealousy or peculiar stupidity, spreads far beyond the circle of her acquaintance. Astute remarks and clever puns, to which the Turkish language readily lends itself, are soon widely broadcast. Births, circumcisions, marriages, parties, all the small events that take place in the European colony and in the Seraglio form the subject of endless chatter. "Have you seen the new bonnet of the French ambassador's wife? Is anything known about the beautiful Georgian slave that the Sultana Valide is going to give the Sultan as a Bayram* gift? Is it true that Ahmet Pasha's wife was seen yesterday in a pair of European boots trimmed with silk ribbons? Have the costumes for the *Bourgeois gentilhomme** at the Seraglio theatre finally arrived from Paris? Mahmut Effendi's wife has been going to the Beyazit Mosque every morning for a week to pray for twins. There was a to-do at a certain photographer's studio in Pera, because Ahmet Effendi came across his wife's portrait there. Madame Ayesha drinks wine. Madame Fatma has had visiting cards printed. Madame Hafiten was seen going into a European shop at three and coming out at four." All this malicious gossip spreads rapidly around the houses, flows into the rumours emanating from the court, expands through Scutari and along the Bosphorus as far as the Black Sea, frequently making the journey to the main provincial towns, from where it returns, embroidered with new details, which provoke new laughs and more gossip in the thousand harems of the metropolis.

\* \* \*

It would be curious and amusing if the Turks had a type common among us: those gossips of the beau monde who know everyone and everything, and talk of nothing else. And it would be both amusing and instructive for a study of Constantinople's social behaviour to accompany one of these on a holiday to the Sweet Waters of Europe and stand at the entrance listening to their commentary on all the notabilities as they walk by. But what does it matter if such a person doesn't exist? We know what there is to gossip about and it's easy to conjure up the characters. I can already see and hear them walking along as the Turk points them out. That lady there has just left her husband and gone off to live in Scutari, where all unhappy wives go to sulk. She's staying with a friend until her husband, who's really fond of her at heart, comes and tells her he's thrown out his mistress, who was the reason for their quarrel, so they can go home in peace. This gentleman now going by works at the Ministry of Foreign Affairs: in order to get away from his extended family and all the uproar they create he's gone and married an Arab slave who's now just started to learn Turkish from his sister. This pretty little woman is divorced, and she's only waiting until a certain gentleman has got rid of one of his four wives, to go and take her place as he's long been promising she can. That one over there is a lady who has been twice divorced from the same husband, and now wants to marry him a third time, with his agreement; she's getting married in a day or two, as the law demands, to another man, from whom she can get divorced the following day, after which the giddy girl will be free to try for the third time round with her first husband. The brunette with the lively eyes is an Abyssinian slave who was given by a great lady of Cairo to a great lady of Stamboul, who, when she died, left her mistress of the house. That fifty-year-old man has already had ten wives. That little old woman in green can boast she's been the legitimate wife of twelve husbands. Here comes a lady who's making a fortune by buying girls of fourteen, teaching them music, singing, dancing and etiquette, and then selling them on at a fifty per cent profit. Ah, as for this beauty here I can tell you exactly how much she cost: she's a Circassian who was bought at Tophane for one hundred and twenty Turkish lira and sold there three years later for no less than four hundred! This one – the one adjusting her veil – was first a slave, then a concubine, then a wife, then divorced, then married again, and now she's a widow and on the lookout for a new marriage. You see that man there – well, you'll never believe his story – his wife's fallen in love with a eunuch and they say she's capable of poisoning her husband's coffee just to be able to elope with him – there's platonic love for you! That man's a merchant who's married four wives for business reasons – there's one in Constantinople, one in Trabzon, one in Salonika, and the fourth in Alexandria – so he's got four cosy love nests waiting for him whenever he's travelling... Only a month ago that handsome young pasha was just a subaltern officer in the Imperial Guard when the Sultan suddenly promoted him so he could marry him off to one of his sisters; but life with a royal is no bed of roses, you know, the poor chap's wife is said to be "as jealous as a nightingale" – she's probably got a slave following him now to see who catches his eye and who doesn't. Just take a look at that splendid woman. You don't need to be a connoisseur to tell she's been recycled from the Seraglio: she was one of the Sultan's favourites and has been married for some months to an official in the Ministry of War, who with her help has already got a foothold in the court and is sure to go on to higher things. Look at that little girl! She's five years old and

got engaged this morning to a boy of eight. Her husband-to-be was
taken by his parents to pay her a visit, took a liking to her, and threw
a tantrum because his slightly taller cousin gave her a kiss in front of
him. That old hag slaughtered two rams the other day in thanks to
Allah because he managed to get rid of her hated sister-in-law. And
there's the female quack who was asked by some lady to make sure
one of her slave-girls, who'd been carrying on with her husband, had
a miscarriage, since if she'd had a baby she couldn't be sold and the
husband would have to keep her. And here's another of the same kind,
who gets asked every now and then by effendi to do an on-the-spot
check to see whether the slave-girls they've got their eyes on might be
shop-soiled goods. That one with the veil and the lilac feredgi is the
wife of a Turkish friend of mine, but she's a Christian and goes to
church every Sunday morning, but don't tell anyone, out of respect –
for her, I mean, not for her husband – after all, the Koran says nothing
against marrying Christian women, all you need to do after making
love to an infidel is just wash your face and hands. Ah! We've just
missed a Seraglio carriage – and the Sultan's third wife was in it; I
recognized it by the pink ribbon round the attendant's neck. She was
given to him by the Pasha of Smyrna; she has the largest eyes and the
smallest mouth in the whole of the empire – in fact a bit like the little
woman over there with the arched nose, who yesterday did what she
shouldn't have done with an English artist of my acquaintance. The
wretch! To think that when the angels Nakir and Munkar come to
judge her soul, she'll try to get off with the usual fib: "I had my eyes
shut and I didn't recognize him!"

\* \* \*

So there are unfaithful Turkish wives? Of course there are! Despite their
husbands' jealousy and their eunuchs' vigilance, despite the hundred
lashes threatened in the Koran, despite the fact that Turkish husbands
form a kind of mutual assurance society, and the fact that everything
is ordered differently from other countries, where it sometimes seems
as if there's a silent conspiracy to undermine marital happiness. It's
possible to state that the "veiled" women of Constantinople commit
just as many sins as the "unveiled" ones of Christian countries. If
that weren't the case, Karagöz would not have the word *kerata* on
his tongue all the time – a term which, historically rendered, signifies

"Menelaus".* But how do they manage it? In a hundred different ways. It has to be said that women are no longer thrown into the Bosphorus – inside a sack or not – and that starvation, solitary confinement, hair shirts and beatings are no longer practised even by the most enraged *kerata*. A constitutionally jealous husband might try to prevent his wife from betraying him, but when he doesn't succeed, he doesn't go mad with anger and seek revenge as used to be the case – it's much harder now to keep domestic turmoil a secret within the home. The force of ridicule, as with so many other European tendencies, has found its way into Muslim society, and even jealousy is afraid of that. Besides, Turkish jealousy is cold and material, more the effect of self-love than of love itself. While it is certainly powerful and vindictive enough, it is incapable of the untiring vigilance and investigation which a lover whose very soul is in the grip of passion can undertake. Besides, who supervises the women who live separately from their husbands – or even those who don't – in another house, where he doesn't necessarily pay a daily visit? Who follows them through the winding alleyways of Pera and Galata and across distant neighbourhoods? What's to prevent one of the Sultan's handsome aides-de-camp doing what I once witnessed: galloping up alongside a carriage just as it was going round a bend in the road – so that the eunuch walking in front of it had already got his back turned and the one behind couldn't see because the carriage was in the way – and passing a note through the window? On the evenings during Ramadan when women are allowed to stay out until midnight? And the complaisant *kokonas* – especially those who live on the borders between Christian and Muslim neighbourhoods and are allowed to receive as guests both the veiled Muslim lady and the European gentleman? But it is true that the bizarre and terrible escapades of earlier times no longer occur. No great lady nowadays – as a sultana in the eighteenth century once did – enjoys the services of a shop boy who had brought her some cloth to sample in the morning and then gets rid of him at night by pushing him through a trapdoor into the Bosphorus. Now things are done rather more prosaically: the initial rendezvous usually take place in the back rooms of shops – after all it's well-known that there are shopkeepers who are prepared to sell anything. The Turkish authorities do their best to prevent these abuses. It is enough to say that most of the police force's efforts at keeping law and order on holidays relate to women, either in the form of advice or threats. They are forbidden, for example, to enter the back rooms of shops; they must stay where they can be seen from the street. They are not to ride on trams for amusement – that is, they are not to get out at the terminus and then get straight back on. They are not allowed to make gestures to passers-by, to stop here and go there, or to loiter in certain places. It's not hard to guess how assiduously these rules are respected or how easily they're enforced. And then there is the veil, of course, which was originally intended to protect the husband but now protects the woman. They wear transparent ones when they want to make men notice them and thicker ones to conceal themselves when an affair is in progress. You hear many bizarre stories: of lovers who still don't know who their beloved is after several months, of women who conceal themselves under another's name in order to take revenge, who perform hoaxes and unmaskings which give rise to endless gossip and bickering.

\* \* \*

The bathhouses where Turkish women usually meet are the places where gossip is most widespread and most intense. The baths are in a certain sense their theatre. They go in pairs and in groups with their slaves, carrying cushions, carpets, toiletries, delicacies to eat and often their entire lunch so they can stay there all day. There, in those dimly lit marble halls, round the fountains, sometimes more than two hundred women gather, naked as nymphs, or semi-naked, presenting, according to the testimony of European ladies who've been there, a spectacle which would make a hundred painters drop their brushes in astonishment. Here the snow-white *hanım* can be seen next to the ebony-black slave; the buxom matron who represents the old-fashioned Turkish ideal of beauty; slender brides hardly out of girlhood with short curly hair, looking like boys; fair-haired Circassians with long golden tresses falling to their knees, and Turkish women with their thick black hair hanging loose over breasts and shoulders, or in a frizzled tangle like an enormous wig; one with an amulet round her neck, another with a garlic clove tied to her head as a charm against the evil eye; half-savages with tattooed arms, and fashionable ladies whose waists and ankles are still red from their corsets and boots; and sometimes poor slave-girls with weals on their shoulders from the eunuch's whip. A hundred different elegant or unusual poses and groupings can be seen. Some are stretched out smoking upon their mats, some are having their hair combed by their slave-women, others are embroidering or singing; they laugh, splash and chase each other, shrieking in the showers, or sit in a circle eating and drinking or criticizing their fellow bathers in nearby groups. Just as their bodies are uncovered, so too their essential childishness is seen more clearly at the baths. They measure their feet, pass remarks and judgements on each other. One asserts: "I'm beautiful," another: "I'm not so bad," while another complains about some flaw or turns to her neighbour and says, "Do you know you're better-looking than I am?" One will turn reprovingly to her friend and say, "Just look how plump Feride is on a diet of potted prawns – you've always told me rice balls were the best way to put on weight." And whenever they find a *kokona* among them they gather round her and ply her with questions: "Is it true you go to the ball with your shoulders bare? And what does your husband think of that? And what do the other men say? And how do you dance? That way? Really? Well, I never!"

\* \* \*

They try to make the acquaintance of European women not only at the baths but everywhere and at every opportunity: they're always pleased to engage one in conversation and even more gratified when they can invite her as a guest into their homes. On such occasions they celebrate by asking their friends to come too; they make sure all their servants are on display, load the visitor with sweets and fruits, and seldom let her go without giving her a present. All this is more inspired by curiosity than benevolence, of course; indeed, as soon as they have entered into a little familiarity with their new acquaintance they get her to tell them a thousand details of European life, they examine her dress minutely from bonnet to boots, and are not satisfied until they have taken her to the bath, where they can find out how a Christian woman is put together, one of these extraordinary creatures who study and paint and write for the newspapers, who work in offices and ride horses and climb mountains... The strange ideas they had about European women before the Sultan's reforms have long disappeared, however; they no longer think, for example, that the corset is a kind of chastity belt which husbands attached to their wives to ensure they remained faithful and to which they alone had the key; nor that European women belong to every man they go arm in arm with; because of which they distrusted them and spoke of them with contempt, not even envying their education, of which they had no idea or were incapable of appreciating. Now their feelings are very different and they have become diffident in another sense: they are ashamed of their own ignorance when they meet European women and worried whether they might appear coarse or silly or childish; many have lost their former attitude of trusting naivety. They seek to imitate their dress and manners in every way. If they study a foreign language, it is only for imitation's sake – not because they want to speak it – or they learn it to be able to converse with Christian women. They try to insert a few French words into their Turkish and those who know no French pretend they speak it or at least understand it. They are thrilled if they are addressed as "Madame", and go into certain European shops just for the pleasure of hearing this greeting. They are attracted to Pera like moths to a flame: their fantasies, their purses and, on occasion, their sins all circle round its streets. For this reason they are keen to know European women, who reveal a new world to them. They get them to describe the grand spectacles in Western theatres, the splendid balls, the great banquets and sumptuous receptions given by aristocratic ladies, the carnivals and the grand tours – all these images of light put their bewildered heads into a whirl in the tedium of the harem and the melancholy shade of their gardens. Just as European women dream about the vast serene horizons of the Orient, so they long for the varied and frenetic life of our countries, and would give all the marvels of the Bosphorus for fog-bound streets in Paris. Yet it is not only the varied and feverish life of gaiety that attracts them; it is also domestic life which they more often and more inwardly wish to know about: the small world of a European house, the circle of loyal friends, the dinner table surrounded with children, the respect shown to elderly female members of the family; that sanctuary full of memories, trust and tenderness, that can make the union of two people a fine thing, even if they do not love each other; the place to which we return burdened with our faults and mistakes after a long life; where, even among the turbulence of youth or our present afflictions, the mind finds refuge and the heart consolation, as though it held out the promise of peace in later years, like the beauty of a serene sunset seen from the depths of some dark valley.

\* \* \*

But there is one great thing to be said to comfort those who lament the destiny endured by Turkish women: it is that the practice of polygamy is in daily decline. The Turks themselves have always regarded it as an abuse to be tolerated rather than a natural right. Mohammad said: "The man who marries a single wife should be praised" – although he himself had several – and all those who wish to set an example of upright and austere manners always marry just one wife. He who has more than one is not openly blamed, but neither does he meet with approval. Turks who support polygamy openly are rare, still fewer those who approve of it in their hearts. Almost all are aware of its injustice and deleterious consequences; many fight openly and ardently to have it abolished. All those who are in a social position which imposes a certain respectability and decorum in their way of living have only one wife – senior civil servants, army officers, judges and clerics, as well as all poor Turks and most middle-class men. Four-fifths of the Turks of Constantinople are no longer polygamous. It is true that many marry only one wife in order to imitate European ways, while numerous other men might have one wife but also keep concubines. But the desire to imitate Europe is rooted in a sense that Muslim society needs to change, and the use of concubines is bound to diminish – as the trade in slave-women, which is still allowed, gradually disappears – until it resembles the ordinary sexual corruption found in all European societies. Or is this itself a greater form of corruption? Let others decide. The fact of the matter is this: the European transformation of Turkish society is not possible if Turkish women are not liberated and this liberation can only come about if polygamy ceases to exist... It is probable that not a single protest would be heard if the Sultan issued a decree banning it tomorrow. The edifice has already collapsed, but the ruins need to be cleared. The rosy light of the rising sun already tinges the terraces of the harem. There is hope for you, O lovely *hanim*! The doors of the selamlik will open, the grating will fall from the windows, the feredgi will go to fill the old-clothes shops in the Grand Bazaar, the eunuch will become a childhood bogeyman, and you will be free to display to the world the beauty of your faces and the qualities of your souls; and then, whenever "the pearls of the Orient" are spoken of in Europe, the allusion will be to you, O white *hanim*, to you, beautiful Muslim women, gentle, intelligent and cultivated; not to the useless pearls that shine on your hair in the heartless ceremonies of the harem. Courage then! – for the sun is rising. As for me – let my incredulous friends just listen – even though I'm getting on in years, I have not yet given up hope of giving my arm to a visiting pasha's wife in Turin and taking her for a stroll along the banks of the Po, while reciting to her a chapter from *The Betrothed*.*

## *"Yangın var!"*

I was half asleep and dreaming about this very walk towards five o'clock in the morning in my bedroom at the Hotel Byzantium. I could see the hill of Superga* in the distance and had just started to recite to my Turkish lady visitor: "That branch of the lake of Como which turns towards the south between two uninterrupted chains of mountains" – when my friend Junck suddenly appeared before me, dressed in his nightgown and carrying a candle, and exclaimed in astonishment: "What's going on in Constantinople tonight?" Listening, I could hear a confused and muffled sound coming from the street, a noise of hurried footsteps on the stairs, a murmur and bustle, as if it were day. From my window I could make out in the darkness a crowd of people hurrying towards the Golden Horn. I ran out on the landing and seized a Greek waiter who was rushing down the stairs, and asked him what was happening. He tore himself away, yelling: "*Yangın var,** for heaven's sake! Haven't you heard the shout?" and then vanishing he called back, "Look at the top of the Galata tower." I returned to the window, and looking towards Galata saw all the upper part of the tower lit up by a vivid crimson light, and a huge black cloud within a great vortex of sparks billowing up from the neighbouring houses and rapidly covering the starry sky.

Suddenly we thought of the great fires of Constantinople in the past, and especially the terrifying conflagration which had broken out four years previously,* and our first reaction was one of terror and compassion. But immediately afterwards – I am ashamed to confess it – a crueller, more egotistical feeling arose in me, the curiosity of the painter and the writer and – this too I must confess – Junck and I exchanged a smile that Doré* could have used for one of the demons in Dante's *Inferno*. If someone had opened our bodies up at that moment he'd have found only an inkwell and a palette inside.

We dressed in furious haste and went down into the main street in Pera. But our curiosity, fortunately, was disappointed. The fire had already been extinguished even before we reached the Galata Tower. Two small houses were still burning a little; people were beginning to go home; the streets were running with water from the pumps and encumbered with furniture and bedding, in the middle of which, in the grey light of dawn, men and women in their underclothes were coming and going, shivering with cold, and shouting in a dozen different languages, in a tone of voice in which only just enough of the terror at the danger they had recently passed remained to animate their talk about it. Seeing that everything was over, we went towards the bridge to console ourselves, for our wicked disappointment, with the sunrise, which, as a spectacle, proved to be quite equal to a conflagration. The sky was beginning to grow light beyond the hills of Asia. Stamboul, which had only taken fright a little at the first announcement of the fire, had already sunk back into nocturnal calm. The shores and bridge were deserted; the Golden Horn slept on, covered with a light mist and immersed in deep silence. No boat moved, no bird flew, no leaves rustled, not a breath disturbed the stillness. The vast azure city, mute and veiled, seemed painted on the air, and looked as though it would vanish in a trice if we gave a shout. Constantinople seemed utterly ethereal and mysterious: never before had it looked so much like one of those magical cities in oriental fables, which rise up suddenly in front of the traveller, and where he finds on entering all the inhabitants motionless, frozen in all the attitudes of busy cheerful daily life, turned to stone by the vengeful spell of some genie king. We leant upon the parapet of the bridge, contemplating the marvellous scene and forgetting the fire, when from beyond the Golden Horn came first a faint confused sound, like the voices of people in distress, and then a burst of screams, shrill and piercing: "Allah! Allah! Allah!" – which suddenly filled the immense and silent emptiness of the roadstead with its clamour. At the same moment a yelling and sinister-looking mob of people appeared upon the opposite shore and rushed onto the bridge in our direction.

"*Tulumbacı!*" ("Firemen!"), cried one of the watchmen on the bridge.

We drew back to one side. A horde of half-naked savages, with bare heads and hairy chests, dripping with sweat, old and young, blacks, dwarves and giants, hirsute or shaven-headed, looking like murderers and thieves, four of whom were carrying on their shoulders a small pump that looked like a child's bier. Armed with long hooked poles, coils of rope, axes and picks, they rushed by us, shrieking and yelling, with dilated eyes, flying hair and trailing rags, pressed close together, impetuous and grim, leaving a stench of wild beasts in their wake, until they disappeared into Galata, from where their last faint cry of "Allah!" reached our ears, at which point a deep silence fell again. The impression made on me by that sudden tumult in the quiet sleeping city is indescribable. In a flash I seemed to see and understand a thousand scenes, in faraway countries and in distant times, of barbarian invasions, of cities being sacked, of warlike horrors which until then I had struggled to picture to myself. I wondered if the spectacle I had just witnessed had taken place in the same city and on the same bridge where every day European ambassadors made their way along with ladies dressed in the latest Parisian fashions and paper boys selling French newspapers.

A minute later the silence was broken again by a distant cry, and another bare-chested, wild crowd rushed in front of us like a whirlwind over the rocking groaning bridge, shouting, puffing and panting, and laughing in a sinister fashion, and again the long, drawn-out, lamenting cry of "Allah!" faded as they stormed into Galata, followed again by a deathly hush. Presently the silence was again broken, and a similar crowd sped by, followed by a fourth, and then two more mobs, and then, bringing up the rear, the madman of Pera – naked from head to toe, half dead with the cold, and uttering piercing yells – followed by a gang of Turkish boys who vanished with him and the firemen behind the houses on the European shore; and over the great city, gilded by the first rays of the rising sun, a deep calm settled once more. In a little while the sun rose, the muezzins' cry was heard from the minarets, caiques set forth from the shore, the port started to come to life, people began to pass over the bridge, the low murmur of daily activity began to spread through the streets, and we returned towards Pera. But the image of that great sleeping city, of the dawn-flushed sky, the solemn peacefulness, and those wild crowds remains so deeply stamped upon the memory that Junck and I never meet even now without recalling it, with a mixture of fear and astonishment, like a scene from the old Stamboul of centuries past, a vision seen in an opium haze.

So I never did get to see an actual outbreak of fire in Constantinople, yet I knew many people who had witnessed the fire which destroyed Pera in 1870, and the accounts which I gathered were so detailed that I can say I was present in imagination and can describe the scene almost as if I had observed it with my own eyes.

\* \* \*

The first flames broke out in a small house on Feridiye Street in Pera, on 5th June, at a time of year when most of the well-to-do residents were out of town in their villas on the Bosphorus, and just after midday, when almost all the inhabitants of the city, including the Europeans, are indoors taking their siesta. There was no one in the house but an old servant woman – the owners had left that morning for the country – who as soon as she saw the flames rushed out into the street screaming "Fire! Fire!" The people in the neighbouring houses ran at once with buckets and small pumps – the nonsensical law which forbade anyone from trying to extinguish a fire before officers arrived from the Seraskerat had by now fallen into disuse – and as usual everyone rushed to the nearest fountain for water. The public fountains in Pera, from which the water-carriers at fixed hours fetch the water which they then supply to the inhabitants in each neighbourhood, were locked since the distribution had already taken place that day, and the official who held the keys couldn't open the fountains without the permission of the authorities. There was in fact a Turkish guard from the municipality in Pera standing next to the fountain with the keys in his pocket, watching impassively the progress of the fire. The excited crowd surrounded him and asked him to open up the fountain. He refused to do so without the necessary authority. They pressed about him, threatened him, seized him; he struggled and resisted, declaring they would get the keys only off his dead body. By now the entire house was ablaze and the flames were already attacking neighbouring houses. The news of the conflagration was spreading rapidly through Pera. From the top of the Galata and Seraskerat towers the watchmen had seen the smoke and had hung out the great red baskets which are used as a sign that a fire has broken out in the city. The watchmen ran about the streets, beating their long staves on the cobblestones and calling out the sinister cry: "*Yangın var!*" – answered by deep brisk drum rolls from the barracks. The Tophane cannon announced the danger with three tremendous explosions, which resounded from the Black Sea to the Sea of Marmara. The Seraskerat, the Seraglio, the embassies, all Pera and all Galata were plunged into chaos. After a few minutes the Minister of War, with a group of officers and an army of firemen, arrived hotfoot in Feridiye Street, and they set hastily to work. But as usual in such cases, the first attempt proved futile. It was impossible to manoeuvre freely in the narrow street, the pumping engines didn't work, there was too little water and it was too far off, the firemen were ill-disciplined and seemed more intent on increasing rather than reducing the chaos in order to take advantage of it. What is more, there were almost no porters to carry things away since most of them had gone to celebrate an Armenian national holiday at Beykoz. There were at that period many more wooden houses than there are now, and even the stone and brick buildings had thin, sparsely tiled roofs which caught fire easily. The inhabitants of the quarter were almost entirely Christian and panicked immediately, whereas the natural fatalism of Muslims in the face of misfortune means they are never unduly alarmed in a fire – even if they don't do much to help they don't get in the way of the rescue efforts. So far only a few houses had caught fire, but already in all the surrounding streets there was an indescribable tumult, with furniture being thrown out of the windows and terrified people everywhere crying and shouting and blocking the way. Threats and force and even gunfire didn't succeed in calming them down. Barely an hour had gone by since the first appearance of the flames and already the whole street was ablaze, and the officials and firemen were in retreat, leaving behind the dead and wounded: any hope of extinguishing the fire before it spread any further was gone. As ill luck would have it, a strong wind was blowing that day which beat the flames in great horizontal waves, like undulating curtains, across the roofs of neighbouring houses which then caught fire inside, as if streams of molten lava from a volcano had been poured into them. The blaze moved so rapidly that families who were confident they had time to save some of their belongings suddenly heard the roof crackle over them and barely escaped with their lives. The houses caught fire as quickly as if they'd been covered in pitch, and immediately long, agitated tongues of flame stretched from the windows like snakes hunting their prey, even curving down into the street as if searching for human victims. The fire did not run, it flew, it enveloped and overwhelmed like a great tidal wave. From Feridiye Street it burst into Tarlabaşi Street, then turned back and poured like a torrent through Mis street, after which the Ağa Camii neighbourhood went up in flames like dry tinder, then Sakızağacı street, then Kalyoncu Kulluğu, and then street after street, until the whole hillside of Yenişehir was enveloped, and the flames crossed the vortex of fire which was coming down the hill along the street in Pera, roaring and moaning. It wasn't simply a question of a thousand different fires to put out like a thousand different enemies to combat: they resembled the decoys and the sudden unexpected movements deployed by a great army under the astute control of a single command, with the aim of trapping the whole city within its net and closing off every escape route. They were like so many streams of lava flowing and mingling together, pouring and expanding into huge lakes of fire, with a swiftness which made any attempt at rescue futile. Within three hours one half of Pera was in flames. Hundreds of columns of sulphurous smoke – red, white, black – swept across the roofs and stretched out as far as the eye could see over the hills, darkening all the towns along the Golden Horn with sinister colours. Everywhere there was a furious vortex of ashes and sparks; embers and smouldering bits driven by the wind rained down like hail on the still intact houses in the quarters lower down the hill, and raked the streets like rifle fire. The streets where the fire was raging were now huge furnaces over which the flames formed a kind of tent, while inside, the pine-wood beams in the roofs and the glazed balconies crashed and splintered with an ear-splitting sound, and the wooden minarets of the smaller mosques crumbled to pieces as if in an earthquake.

In the streets which were still accessible, lancers on horseback sped by, spectral shadows lit by the fires of hell, carrying orders from the Seraskerat in every direction. Officers from the Seraglio, with bare heads and scorched uniforms, riderless horses, troops of porters laden with household goods, packs of howling dogs, streams of people fleeing and tumbling down the slopes over the wounded and the dead, appeared and disappeared among the smoke and flame like the legions of the damned. For one instant, at the entrance to a burning street in the Ağa Camii quarter, the Sultan Abdülaziz was glimpsed on horseback, surrounded by his courtiers: he was deathly pale, and gazed fixedly upon the flames as if he were repeating to himself the words of Selim I: "I feel the burning breath of my victims! It will destroy my city, my Seraglio and myself!" Then he disappeared in a cloud of ashes, carried off by his courtiers. The entire army along with huge numbers of firemen were at work, in groups, stretched out in long human chains, or arranged in vast semicircles around entire neighbourhoods, supervised and directed by viziers, court officials, pashas, ulemas; in some places desperate battles were being waged to prevent the fire spreading into certain streets, and house after house was rapidly demolished with axe blows. The roofs were swarming with people who'd plucked up their courage and faced the flames head on; some fell headlong into the great holes which suddenly opened up under their feet and others chased after them grimly, as if they were brawling, shouting wildly and waving their scorched fezzes in the middle of the red smoke. And still the flames advanced triumphantly despite a thousand water jets, leaping through squares and gardens, great stone buildings and small graveyards, driving back firemen, soldiers and citizens on every side, like a routed army, stinging their backs as they retreated with showers of burning embers. Even in that horrible confusion there were moving deeds of courage and humanity. The fluttering white veils of the Sisters of Charity could be seen everywhere among the smouldering ruins of the houses, bending over the dying; there were Turks who dived into the flames and emerged carrying Christian children in their scorched arms; other Muslims, standing quietly in the middle of a group of despairing Christians, were calmly offering large sums of money to anyone who would go in and save a European boy trapped in one of the burning houses; others scoured the streets to rescue lost children, tying them together with the cloth of their unravelled turbans in order to lead them back safely to their parents; others opened up their homes to the half-naked fugitives; and more than one gave an example of courage and contempt for worldly goods by remaining seated on a rug in the street tranquilly smoking, while their house was burning down in front of their eyes, retreating slowly and with supreme indifference as the flames advanced towards them. But courage and stoicism were worth nothing in the face of that storm of fire. At times it seemed that the wind died down a little and the fire abated, but then the wind started up again with even greater force and the flames sprang up too, bending and lashing their tips, pointed and implacable like arrows, accompanied by a deep rushing roar, interspersed with the sudden explosions of petrol in chemists' shops and of gas inside the houses, where the lead piping melted and flowed in streams. Roofs suddenly caved in as if under the weight of an avalanche; cypress trees crackled and twisted as they caught fire, disintegrating in a shower of burning resin; clusters of old wooden houses exploded like fireworks, letting off huge balls of white flame, as if a hundred factory bellows were being blown. It was a scene of wild destruction and ruin, as if a fire, a flood, an earthquake and enemy pillage had hit the city all at once. Such horror had never been seen or even imagined. The inhabitants were like madmen. The streets of Pera were full of desperate crowds screaming in panic, as on a boat just before it capsizes. Furniture was being wheeled away, the officers' swords were glinting, porters and the men carrying water were shouting and bumping into each other, pashas on horses and hurrying firemen were knocking over everything and everyone in their way as they rushed along; in the middle of all this, families of Italians and French, Greeks and Armenians, rich and poor, women and children, lost and disoriented, groped for each other and shouted each other's names, suffocated by the smoke and blinded by the flashes; ambassadors hurried through, followed by their servants clutching piles of papers and books; friars lifted crosses above the heads of the crowd; Turkish women fled carrying all the precious objects from the harem; people bending under fittings from churches, theatres, schools, mosques. Every now and then a sudden gust of wind would blow a huge cloud of sooty smoke over everyone and plunge them into darkness, increasing their terror and confusion. What made the horror even worse – as always but particularly so on that occasion – were the numbers of thieves of every nationality who emerged from every low den in the city; they roved about together, dressed as porters or gentlemen or soldiers, entered the houses and, completely undisturbed, plundered whatever they wanted, after which they would run to Kasımpaşa and Tatavla to deposit their booty. The soldiers gave chase, trying to block their movements or attacking them head on, at which point there were pitched battles, routs and pursuits which only added to the general terror. Firemen, porters, water-carriers working in gangs backed up by their families would stop work and demand money to continue. The piled-up heaps of furniture across the streets were attacked by looters, although the owners tried to defend them, and then defended them again, like barricades, against new waves of thieves. People trying to escape with all their stuff would fight fiercely over who would go first through narrow passageways, trampling and wounding each other. But after the fire had been raging for only four hours, people realized it was no longer a question of saving their belongings, but rather of saving their own skins. Two thirds of Pera was on fire and the flames were racing so fast in every direction and surrounding such huge areas that people suddenly found themselves trapped. Hundreds of these unfortunate people poured into narrow streets trying to find a way out, only to turn a corner and see a huge wave of flame and smoke coming towards them, driving them back, out of their minds with terror, to find another escape route. Entire families – one with twenty-two people – were suddenly engulfed, asphyxiated, burnt alive. Despair drove them to take shelter in cellars – where they suffocated – to throw themselves down wells and cisterns, to hang themselves from trees, or, after they'd searched in vain for some hiding place inside, to race out and in their madness run directly into the flames. Looking down the hillside from Pera, you could see families kneeling on their terraces, surrounded by the flames, with their arms stretched out and hands joined in prayer, asking Heaven for the help which would not come from their fellow men. As if the flames were in pursuit, terrified crowds of people, pale, their hair streaming behind them, ran down from Pera and spread out through Galata, Tophane, Fındıklı and the cemeteries on the lower slopes, trying to find a refuge: children streaming with blood, women with their faces torn and hair burnt carrying their babies, dead or blinded, in their arms, men writhing in agony on the ground with the skin peeling from their faces and arms; old men sobbing like children, the wealthy banging their heads against the wall in despair at the loss of their fortune, delirious youths falling exhausted on the banks of the Golden Horn, families carrying blackened corpses, people driven mad with terror, dragging stools by a piece of string or wearing rags and broken bits of pottery about their necks, shaking with piteous howls or wild laughter. All the while troops of nizam, gangs of looters, hosts of firemen, army officers, dervishes, court messengers, families returning to search for their lost relatives, villains and heroes – all human life, all its accidents and charities and crimes – continued to surge up the hill, away from the low-lying areas, from the arsenals of Tophane and Tersane, the barracks and the mosques, the Sultan's palaces, running as if they were launching an attack, shouting "*Yangın var!*" and "Allah!" at the top of their voices, in the midst of swirling ashes and sparks, under a thick shower of soot, through streets piled with burning embers and debris: a terrifying mass roaring like the sea in a storm, reddened in the glow from the huge furnace which the city had become. Only a short distance from this hell, the majestic serenity of Stamboul and the springtide loveliness of the Asian shore looked on smilingly, mirrored in the waters of the Sea of Marmara and the Bosphorus, where the ships lay calmly at anchor, while an immense crowd that covered both shores gazed silently and impassively at the terrifying scene; the muezzins announced in slow musical chants the hour of sunset; birds circled happily round the mosques of the seven hills, and old Turks seated under the plane trees on the green heights of Scutari murmured in low calm voices: "The last day of the City of the Sultans has come! The destined hour has come! The sentence of Allah is fulfilled! So be it! So be it!"

Fortunately the conflagration did not continue into the night. At seven in the evening the British embassy was the last building to catch fire, after which the wind suddenly dropped and the flames died out or were extinguished on every side. In six hours two thirds of Pera had been razed to the ground, nine thousand houses reduced to ashes, and two thousand people killed.

Such a terrible disaster had not been seen since the famous fire in 1756, under the reign of Osman III, which destroyed eighty thousand houses and razed two thirds of Stamboul, and no fire, from the conquest of the city to this day, has caused the loss of so many lives.

On the following day the spectacle of Pera was less terrifying but no less saddening than during the fire itself. The passage of the fire had left whole areas destroyed, and the bare sinister outlines of the great hill could be seen; new views had opened up, the light fell differently, there were huge empty spaces covered in ashes, in which only blackened chimney stacks were left standing like tombstones. Whole neighbourhoods had disappeared like Bedouin camps swept away by a hurricane; only the black and still-smoking traces of streets and crossroads could be seen in the earth, over which thousands of the dispossessed wandered about in rags, begging for charity in the middle of a busy crowd of soldiers, doctors, nuns, clerics of every religion and civil servants of every grade distributing bread and money and directing long lines of carts carrying mattresses and blankets, which had been sent by the government for those left homeless. Army tents had also been distributed. Tatavla and the large Armenian cemetery had been turned into vast camps round which huge crowds of people were milling. Everywhere household goods were piled up, on which exhausted, dazed families were sitting. The cemetery at Galata looked like a ransacked bazaar: in random heaps and stacks, along the paths and round the tombs, there were sofas, beds, cushions, pianos, pictures, books, dented carriages, wounded horses tied to cypresses, gilded sedan chairs belonging to ambassadors and parrot cages from

EDMONDO DE AMICIS

the harems, all watched over by servants and porters black with soot and dropping with exhaustion. An unbelievably numerous throng of the poor, dressed in filthy rags, roamed the streets rummaging for nails and iron bolts among the rubble, stepping over the soldiers and firemen stretched out asleep after the night's labours. Everywhere people could be seen busily constructing shelters out of tents and wooden boards on the ruins of their former houses, families kneeling in burnt-out roofless churches in front of blackened altars, men and women running up and down long rows of burnt and deformed corpses, their heads bent to scrutinize the faces, shouting and weeping desperately when they recognized one, and staggering as if hit by a thunderbolt. All around, stretchers and coffins, thick dust and heat, a stench of burnt flesh; as the diggers worked with their spades and picks, sudden flurries of sparks would shoot up and then fall onto a dense, slow-moving, silent, stunned mass of people who had come there from every part of Constantinople. The serious pale faces of ambassadors and consuls could be seen moving on horseback through the crowd, stopping at the crossroads and gazing round, astonished at the scale of the disaster.

* * *

And yet, as always happens in oriental countries, even this huge disaster was soon forgotten. When I was in Constantinople four years later there was hardly a trace of it to be seen, apart from some razed areas at the far end of Pera, just before the hill of Tatavla. The fire was talked about as if it had happened in the remote past. While the ashes were still smouldering the press had demanded action from the government: it must reorganize the firemen, acquire new pumps, ensure a better water supply and regulate the building of new houses. The government had ignored all these demands and the Europeans in the city had resigned themselves to going on living in the Turkish manner – in other words, putting some of your trust in the Good Lord and some in your own good luck.

So, since nothing, or almost nothing, has changed after the great fire of 1870, one can be certain that it won't be the last of the conflagrations which, as the city's "destiny" would have it, break out periodically. It is true that almost all the houses in Pera are now made of stone, but they are almost all shoddily designed by unqualified and inexperienced architects, working without government supervision – and often constructed by any available builder in such a way that they collapse before they've been finished, while those that remain standing are not fireproof. Water is still in short supply, especially in Pera, and subject to a disgraceful monopoly. Most of it comes from the ancient Roman reservoirs in the Belgrad village, which dry up when there's no heavy spring or autumn rainfall: when this occurs the wealthy pay through the nose for water and the poor drink muddy dregs. The city's firemen are still more like a great criminal rabble than a well-organized body of public servants; their ranks include men of all nationalities and they are only nominally under the control of the municipal authorities, from whom they get nothing more than a daily ration of bread. They are untrained, ill-disciplined and thievish; the inhabitants hate and fear them almost as much as the outbreaks of fire they are incapable of extinguishing, and also suspect them, not without reason, of welcoming fires as an opportunity for looting. It is true that the number of pumps has been increased and the Turks are as proud of them as though they were miracle machines. In actual fact they are absurd contraptions, holding about a dozen litres of water, and produce a thin jet more suitable for watering gardens than putting out fires. And yet these deficiencies are nothing compared to far more serious failings. The widespread belief that the government starts fires as a way of widening the streets is certainly unfounded: the dangers and the resulting damage would be too high a price to pay for such improvements. Nor does the "party of opposition" start a fire in a neighbourhood to terrify the Sultan, as used to happen in the past, or the army set a whole district ablaze in order to get a pay increase. But there is still a strong suspicion that fires are encouraged by those who stand to profit from them, and too often the facts themselves seem to bear this out. This is why the population of the city is perpetually anxious. They fear water-carriers, porters, architects, building merchants, but most of all servants, the scum of Constantinople: most have close contacts with organized crime, which is linked in its turn with other secret gangs responsible for selling the stolen goods and making various facilitating arrangements. The local police are weak, not to say indulgent, when it comes to dealing with these men, and the effects are much the same as though they were complicit. No arsonist has ever been arrested and charged, and after a fire the looters are rarely caught and punished. It is even more exceptional that the stolen items sequestered by the police are returned to their owners. Moreover, since Constantinople teems with the low life from half the countries in the world, attempts to bring them to justice invariably come up against the obstacles imposed by a hundred international treaties. The national consulates claim rights over their own wrongdoers; trials drag on for ages; many of the accused manage to abscond; the fear of punishment has almost no effect on criminals, who regard looting during a fire almost like a privilege conceded to them by the authorities just as victorious armies in the past were allowed to sack the cities they had conquered. For this reason the word "fire" strikes fear into the hearts of the inhabitants of Constantinople and their bowels shudder at the tremendous cry of *"Yangın var!"* as if it were a declaration of imminent divine punishment. Who knows how many times the great metropolis will be burnt down and rise again from its ashes before the flag of European civilization is raised over the imperial palace of Dolmabahçe!

In former times, when a fire broke out in Constantinople and the Sultan was in his harem at the time, the news of the danger was brought to him by a concubine dressed in red from head to toe, who had orders to present herself before him wherever he might be, even if he were in bed with his favourite mistress. She had only to appear in the doorway; her fire-coloured robes served as the mute announcement of disaster. Who would believe that of all the grand and terrible images which come to my mind whenever I think of the fires of Constantinople, the figure of this concubine is always the most striking and compelling? I wish I were a painter in order to show the scene and I shall never cease to entreat all the artists I know until I find one who warms to the subject, and so earns my undying gratitude. He will depict a room in the imperial harem, hung with satin and softly lit, where, upon a large divan, beside a fifteen-year-old blonde Circassian girl swathed in pearls, the great Sultan Selim I is seated. He has torn himself abruptly away from her embrace and fixes his terrified gaze upon the crimson-robed concubine who stands upon the threshold, silent, sinister, as still as a statue, with her pale face full of dread and awe, which seems to say: "King of Kings! Allah calls to you, and your desolate people are waiting for you!" She lifts the curtain from the door and points into the distance beyond the terrace where the vast city lies burning.

Firemen

After the fire

Section of the walls in ruins

## The Walls

I chose to walk the circuit of the old walls of Stamboul alone, and I should advise my fellow Italians going to Constantinople to do the same, because the spectacle of those grand solitary ruins will only leave a deep and enduring impression on those who are ready to receive it, and are free to follow the course of their own meditations in silence. It is a walk of about fifteen Italian miles, through deserted streets, under a hot sun. "Perhaps," I said to my friend, "I will be overcome by sadness on my solitary way and call on your aid like a saint, but, be that as it may, I want to go alone."

I reduced the contents of my wallet in case any local thief should take a fancy to examine them, thrust a morsel into "those gaping apertures" – so I could say to myself later on: "Be quiet, cursed wolf!"* – and set off at eight o'clock in the morning, under a fine sky washed clear by a shower of rain in the night, towards the bridge of the Sultana Valide.

My plan was to leave Stamboul by the Blachernae gate, to follow the line of the walls from the Golden Horn as far as the Castle of the Seven Towers, and then return along the shore of the Sea of Marmara, in this way walking the entire extent of the three sides of the Muslim city.

Turning right after crossing the bridge, I found myself in the large area known as *Istanbul dışında*, or Stamboul "outside the walls", which is a long, built-up strip of land between the walls and the port, with small houses and stores for oil and wood, which have more than once been destroyed by fire. The area between the narrow alleys and the shore of the Golden Horn is lined with small landing stages and inlets where ships and boats are moored, and was busy with porters and donkeys and camels, strange-looking men bustling about with dirty bundles of goods, shouting incomprehensibly in a dozen different languages – it made me think of those extraordinary ports on the Indian and China Seas where the races and merchandise from two hemispheres meet and mingle. The walls still standing on this side of the city are about five times the height of a man, crenellated and flanked at regular intervals by small square towers, and in many places falling into ruin – but this is the least noteworthy stretch of the walls of Stamboul, both from an artistic and historical point of view. I crossed the district of Fener, walking along the shore crowded with

fruit and pastry vendors, sellers of anisette and rosolio, and open-
air kitchens, among handsome Greek sailors looking like statues of
their ancient gods, and then I skirted the huge ghetto of Balat, crossed
through the silent quarter of Blachernae, and finally emerged from the
city by the gate called Eğri Kapı, not far from the shore of the Golden
Horn.

All this is quickly narrated, but it took me one and a half hours to
walk it, uphill, downhill, stepping over great puddles of mud, over
enormous cobblestones, down endless alleys and under dark vaults,
across wide empty spaces, with only the pinnacles of the minarets on
Selim's Mosque to guide me. At a certain point no more European faces
or clothes are seen; then European-style houses disappear, followed by
cobblestones, shop signs, street names, sounds of people at work. The
further you proceed the more fiercely dogs look at you, the bolder the
Turkish ragamuffins become, the more care the common women take
to cover their faces – until you are in the midst of complete Asiatic
barbarity. The two-hour walk began to seem like a two-day journey.

Turning to the left as I came out of the Eğri Kapı gate I came
unexpectedly upon a large tract of that famous wall that defends
Stamboul on the land side. Three years have passed since that day,
but I can still feel the amazement which overcame me. Where else
in the whole of the Orient could one find in such a combination the
grandeur of human achievement, the majesty of power, the glory of
antiquity, the solemnity of things past, the melancholy of ruins, the
beauty of nature? The sight inspires wonder, reverence and awe in
the onlooker: it is worthy of Homer. When you first see it you feel
like throwing your hat in the air and shouting out "Glory be!" – as
if faced by an immense army of wounded giant heroes. The line of
walls and enormous towers stretches as far as the eye can see, rising
and descending with the lie of the land; in places they are so low they
seem to sink into the earth, in others they are so lofty they appear
to crown the summit of a mountain; in infinite forms of decay and
ruin, built in limestone – which ranges from a sombre, almost black
hue to a warm and almost golden-yellow colour – and covered by a
luxuriant dark green vegetation which climbs up the walls, crests the
tops of the towers and falls in hanging garlands from the battlements
and loopholes, filling every breach, crack and fissure, and even spilling
onto the road alongside. There are three ranges of walls which form
so to speak a sequence of giant broken steps; the inner wall – which is

the highest – is flanked at short intervals with square thickset towers; the middle wall is reinforced by small round towers; while the external wall is very low, has no towers and is defended by a deep wide moat that was once filled with sea water from the Golden Horn and the Sea of Marmara, but is now dry and covered with grass and scrub. All three walls remain in much the same condition they were in the day after the capture of Constantinople: the restorations which were carried out by Mehmet and Beyazit II are very insignificant. The breaches made by the great cannon of Urban may still be seen, as well as the places where rams and catapults battered and mines exploded; all the parts where the assaults were fiercest and the resistance most desperate are clearly visible. The round towers in the middle wall are almost all in a state of complete dilapidation; those of the interior wall are nearly all standing, but so broken and lopped at the sides and top that they resemble huge tree trunks with all the branches hewn off and split from top to bottom, or great rocks that have been hollowed out by sea currents. Massive fragments of masonry have rolled down from the curtain wall, and are strewn along the platforms of the middle and external walls and in the moat. Narrow footpaths wind here and there among the rubble and the weeds, and are lost in the tall dark undergrowth between the rocks and the bare depressions uncovered by the fallen walls. The bastions between the towers present a wonderful picture of ruin, full of majesty and grandeur. It is all colossal, wild, jagged, threatening and full of an imposing, melancholy beauty which inspires awe. It's like the ruins of a great chain of feudal fortresses or the extraordinary fortifications which walled in the legendary empires of the Far East. The Constantinople of today vanishes and the city of the Constantines is before us; we breathe the air of the fifteenth century; the thought of the day when the great city fell fills our minds: you are for a moment utterly overwhelmed and lost.

The gate by which I had left, called Eğri Kapı by the Turks, was the famous Kaligaria gate by which Justinian made his triumphal entry, and Alexius Comnenus came to take possession of the throne. In front of it there is now a Muslim graveyard. In the first days of the siege Urban's great cannon, which needed one hundred oxen to move it and four hundred artillerymen to work it, was placed here. The gate was defended by Theodore of Karystos and John Grant* against the left flank of the Turkish army which extended as far as the Golden Horn. From here to the Sea of Marmara there is not a single house.

EDMONDO DE AMICIS

The road runs straight between the walls and open country. There
is nothing to distract your attention from your contemplation of the
ruins. I set off and walked for some distance between two graveyards,
a Christian one on the left under the walls and a Muslim one on the
right, very large and shaded with cypress trees. The sun beat down;
the road stretched white and lonely before me, gradually climbing in
a straight line to meet the clear blue sky. On one side tower followed
tower, on the other, tomb succeeded tomb. The only sounds were my
own footsteps and the occasional rustle of a lizard among the bushes.
At length I unexpectedly found myself in front of a fine square gate
under a high round arch and flanked by two large octagonal towers.
It was the Adrianople gate, the polyandrium of the Greeks – the same
gate which in 625 AD, under Heraclius, held back the formidable attack
of the Avars – which was defended against Mehmet II by the brothers
Paolo, Antonio and Troilo Bocchiardo,* and which subsequently
became the principal gate for the triumphal entries and sorties of
the Ottoman army. Not a living creature was around. Suddenly two
Turkish horsemen galloped out, enveloped me in a cloud of dust, and
vanished on the road towards Adrianople; then deep silence reigned
once more.

Turning my back to the wall at this point, I followed the Adrianople
road, and descending into the valley of the Lycus, climbed a hillock
and found myself looking out over the wide undulating arid plain
of Davutpaşa, where Mehmet II set up his headquarters during
the siege of the city. I stayed some time looking out, with my hand
shading my eyes, as if to search out the traces of the Ottoman camp
and imagine the extraordinary sight as it was at the end of spring in
1453.* Here beat the heart of that enormous army which held in its
formidable embrace the great city in its dying throes. From here sped
the orders that set a hundred thousand labourers to work, dragging
two hundred galleys overland from the bay of Beşiktaş to the bay of
Kasımpaşa; that sent armies of Armenian miners into the bowels of
the earth, that unfurled in a hundred parts of the field the heralds'
banners as a signal to launch an attack, and, in the time it takes to
count the beads on a *tesbih*, drew three hundred thousand bows
and unsheathed as many scimitars. There the pale messengers of
Constantine met the Genoese from Galata coming to sell their oil to
lubricate Urban's cannon, and the Muslim lookouts scanned the Sea
of Marmara for a fleet of European ships carrying a final possibility

of aid from Christendom to the last stronghold of the Byzantines. There renegade Christians, Asiatic mercenaries, aged sheikhs and famished dervishes swarmed busily about the tents of the fourteen thousand janissaries, mingling with endless troops of horses and long lines of camels, broken catapults and ramming engines, shards of exploded cannon and heaps of granite cannonballs, while dusty toilworn soldiers working in pairs carried the mutilated corpses and the writhing bodies of the wounded from the walls into open country, surrounded by clouds of smoke which never lifted. In the midst of the janissary encampment rose the many-coloured tents of the court, and above these the flame-coloured pavilion of Mehmet II. Every morning at sunrise he stood at the entrance to his tent, pale from sleepless nights, in his long blood-red kaftan, and his turban plumed with yellow, fixing his eagle gaze upon the doomed city, combing his fingers repeatedly through his thick black beard and twisting the silver hilt of his curved dagger in the other hand. Around him stood Urban, the inventor of the miraculous cannon, which in a few days would explode and scatter his bones as far as the Hippodrome; the admiral, Baltaoğlu, already disturbed by the presentiment of a defeat which would bring down on his head the golden rod of the wrathful *Grand Signor*; the brave commander of the Elepolis,* a mobile fortress with towers and cased with iron which would be burnt to the ground in front of the St Romanus gate; a circle of poets and jurists, their faces bronzed and battle-worn; an entourage of pashas with scarred limbs and kaftans torn by arrows; a swarm of brawny janissaries clutching naked swords and *çavuş* armed with steel rods, ready to behead and strike down mutineers and deserters; and the flower of that vast Asiatic horde, brimming with youth and strength and warlike ferocity, ready to rush like a river of steel and flame upon the decrepit remnant of the Byzantine Empire. All, motionless as statues in the first rosy rays of dawn, gazed at the thousand silvered domes of the city promised to them by the Prophet, under which at the very same hour its cowardly inhabitants were praying and sobbing. I saw them all, their faces, their poses, the daggers, the folds of their caps and kaftans, and the long shadows they cast over the earth marked by the wheel-ruts of cannon and assault towers. Suddenly my eyes fell upon a large stone at my feet on which I read a roughly carved inscription, and the great picture I had painted in my mind vanished, only to give place to another. Under a hot sun the plain swarmed with a cheerful throng of Chasseurs de

Vincennes, Zouaves and infantrymen in red trousers; I heard the songs of Provence and Normandy; I saw Marshals Saint-Arnaud, Canrobert, Espinasse, Pelissier;* I recognized a thousand faces and uniforms vivid in my memory and dear to me from childhood – and read once more with pleasure and surprise the simple inscription: "*Eugène Saccard, caporal dans le 22ème léger, 16 Juin 1854.*"*

From there I recrossed the Lycus valley and returned to the road which skirts the walls, still empty and winding between the ruins and the graveyards. I passed the ancient military gate of Pempton, now walled up. I crossed the river Lycus which enters the city at that point, and finally arrived before the Cannon gate – so called after Urban's great cannon which was positioned opposite it – against which Mehmet's army made their final assault. Lifting my eyes, I saw behind the battlements horrible black faces with tangled hair peering down at me with an amazed expression. They turned out to belong to a group of gypsies who had put up their tents among the ruins of the curtain walls and towers. Here the traces of the struggle in 1453 are very marked and on a giant scale: the walls are torn away, shot through, reduced to pieces; the towers half toppled and shapeless; the battlements buried under a mountain of rubble, the loopholes smashed, the earth churned up, the moat full of colossal fragments of masonry, like boulders fallen in a mountain avalanche. The terrible encounter could have been fought yesterday, and the ruins tell better than any words could of the horrible slaughter which they witnessed. All the gates the whole length of the walls could tell the same tale. The battle was joined at dawn. The Ottoman army was divided into four huge columns, and preceded by a vanguard of a hundred thousand irregular troops, all destined to die. All this cannon fodder – this wild, undisciplined mob of Tartars, Arabs, Caucasians and Negroes, led by sheikhs, goaded on by dervishes, and whipped on by an army of *çavuş* – led the attack, carrying fascines and grubby with soil, forming an unbroken chain and raising a single shout from the Sea of Marmara to the Golden Horn. When they reached the edge of the moat, a hailstorm of stone and iron stopped them short and mowed them down in their hundreds; old men, boys, slaves, robbers, shepherds, brigands, crushed by boulders, pierced by arrows, riddled with bullets, set ablaze by fire-launching springalds; but other hordes took their place, driven on by still more behind them, until in a little while the moat and its slopes were filled with a bloody writhing mass of men, over which more soldiers rushed in a torrent, beating against the walls and towers, with javelins and stones raining down upon them in a dark cloud which hid the walls, the defenders, the corpses and the road, until the savage blare of a thousand Ottoman trumpets was heard above the din of battle, and the great vanguard, its ranks decimated and covered in blood, retreated in confusion all along the line. Then Mehmet II unleashed his main troops. Three great armies, three human torrents, led by a hundred pashas, with a thousand standards fluttering over their heads, advanced, fanned out, swarmed over the heights and filled the valleys – with a deafening noise of trumpets and cymbals and swords, and a great shout of *"Lailahaillallah!"*, echoing like a roll of thunder from the Golden Horn to the Castle of the Seven Towers – picked up speed and threw themselves against the walls, like sea waves in a storm breaking on a rocky coast. Then the great battle was joined, or rather a hundred battles, at the gates and at the breaches, in the ditches, on the battlements, beneath the curtain walls, from one end to the other of the great and ancient bulwarks of the city. Death arrived for two hundred thousand souls from ten thousand loopholes. Rocks, wooden beams, barrels filled with earth, blazing fascines were rolled down from the tops of the walls and the towers. The steps collapsed under the hordes of attackers; the drawbridges of the siege towers gave way; the burning catapults flared. Troop after troop rushed up only to fall back on the stones, on shattered corpses, on the dying, in pools of blood, in the water, on the weapons of their comrades, enveloped in thick smoke, lit here and there by the flashes of Greek fire, surrounded by the furious whistle of bullets and the explosions of mines, the cries of the wounded, the deafening booms of Mehmet's eighteen artillery batteries which targeted the city from the raised ground where they were positioned. From time to time the battle paused as if to take breath and then, against the wide breach at the St Romanus gate, Constantine's purple cloak could be seen billowing through the thinning smoke, or the gleaming armour worn by Giustiniani or Don Francisco of Toledo,* or the movements of three hundred Genoese archers. Then the struggle starts again, once more smoke covers the breaches, the ladders are placed against the walls and the stones and the corpses begin again to pile up at each of the gates, the Adrianople and Golden Gates, Selymbria and Tetarton, Pempton and Rhusion, Blachernae and Heptapyrgion. Wave after wave of armed forces seem to emerge from the earth – rushing against the walls, crossing the moat, climbing the outer walls – fall back, rise again, clamber over the rocks, slither over the corpses, with arrows and bullets and fire raining down on them. At last the assailants, their ranks thinned out and exhausted, began to give way, retreat and disperse; a great shout of victory and a solemn chorus of thanksgiving rose from the walls. From the heights before St Romanus, Mehmet II, surrounded by his fourteen thousand janissary troops, watched and for a while was uncertain whether he should withdraw or renew the attack. But after he had taken one look at his formidable soldiers, who shook with impatience and anger as they watched his face, he rose in his stirrups, and once more shouted his battle cry. Then the vengeance of God was unleashed. The janissaries answered as one; the columns moved; a throng of dervishes spread out through the camp to revive the spirits of those who had become dispersed, the *çavuş* rounded up the deserters, the pashas reformed their lines, the Sultan, brandishing an iron mace, advanced in a thick forest of glittering scimitars and bows, and a sea of helmets and turbans. The St Romanus gate once more found itself under a hail of arrows and bullets; Giustiniani was wounded and disappeared while the Italian archers were disheartened and broke up. The giant janissary Hasan of Ulubat was the first to scale the rampart. Constantine, fighting in the midst of the last survivors of his brave Morean troops, was thrown from the battlements, but continued to fight by the gate, surrounded by corpses, wielding wild blows. The Empire of the East had fallen. Tradition says that a great tree marks the spot where Constantine's body was found, but there is no trace of it. There, where rivulets of blood once ran, the ground was white with daisies and saxifrage, over which butterflies were fluttering. I picked a flower for remembrance, under the astonished eyes of the gypsies, and went on my way.

The walls still stretched before me as far as the eye could see. At the highest points they hid the city completely, making it difficult to believe that behind those solitary and silent ruins lay an immense metropolis, with great monuments and a huge population. Where they were lower, on the contrary, the silvery tops of minarets and domes, the roofs of Greek churches, and the topmost boughs of cypresses could be seen through the crenellations. Here and there through an opening in the curtain walls you could catch a sudden glimpse of a part of the city, as if a door had quickly opened and shut: clusters of houses which looked abandoned, little valleys, orchards, gardens, and, further off, hazy in the white glare of the noonday sun, the fantastic outlines of Stamboul. I passed by the walled-up Tetarton gate, only distinguishable because of the two towers on either side. This stretch of the walls is better preserved. There are long portions of the curtain walls of Theodosius II which are almost intact; beautiful towers from the period of the Praetorian Prefects Anthemius and Cyrus Constantinus, still gloriously undamaged and lofty after fifteen centuries, ready to meet a new assault. At some places, on the battlements, peasants have built huts, which seem small and fragile against the majestic solidity of the walls, and look like birds' nests on a rocky mountain side. On the right there were yet more cemeteries, cypress groves on hillsides, small valleys scattered with tombstones. I glimpsed a dervish monastery half hidden among plane trees; a solitary café, with a fountain behind it in the shade of a willow tree; and further off, beyond small woods, white paths leading across the parched highlands, under a dazzling bright sky across which vultures slowly wheeled.

After another quarter of an hour I reached the gate called Yeni Mevlevihane, so called after the famous dervish monastery nearby. It is a low gate in which four marble columns are set, and on either side are two square towers, with an inscription of Cyrus Constantinus dating from 447 AD, and the other with an inscription of Justin II and Sophia, in which the imperial names are misspelt – a curious instance of the barbarian ignorance of the fifth century. I looked inside the gate, on the walls, around the monastery and in the graveyard – not a living soul was to be seen. I rested a little while leaning against the piers of a small bridge which crossed the moat and then continued on my way.

I would give up the memory of one of the most beautiful views in all Constantinople if I could convey to the reader even a pale shadow of the deep and peculiar emotion which I experienced as I walked on between two endless lines of ruins and of tombs, under the sun, in that austere solitude, surrounded by that immense peace. Many times in my life, on melancholy days, I've wished I were part of some silent and mysterious caravan forever wandering onward, through unknown countries, towards an unknown end. Well, that road was like my dream come true. I wish it could have gone on forever. It did not make me sad, but rather filled me with serenity and courage. The vivid colours of the trees and plants, the Cyclopean forms of the walls, the long lines of open country, like waves on a rough sea, the solemn memories of emperors and armies, of titanic struggles, of scattered peoples, of dead generations, alongside that vast city – in that deathly silence broken only by the powerful beat of eagles' wings as they took flight from the towers – aroused overweening fantasies and desires which redoubled my sense of life. I wished I were three metres tall and wearing the giant armour of the Grand Elector of Saxony which I'd once seen in the armoury in Madrid, and that my steps echoed in the silence like the march of some troop of medieval halberdiers. I wished I had the strength of a Titan so that I could lift the huge boulders from those proud walls. I walked along with my head held high, frowning and my right hand clenched in a fist, calling in blank verse on Constantine and Mehmet, drunk with a kind of warlike rapture, my soul entirely absorbed by the past. My mind and my blood were racing with youthful energy; I derived deep enjoyment from my living solitude; such was my anxiety that it remained undisturbed that I would not have wished at that moment to meet even the closest of my friends.

The next gate I saw was the ancient military one of Triton, now closed. The curtain walls and towers show traces of heavy bombardment from some of Urban's large cannon, and it is also thought that this was one of the three large breaches which Mehmet II pointed out to his army before the assault, saying: "You can enter Constantinople on horseback by the three breaches which I've opened." Next comes an open gate, flanked by two octagonal towers, and recognizable from its small bridge with three arches built in a beautiful honey-coloured stone as the Silivri gate, from which the main road to the city of Selymbria left, a name changed by the Turks to Silivri. During the siege this gate was defended by the Genoese captain, Maurizio Cattaneo. The road still retains some traces of the paving laid down during Justinian's reign. In front there is a very large cemetery and on the other side of the cemetery there is the famous monastery of Balıklı.

Near the entrance into the cemetery I came upon the solitary spot where the heads are buried of the famous Pasha of Janina, Ali of Tepelenë* with those of his sons, Veli, governor of Trίkala, Mukhtar, commander of Alonia, Saleh, commander of Lepanto, and that of his nephew Mehmet, son of Veli, commander of Delvinë. There are five small columns surmounted by turbans, all bearing the date 1827, and a simple inscription, written by the poor dervish Süleyman, Ali's childhood friend, who purchased the heads after they had been removed from the battlements of the Seraglio, and buried them with his own hands. The inscription on the cippus of Ali says: "Here lies the head of the famous Ali Pasha of Tepelenë, governor of the sanjak of Janina, who strove for the independence of Albania for more than fifty years." Which just goes to show that pious falsehoods can also be found on Muslim tombstones. I stopped for a moment to contemplate the handful of earth that covered that formidable head, and Hamlet's words to Yorick's skull came into my mind. Where are your palikars now, Lion of Epirus? Where are your brave Arnauts, your palaces bristling with cannon, and the beautiful kiosks reflected in the waters of lake Janina, and your treasures buried among the rocks, and the lovely eyes of your Vassiliki?* And I was musing on that poor beautiful lady wandering through the streets of Constantinople, impoverished and desolated by the memories of her lost happiness and greatness, when I heard a slight rustle behind me, and, turning, saw a tall angular figure, dressed in a long dark gown, bareheaded, who was looking at me with a questioning air. He made a sign and I understood that he was a Greek monk from Balıklı who wished to show me the miraculous fountain, so I followed him towards his monastery.

He led me across a silent courtyard, opened a small door, lighted a taper and beckoned me to accompany him down a flight of steps into a damp dark cellar; there he halted before a kind of cistern, where, shading the candle with his hand, he pointed out to me the goldfish darting through the water. As I looked, he was mumbling something incomprehensible which I took to be the story of the famous miracle of the fish. While the Muslims were making their final assault upon the walls of Constantinople, a Greek monk in this monastery was frying fish. Suddenly at the door of the kitchen another monk appeared, in a state of terror, and called out: "The city's fallen!" "Come off it!" the cook replied, "I'll believe that when I see these fish jump out of the pan." And immediately the fish jumped out alive, half brown since only one side had been cooked. As you might expect, they were piously replaced in the cistern from which they'd been taken, and where they may be seen to this day. When he had finished mumbling, my monk sprinkled a few drops of holy water in my face – which I duly converted into a tip – and after he'd led me to the door, he stood for a moment looking after me with his sleepy little eyes.

And so I continued, with walls and towers on one side and shaded graveyards on the other, a few green fields and vineyards, an abandoned house or two, and beyond, emptiness. Sometimes, looking up at the walls from a dip in the road I thought I could see where they ended, but once the road had climbed a little, I saw them once more stretching endlessly away. With every step I took towers seemed to emerge in the distance, one after the other, as if they were crowding the side of the road to see who was disturbing their solitude. The vegetation in this part of the walk was extraordinary. Leafy trees rise up from the towers as from gigantic vases; red and yellow blossoms and garlands of ivy and honeysuckle hang from the battlements, and below grows an inextricable tangle of wild strawberry and mastic trees, nettles and wild plums, in the midst of which plane trees and willows grow, which shelter the moat and the banks with their shady foliage. Large stretches of wall are completely masked by ivy, which holds the bricks and crumbling mortar together like a net and hides the gaps and fissures. The moat has been transformed into kitchen gardens, and on its banks goats and sheep graze, watched over by Greek boys lying in the shade of the trees; flocks of birds fly out from the walls; the air is full of the pungent fragrance of wild herbs; and a sort of springlike joyousness seems to breathe over the ruins which look as though they were festooned with flowers for the triumphal passage of some sultana. Suddenly I felt upon my face a gust of salt air, and raising my eyes saw the blue waters of the Sea of Marmara in front of me. At the very same moment I seemed to hear a low voice murmuring in my ear: "The Castle of the Seven Towers" – and I halted in the middle of the road with a vague sense of apprehension. Then I went on, passing by the ancient gate of Deuteron, and that of Melandesia, to arrive in front of the castle.

This building of ill repute, erected by Mehmet II upon the ancient Cyclobion of the Greeks in order to protect the city at the point where the defensive land wall joins the defensive sea wall, was converted into a state prison as soon as his subsequent conquests had ensured Stamboul against the dangers of a siege and meant it was no longer needed as a fortress. It is now nothing but the ghost of a castle, guarded by a handful of soldiers; a ruin, full of painful and atrocious memories that live on in sinister legend among the inhabitants of Constantinople, and is seldom seen by travellers except for a moment from the prow of the vessel that is carrying them to the Golden Horn. The Turks call it Yedikule, and it is for them what the Bastille is to the French, and the Tower of London to the English, a monument recalling the worst periods of the Sultans' tyranny.

The city walls conceal it from those who approach it from the road, except for two of the seven great towers which gave it its name and of which only four survive intact. In the outer wall two Corinthian columns remain which came from the ancient Golden Gate through which Heraclius and Narses* made their triumphal entries; according to a legend common to both Muslims and Greeks, the Christians will re-enter Constantine's city by this gate when they return victorious. The entrance is inside the walls in a small square tower, where you find a slippered sentinel taking a nap; as long as you make sure a coin goes into his pocket, you can enter too.

On entering, I found myself alone in a large enclosure, as gloomy as a prison or a cemetery, which made me hold back for a moment. There were high black walls all round, forming a pentagon, crowned with massive square and round towers, some high, some low, some crumbling away while others were still intact, covered with conical lead roofs, and with numerous dilapidated flights of steps leading up to the battlements and lookouts. Tall close-set trees grow within the enclosure, dominated by a group of cypresses and plane trees, above which the minaret of a small hidden mosque could be made out; lower down there were the roofs of a group of huts where the soldiers sleep; in the middle the tomb of a vizier who was strangled in the castle; here and there the shapeless remains of an ancient redoubt; and among the undergrowth and along the walls, fragments of bas-reliefs, broken column shafts and capitals sunk in the ground, half covered with grass and submerged in brackish water; an eerie, gloomy confusion, full of mystery and menace, which made me reluctant to go on. I stood awhile looking around uncertainly and finally advanced with some trepidation, as though afraid I might step in a pool of blood. The soldiers' huts were locked, the mosque shut up, everything was still and deserted, as in an abandoned ruin. On the walls could still be made out traces of Greek crosses, fragments of Constantine's monogram, the broken wings of Roman eagles, and the remains of friezes from the original Byzantine edifice, blackened with the passage of time. On some stones Greek sentences roughly incised in tiny characters could be seen: almost all carved by Constantine's soldiers, who were guarding this fortress under the Florentine commander Giuliani, on the day before the fall of Constantinople; poor souls resigned to death, praying to God to save their city from pillage and their families from slavery.

There are two towers behind the Golden Gate: in one, the ambassadors from states which were at war with the Sultan were incarcerated. There are numerous Latin inscriptions on the walls, of which the most recent was carved by the Venetian ambassadors who were imprisoned there in the reign of Ahmet III, when the war in the Morea broke out.* The other is the notorious tower which has given rise to all the most dismal tales associated with the castle; a labyrinth of horrendous dungeons, tombs where the living were immured, where viziers and other court dignitaries waited for the executioner to come, praying in the darkness or mad with despair, clawing the walls and beating their heads against them. In one of these dungeons was the great mortar in which the bones and flesh of the ulemas were crushed to powder. On the ground floor there is a large circular chamber, called the prison of blood, where the condemned were secretly decapitated, and their heads thrown into a well, called the well of blood, the opening of which may still be seen in the uneven paving, covered by two stone slabs. Beneath this was the so-called rocky cavern, lit by a lantern hanging from the roof, where those condemned to torture had their flesh peeled off in strips, burning pitch was poured into the wounds made by the whip, feet and hands were crushed with clubs, and from where the terrible howls of the dying only reached the ears of the prisoners in the tower above as faint lamentations. In one corner of the inner courtyard the traces of a smaller enclosure are still visible; here the heads of ordinary folk who had been condemned to death were struck off in the night; and nearby, not so very long ago, you could still find a heap of human bones that rose nearly as high as the castle battlements. Near the entrance is the dungeon of Osman II, the first imperial victim of the janissaries. This is the room where the poor eighteen-year-old Sultan, with a strength born of despair, struggled furiously against the four assassins sent to kill him, until one of them, with a cruel and cowardly hand used to turning men into eunuchs, grabbed his genitals and caused him to scream at the top of his voice until he was throttled by the rope. In all the other towers and in part of the walls there is a network of dark corridors, secret stairways, and low doors barred with beams of iron or wood, under which pashas, imperial princes, governors, chamberlains, high officials in the flower of their youth and at the height of their power who were to lose everything in an instant, stooped their heads for the last time; their severed heads were already dripping blood down the outer wall of the castle as their brides, still dressed in their ceremonial gowns, waited for them amid the splendours of the harem. Soldiers and assassins and messengers from the Seraglio, carrying the Sultan's final refusal of clemency to the condemned men still vainly grasping at some ultimate glimmer of hope, went down those damp passageways and staircases, dark as a tomb, at night, by the light of a lantern, and their corpses were removed, eyes half out of the sockets, the dreadful silk cord twisted round their necks by hurrying çavuş, exhausted by the long struggle in the dark with men fighting with the fury of despair. At the other end of Stamboul, on the hill of the Seraglio, stood the terrifying Palace tribunal. Here was a huge machine for torture, surmounted by its seven stone towers like scaffolds, which received a supply of victims – by sea and by road, in the moonlight – on whose skulls and corpses the sun would rise the following day. The night sentinels posted on the towers where these men were dying could see in the distance the kiosks of the Seraglio lit up for some imperial festival. Today there is a certain satisfaction in seeing this infamous castle in such a state of decay, as though all its victims had come back to life and gnawed and scratched away at its walls with their teeth and nails to take their revenge on the stones at least, if they couldn't on the men who'd tortured them. The now defenceless and decrepit monster gapes with the hundred mouths of its loopholes and collapsed doorways, reduced to a mere scarecrow; thousands of rats, snakes and yellow scorpions pullulate like worms in its dirty carcass and swarm in its hollow stomach and broken loins, among the insolently riotous trees and plants which wreath and plume its hideousness, as if in mockery. After looking in at various doors without seeing anything but rats scuttling away, I mounted by an old mossy flight of steps to the battlements on a section of the western wall. From there you can look down on the whole castle: a chaos of ruins, towers, crenellations, stairs, battlements – all built of blackish or reddish stone with the intense green of the trees and bushes in the middle. Beyond the castle the towers and battlements of Stamboul's eastern walls could be seen. If I half-closed my eyes the castle and the walls seemed to form one immense abandoned fortress standing out against the blue sea. Looking to the left large areas of Stamboul could be made out, crossed by many long roads gradually winding towards the ancient triumphal way used by the Byzantine emperors, which led straight from the Golden Gate through the forums of Arcadius and Constantine to the palace. It was an ample, lovely view which only made the heap of infamous ruins at the foot of it seem even more sinister. I remained a long time sitting, dazzled by the bright light, on a merlon which was baking hot under the sun, contemplating that huge open sepulchre of a castle with the kind of hesitant, brooding curiosity one looks at the site of a recent crime. A deep silence lay over the place. Large lizards scampered over the walls, toads croaked down in the moats, crows wheeled above the towers, clouds of gnats from the marshy ground inside the castle flew round my head, and a slight breeze carried the stench of the rotting carcass of a horse at the bottom of the outer moat. A sensation of disgust and nausea came over me, yet I remained rooted to the spot, as if hypnotized, plunged into a kind of torpor. Through the monotonous buzz of the gnats I thought I could hear the splash of skulls thrown into the wells, the agonizing cries of the dying in the underground cellars, and the voice of Brancovan's little boy who cried out to his father as he felt the cold noose against his neck. As I was tired and dazzled by the light, I closed my eyes and stayed still for a while, and then all those horrible images sprang up before me with terrifying clarity. I was startled out of this reverie by a loud penetrating cry: looking down I saw the muezzin on the terrace of the little minaret in the castle mosque. That slow, sweet, solemn voice, chanting of God, in that place and at that moment, spoke to the very depths of my soul! It seemed to speak in the names of all those who had died within its walls, to say that their sufferings had not been in vain, that their last tears had been gathered up, that their tortures had been recompensed, that they had forgiven and that we should forgive, we should pray and trust in God even when the world abandons us, and that all is vanity on this earth except for this infinite feeling of love and compassion. I went out of the castle much moved.

I resumed my walk towards the sea along the outer walls of Stamboul. I soon reached the Adrianople station, where, under the walls, various stretches of railway track meet and cross. I found myself in the middle of long rows of dusty old railway carriages, but there was not a person to be seen. Had I been some Turkish fanatic, opposed to all European innovations, I could have set fire to the whole lot and gone on my way completely undetected. I walked on ahead, along the verge of the road, expecting at every moment to hear the threatening shout of some guard, but no one accosted me, and in a short while I arrived at the end of the walls. I thought that I could enter Stamboul here, but I was proved wrong. The sea walls and the land walls join on the beach, but there wasn't the trace of a gate. So I walked on through the remains of an ancient quay and sat on a rock jutting out into the waves. All I could see was the Sea of Marmara, the Asian mountains, and the blue heights of Scutari which seemed very far away. The shore was deserted: I could have been alone in the universe. The waves broke against my feet and splashed my face. I sat there for a while aimlessly reflecting on a hundred different things. I saw myself on my own coming out of the Kaligaria gate and slowly making my way down the empty street which runs between the cemeteries and the towers; I followed myself as though I were another person. Then I started to look for Junck through the huge city. Then I stood and watched the waves rolling in, one after the other, with a low murmur, only to vanish one after the other into silence. I thought they were like the peoples and armies who had come, one after the other, to attack the walls of Byzantium: Pausanias's and Alcibiades's troops, the legions of Maximus and Severus, the great Persian throng, the hordes of Avars, of Slavs and Arabs and Bulgarians and Crusaders, the armies of Michael Paleologus and Comnenus, of Beyazit the Thunderbolt and Murat II and Mehmet the Conqueror, all gone one after the other into the silence of death. I felt the same pangs of sadness which Leopardi felt on the evening of the holiday when he heard the solitary song of the workman gradually dying away, recalling the songs of ancient peoples, and thought that everything on earth passes away as in a dream.*

So I returned to the gate of the Seven Towers, entered the walls there and traversed the whole of Stamboul along the Marmara shore. I had walked so much my legs were dropping, but there's a point on long treks when one's very tiredness provokes a kind of mule-like stubbornness which revives one's strength. I can see myself walking on and on through those deserted streets, under the burning sun, in a kind of half-waking dream, in which the faces of friends back in Turin, episodes from novels, scenes from other countries and vague thoughts on life and immortality drifted through my mind. It all led back to the dining room in the Hotel Byzantium, bright with chandeliers and lamps, which I could see far off in the distance, beyond a city a hundred times larger than Stamboul, where night had already fallen. I crossed a Muslim neighbourhood that seemed uninhabited – and where I sensed again the gloom of the castle – and entered the large district of Samatya where Greeks and Armenians live, which was similarly deserted. I went on down an endless winding lane, with glimpses between the houses of the crenellated city walls, black against the glittering sea. I walked under the Samatya gate and found myself once again in a Muslim quarter, with latticed windows, closed doors, small mosques, hidden gardens, moss-grown cisterns and neglected fountains. I crossed the site of the ancient cattle market, with the city walls still visible to my right, and encountered no one apart from a few dogs who stopped to watch me pass by and a few Turkish ragamuffins who looked at me with a cheeky stare. A couple of windows opened and suddenly shut again, letting me glimpse a woman's hand or the hem of her sleeve. I skirted the huge gardens of Vlanga above the ancient harbour of Theodosius; I could see large areas marked by the traces of a recent fire, places where the city seemed to finish in the countryside, dervish monasteries, Greek churches, mysterious little squares shaded by great plane trees, under which an old man smoking a narghile was dozing. Going on, I stopped in front of a small café to drink a glass of water which was displayed in one of the windows, but though I called out and knocked on the door, no one answered. I left the Greek quarter of Yenikapı behind and entered another Muslim one, then once more found myself among Greek and Armenian houses in Kumkapı. All this time the walls and the sea could be seen on my right; I met only dogs, beggars, urchins, and heard only the cry of the muezzin at the hour of sunset. It grew dark, and the houses, melancholy mosques, empty crossroads, street openings continued to go by one after the other. My strength began to ebb and I started to think of throwing myself down on a mattress in front of the next café I came to, when I turned a corner and suddenly saw in front of me the huge dome of Hagia Sophia. What a wonderful sight! My strength revived, my mind cleared, I quickened my pace, walked over the bridge and saw the lighted door of the main café in Galata with Junck, Rossasco and Santoro – my small homeland away from home – who came to meet me with their hands outstretched and smiling faces – at which I heaved one of the longest and deepest sighs of satisfaction a gentleman has ever been known to give.

## The Old Seraglio

As in Granada before you have visited the Alhambra, so in Constantinople you feel you have seen nothing until you have been within the walls of the Old Seraglio. A hundred times a day, from all parts of the city and the sea, that greenest of hills is seen, full of secrets and enticements, continually drawing your gaze to it like some novelty and tormenting the imagination like an enigma, and cutting across your other thoughts until you decide to go there before you'd planned to, more to exorcise its presence than for pleasure.

There is not another place indeed in the whole of Europe the name of which alone arouses in the mind so strange a combination of beautiful and terrible images; about which so much has been thought and written and supposed; which has given rise to so much vague and contradictory information; which is still the object of so much insatiable curiosity, of so many absurd prejudices, and so many marvellous tales. Nowadays anyone can enter, and many come out unmoved. But we may be sure that for centuries to come, when Ottoman rule is perhaps no more than a memory in Europe, and the busy streets of a new city cover that lovely hill, no traveller will pass that way without thinking of the old imperial kiosks which once stood there, or without envying us of the nineteenth century, who were still in time to find the grand Ottoman palace full of living memories. Who knows how many archaeologists will patiently seek for the traces of a door or a wall in the courtyards of the new buildings, and how many poets will write verses on the handful of ruins scattered along the seashore! Or perhaps, after many centuries, these walls will still be jealously guarded, and scholars, lovers and artists will visit them, and the legendary life which went on within their precincts will live again all over the world, in the form of a thousand books and pictures.

It is not its architectural beauty which arouses such universal curiosity. The Seraglio is not, like the Alhambra, a great artistic monument. The Court of Lions alone in the Arab palace is worth all the kiosks and towers of the Turkish edifice. The Seraglio is a great historical monument which reveals and illuminates almost the entire course of the Ottoman dynasty: the secret and innermost chronicle of the Turkish Empire is written in the stones of its walls and on the trunks of its centuries-old trees. Nothing is wanting but the record of the last thirty years, and of the two centuries which preceded the conquest of Constantinople. From Mehmet II who laid its foundations, to Abdülmecit who abandoned it to inhabit the palace of Dolmabahçe, twenty-five Sultans have lived there. Here the dynasty established itself immediately on conquering its first European capital, here it rose to the zenith of its fortune, and here its decline began. It was at once a royal palace, a fortress and a sanctuary; here was the brain of the empire and the heart of Islam; a city within a city, a noble and magnificent stronghold, with an entire population of its own, guarded by an army, containing within its walls an endless variety of buildings – places of pleasure or of horror, the urban and the rural, palaces, arsenals, schools, offices and mosques; where feasts and massacres, religious rituals and love trysts, diplomatic ceremonies and outbursts of frenzy all took place; where the Sultans were born, ascended the throne, were deposed, imprisoned, throttled; where all conspiracies began and the cry of every uprising resounded; the point to which the purest gold and the purest blood from the whole empire flowed; where the hilt of the great sword which kept a hundred peoples in subjection was wielded; on which for three hundred years the eyes of anxious Europe, timid Asia and frightened Africa were fixed, as on a smoking volcano which threatened ruin on all sides.

This monstrous palace is situated on the most eastern of the hills of Stamboul, sloping gently towards the Sea of Marmara, the entrance to the Bosphorus and the Golden Horn, on the spot formerly occupied by the Acropolis of Byzantium, by a part of the ancient city, and a wing of the great Imperial Palace. It is the most beautiful of the hills in Constantinople and the most favoured by nature of all the promontories on the European shore. Converging towards it as towards a centre, are two seas and two straits; this was the terminus of the great military and trading routes of Eastern Europe; the aqueducts of the Byzantine Emperors brought water to it; the hills of Thrace shelter it from the north winds; the sea washes it on three sides; Galata watches it from the side of the port and Scutari from the Bosphorus, and the great mountains of Bithynia ring the Asian horizon with their snow-capped summits. It is a solitary, almost isolated eminence sited at one end of the great city, strong and beautiful, as if intended by nature to be the pedestal of a great monarchy and to protect the exquisite and secretive existence of a prince who was regarded as a god.

A high crenellated wall runs round the foot of the entire hill, flanked by large towers. Along both the shores of the Sea of Marmara and the Golden Horn, these are part of the city walls; on the land side they were built by Mehmet II and divide the hill of the Seraglio from the hill on which the Nuruosmaniye Mosque stands. They bend at a right angle near the Sublime Porte, pass in front of Hagia Sophia, and curve down to meet the city walls of Stamboul on the sea. This is the outer boundary of the Seraglio. The Seraglio proper stands on the summit, surrounded in its turn by high walls, forming a kind of central redoubt within the great hill fortress.

But it would be wasted effort were I to describe the Seraglio as it is at present. The railway passes through the outer walls; in 1865 a great fire destroyed many of the buildings; hospitals, barracks, and military schools have been erected in the gardens; of the remaining constructions, many have changed both their appearance and their function; and although the principal walls are still standing so that the form of the Old Seraglio is intact, there have been so many small alterations, and the neglect of thirty years has made such changes to what has survived, that it is not possible to describe the place now without falling short of even the most modest expectations.

It is better for the writer and the reader to see this famous Seraglio as it was in the days of Ottoman greatness. Then whoever could see the entire hill in one glance, either from the battlements of one of the highest towers, or from a minaret of the Mosque of Hagia Sophia, enjoyed an unparalleled view. Against the vivid blue of the sea, the Bosphorus and the port, within the white semicircle formed by the sails of the imperial fleet, there was the green hill, surrounded by walls and towers which were surmounted with cannon and sentinels. On top of the hill, emerging from a wood of tall trees, through which a maze of white paths and colourful parterres could be glimpsed, the vast rectangle of the Seraglio buildings was laid out, divided into three great courts, or rather into three small towns built around three squares of differing sizes, from which arose a plethora of variously coloured roofs, flower-laden terraces, gilded domes, white minarets, airy pinnacles and monumental arches, interspersed with groves and gardens and half hidden by foliage. It was a small white metropolis, dazzling and disordered, as light as an encampment of tents, which had something of the idyllic and the pastoral and the warlike about it; in one part humming with bustle and movement, in another as silent and deserted as a necropolis; here open to the sky and full of sunlight, there inaccessible to every eye and plunged in perpetual shade; cheerful with the splash of water in innumerable fountains, embellished with a thousand contrasts of light and shadow, vivid colours and silvery-bluish tints reflected in the marbled colonnades and the pools, with flocks of doves and swallows circling overhead.

Such was the outward appearance of the imperial city as seen from above, from which viewpoint it does not seem so large; but from within it is so divided and subdivided, and so intricately laid out that servants who lived in it for fifty years never came to know it thoroughly, and the janissaries who invaded it for the third time still managed to lose their way.

The principal entrance was and still is the Bab-ı Hümayun, or "Noble Gate" which opens onto the small square where the fountain of Sultan Ahmet stands behind the Mosque of Hagia Sophia. It is a large gate of black and white marble, decorated with rich arabesques, on which is placed a tall eight-windowed building with a projecting roof. It is an example of that mixed Arabic and Persian style which marks out almost all the buildings constructed by the Turks in the years immediately following the conquest, before they began to imitate Byzantine architecture. Above the door on a marble cartouche the inscription placed there by Mehmet II can still be read:

MAY ALLAH PRESERVE THROUGHOUT ETERNITY THE GLORY OF ITS POSSESSOR.
MAY ALLAH STRENGTHEN THE BUILDING.
MAY ALLAH FORTIFY THE FOUNDATIONS.

It was in front of this door that the people of Stamboul came every morning to see what great statesman or courtier had been decapitated during the night. The heads were suspended from nails inside two niches that still survive undamaged on either side of the door, or were displayed in a silver basin beside which the accusation and the sentence were placed. In the square in front of the gate were thrown the bodies of those who had been hanged; and here detachments from distant armies bringing victory trophies would halt, waiting for the command to enter the first precinct of the Seraglio: they would pile up splendid weapons and banners, skulls and blood-soaked uniforms on the threshold. The gate was guarded by a large company of *kapıcıs*, the sons of beys or pashas in ceremonial dress, who gazed down from the walls and windows at the continual procession of people entering and leaving, or with their broad-bladed scimitars kept back the crowd of inquisitive onlookers who had come to see if they could catch a glimpse of the courtyard, of the second gate, some sudden view of the secretive palace that lay within, the object of so much ambition and so much terror. Passing by, the devout Muslim murmured a prayer for his sublime Master; the poor but ambitious youth dreamed of the day when he too would cross that threshold to have a pasha's horsetail conferred on him; the pretty girl in rags wistfully pictured to herself the splendid life of the harem women; the families of victims looked away as a shiver ran through them; and a strict silence was observed over the whole square, only broken three times a day by the voice of the muezzin calling from Hagia Sophia.

By the Hümayun gate, one entered the so-called Court of the Janissaries, the first precinct of the Seraglio. This great court still survives, surrounded by irregular buildings, very long and shaded by groups of large trees, among which is the enormous plane tree known as the Tree of the Janissaries, whose trunk is so massive ten men holding hands in a ring round it could not encompass it. On the left as one enters is the Church of St Irene, founded by Constantine the Great, and transformed by the Turks into an armoury. A little further on there was once the hospital of the Seraglio, the public treasury, the storeroom where oranges were kept, the imperial stables, the kitchens, the barracks of the *kapıcıs*, the mint, and the houses of the senior court officials. Under the great plane tree there are still two small stone columns where men were beheaded. Through this courtyard all those who were going to the Divan, or to an audience with the Sultan, passed. It was like a vast open-air vestibule, always bustling and full with busy crowds. One hundred and fifty bakers and two hundred cooks and scullions worked in the kitchens and prepared food for the great extended family, "who ate the bread and salt of the *Grand Signor*". On the opposite side guards and servants queued up pretending to be ill so they could be admitted to the luxuriously appointed hospital with twenty doctors on its staff and an army of slaves. Long caravans of mules and camels came in bearing provisions for the kitchens, or weapons from defeated armies to the church of St Irene, where, alongside Mehmet's sabre, gleamed the scimitar which had once belonged to Skanderbeg and Tamerlane's armlets. The tax-gatherers passed through, followed by slaves carrying gold for the Treasury, where there were enough riches, as Sokollu, Süleyman's Grand Vizier once remarked, to build fleets with the anchors made of silver and the rigging from silk. Here too, led by handsome Bulgarian grooms, passed the nine hundred horses of Murat IV, which fed out of silver mangers. From dawn to dusk throngs of uniforms

gleamed, among which you could distinguish the tall white turbans
of the janissaries, the long heron plumes of the solaks, the *peyks*, the
Sultan's bodyguards, wearing silver helmets and dressed in golden
tunics bound at the waist with jewelled belts; the *zülüflü baltacıs*, in
the service of the officers of the household, wearing caps with long
woollen tassels; the *yasakçıs*, holding their ceremonial staves; the
*baltacıs* grasping axes; the Grand Vizier's valets carrying whips with
silver chains, the *bostancıs* or gardeners with large crimson berets;
and a mingled crowd dressed in a hundred colours, bearing a hundred
insignia, of archers, lancers, Treasury guards, the "courageous guards"
and the "audacious guards", black eunuchs and white eunuchs, shield-
bearers and *çavuş*, and haughty ponderous gentlemen moving with all
the dignity of their high office, whose robes filled the courtyard with
perfumed fragrance.

But the disorder was only on the surface, for everyone's business
was regulated by a detailed and inflexible timetable, as if they were toy
automatons controlled by a concealed mechanism. At dawn the thirty-
two court muezzins, who had been chosen for the sweetness of their
singing voices, announced daybreak from the minarets of the Seraglio
mosques, meeting as they came in the astronomers and astrologers
coming down from the terraces, who had passed the night studying
the heavens in order to calculate the most propitious hours for the
Sultan's actions. Then came the chief physician to enquire after the
health of the Padishah; the ulemas arrived, whose duty it was to give
religious instruction to their illustrious pupil; the private secretary,
whose task it was to read to him the petitions which had been handed
in the evening before; the professors of arts and sciences walked
through on their way to the third court to give lessons to the imperial
pages. Each at an appointed time, all the people who were employed
in the Sultan's service came to receive their orders for the day. The
*bostancı başı* or head gardener, who was also the general of the
imperial guard and the governor of the Seraglio and of all the Sultan's
villas on the shores of the Bosphorus and the Propontis, came to ask
if it would please the *Grand Signor* to take a boat trip, because, if so,
it was his duty to steer while the gardeners under him had the honour
of rowing. The grand master of the hunt, accompanied by the grand
falconer, and the head keepers of the white falcons, of the vultures,
and of the sparrowhawks, came to discover their master's wishes. The
chief steward of the Seraglio, together with the stewards of the

kitchens, of the mint, of the forage-stores and the treasury – all came in, one after the other, in a fixed sequence, each with their requests, their prepared speeches, with their own servants wearing special livery. Later the viziers of the Dome would arrive, accompanied by their secretaries and advisors, on their way to the Divan. Men on horseback, in carriages, in sedan chairs, would all have to dismount at the second gate, beyond which one could only proceed on foot. All these people and their roles could be recognized by the shape of their turbans, the cut of their sleeves, the quality of their furs, the colour of the linings of their robes, the ornaments on their saddles, or whether they sported full beards or only moustaches. No confusion was possible in that endless procession. The mufti was in white; the viziers could be distinguished by their pale green robes, the chamberlains by their scarlet gowns; dark blue marked out the six chief law lords, the head of the emirs, and the chief judges of Mecca, Medina and Constantinople; the grand ulema wore purple; the *müderris* and the sheikhs light blue, while the palest blue of all was reserved for the vassal *çavuş* and the agas of the viziers; only the aga of the imperial stirrups and the bearer of the sacred standard was allowed to wear dark green; the men who worked in the stables wore light green; army generals had red boots, officials from the Porte yellow, the ulemas turquoise. The depth of the bows these personages received corresponded to the position they occupied on the colour spectrum. The *bostancı başı,* the chief of police and commander of an army of jailors and executioners, whose title and whose very footsteps struck terror into the onlookers, passed through the courtyard between a prostrate crowd on either side; before the grand eunuch, the marshal of the outer and inner courts, helmets, turbans and plumes went down as if pulled by a hundred invisible strings; the grand almoner was greeted obsequiously. All those whose duties brought them near the person of the Sultan were the recipients of special demonstrations of respect and curiosity: the chief groom who held his stirrups, the valet who fetched his sandals, the *silahtar* aga who polished his weapons, the white eunuch who cleaned the floor with his tongue before unrolling a carpet, the page who poured out water for him to wash, the servant who handed him his musket during the hunt or who dusted his jewelled feathers, the keeper of his turbans and of his garments of black fox fur. A subdued whispering preceded and followed the passage of the court preacher, and the grand master of the wardrobe, who threw coins to

the people on imperial feast days. A thousand curious eyes followed
the fortunate Muslim whose duty it was to shave the imperial head
once every ten days. The crowd was especially careful to make way for
the chief surgeon when he went to a prince's circumcision, the chief
optician who prepared eye lotions for the princesses and concubines
of the harem, the master of the flowers, busy with all the differing
demands of the harem women, carrying his poetically phrased
diploma decorated with gilded roses under his kaftan. The chief cook
received much adulation, and ceremonious smiles greeted the keeper
of the parrots and the nightingales, whose duties took him to some of
the most private kiosks. Thousands of people thronged or processed
through the huge courtyard, each with a precisely defined rank in a
complex hierarchy, adhering to a protocol it would take fifty volumes
to describe, dressed in a thousand picturesque costumes: every minute
brought a new wave of them. Every now and then a messenger would
pass by rapidly and all heads turn to look at him: he was the vizier
*karakulak*\* who carried messages between the Sultan and his prime
minister, on his way to deliver a secret missive to the Grand Vizier; or
a *kapıcı* running to the palace of a pasha whose loyalty was doubted
to summon him to appear without delay before the Divan; or the so-
called "bringer of good news" who was coming to tell the Padishah
that the great caravan had arrived safely in Mecca. Other special
messengers who carried messages between the Sultan and his great
officers of state, each with his own title and some particular feature of
dress to distinguish them, would race through the crowd and vanish
into the gateway. Swarms of coffee vendors made their way to the
court kitchens, of imperial huntsmen bending under the weight of
gilded game bags slung over their shoulders, of porters carrying
cloths, preceded by the grand merchant, the supplier of provisions to
the Sultan, and convicts being led off by the slaves to do the most
menial and exhausting chores in the Seraglio. Twice a day a hundred
scullions emerged from the kitchens, carrying enormous piles of rice,
and whole roasted sheep, which were placed under the trees and the
arcades, whereupon a crowd of guards and servants ran up and the
great court became like a military banqueting hall. Shortly afterwards
the scene changed, and foreign envoys arrived "between two walls of
silk and gold". On such occasions, as Süleyman the Great wrote to the
Shah of Persia, "the entire universe was present". Ambassadors from
Charles V would find themselves alongside those from Francis I;\*

envoys from Hungary, Serbia, and Poland would enter with the representatives from the republics of Genoa and Venice. The *pişkeş başi* who was responsible for receiving gifts would go out to meet the foreign caravans on the threshold of the Hümayun gate, where a huge crowd of onlookers would watch as elephants carrying golden thrones passed by, large gazelles, caged lions, horses from Tartary and the desert, draped in tiger-skins and bearing shields made from elephant hide; Persian envoys holding vases of Indian ink; messengers from the sultans of India with gold boxes brimming with jewels; the ambassadors from the African kings with rugs made from the soft skin of camel foetuses ripped from the mothers' wombs, and great rolls of silvered cloth which made ten slaves stoop beneath the weight; ambassadors from northern lands followed by their servants carrying furs and precious weapons. After victories on the battlefield, the defeated were displayed before the Padishah: army generals bound with chains and captive veiled princesses, with their unarmed and distraught staff, followed by eunuchs of every age and colour, who had been seized as booty or offered up as gifts by the vanquished princes. While these were entering, the officers from the victorious troops were crowding round the doors of the Treasury to deposit the rich brocades and pearled sabres which had been plundered from Persian cities, the gold and gems stripped from the Egyptian Mamelukes, the topaz-decorated golden goblets from the treasury of the Knights of Rhodes, the torsos of statues of Diana and Apollo snatched from Greece and Hungary, and the keys to cities and castles. Others would be taking the young boys and girls abducted from Lesbos through to the second courtyard. The vast quantity of supplies of all kinds which arrived in the Seraglio from the ports of Africa, Karaman, the Morea and the Aegean Sea, passed through or halted within these walls, while an army of major-domos and secretaries busily recorded receipts and payments, organized disposal, placed orders, arranged audiences. Merchants from the slave markets in Bursa and Trabzon waiting their turn to be called found themselves at the second gate alongside poets from Baghdad who had come to recite their poems to the Sultan. Provincial governors in disgrace who had come to plead for clemency with a goblet full of golden coins waited, together with the messengers of a pasha who wanted to offer the Sultan a beautiful thirteen-year-old virgin they had found, after three months' searching, in a tent in Anatolia; surrounded by spies reporting from all parts of the Empire, next to exhausted families who had travelled from some remote province with a petition for justice, among women and children from the common people of Stamboul who wanted their disputes resolved by the Divan. On the days when the Divan was in session the ambassadors from rebel provinces were paraded in front of inquisitive mocking crowds strapped to mules – with their beards shaven off and wearing women's hats – as were the insolent messengers of Asiatic princes who had had the tips of their noses sliced off by the çavuş. Further off, government officials were leaving to take a precious shawl as a gift from the Grand Vizier to a distant governor which, unknown to them, hid in its folds his death sentence. The jubilant faces of men who had successfully plotted to obtain some satrapy could be seen next to the pale faces of those who had just heard in the Divan the veiled threat of their imminent disgrace. Messengers galloped off carrying the hatti sherif, implacable as fate, bearing death and ruin to some viceroy in his palace three hundred miles away. The terrifying mutes of the court were leaving to carry out their orders to throttle some high-ranking prisoner in the Castle of the Seven Towers. And alongside all these there were the ulemas, the beys, the mullahs, the emirs, coming or going to audiences with lowered heads, their eyes fixed on the ground, their hands hidden in their voluminous sleeves; the viziers, with the Koran kept in their pockets just in case they needed to recite a funeral oration; the Grand Vizier himself, a despot whose every move was spied on by torturers, carrying his own will under his robes so that he was ready for death at any moment. All these passed by, at a sedate pace, silent or speaking in low voices and with the formal and circumspect language proper to the place; and there was a continual exchange of serious and searching looks, hands resting on brows or chests, broken whispers, a discreet rustle and shuffle of cloaks and slippers, a subdued clatter of scimitars, which gave them a melancholy and monkish air in contrast to the warlike fierceness of their faces, the vivid colours of their robes, and the splendour of their weapons. In all eyes one thought could be read, all faces expressed the terror of one man, who was above them all, sought out by all, and before whom all alike bowed and prostrated themselves and were as nothing: it seemed as if all objects showed his image and his name could be heard in every sound.

From the first court you entered the second by the great Bab-üs Selam, or Gate of Salutation, which still stands intact between two great towers, and here no one goes through – even today – without a firman or permit. Formerly it was enclosed by two great doors in front and another two within, which when they were closed formed a large dark chamber, where a man could be secretly dispatched. Below it were the cells of the executioners, which connected with the Divan by a dark windowless passage. There high officials and dignitaries who had fallen into disgrace went to hear their sentences, which were often followed by instant execution. On other occasions, a disgraced governor and vizier would be summoned to the Seraglio on some pretext; he would pass, unsuspecting, under the gloomy archway, and enter the Divan, where he was received with a kindly smile or mild reprimand which seemed to imply the prospect, perhaps postponed, of some negligible punishment. Dismissed, he returned tranquilly the way he had come, under the gate. But suddenly he felt a knife in his back or a rope at his throat from an invisible assailant and was done to death before he had time to resist. As he cried out a hundred faces in the other two courts would turn and listen a moment, and then resume whatever they were doing, in silence. The head was placed in one of the niches of the first gate, the body was taken to feed the crows on St Stephen's shore, the Sultan was informed the deed was done, and that was that. You can still see to the right, under the archway, the little iron door of the prison into which victims were thrown when they were not to be executed at once, either in order to prolong their final agony or before being sent into exile.

Coming out through the Bab-üs Selam you find yourself in the second court. Here there is a greater sense of the nearness of the lord of "both seas and both worlds", and an involuntary feeling of fear and reverence makes you pause a moment on the threshold. The second court is a wide irregular space, an immense open-air room, surrounded by graceful buildings with gilded domes, dotted by groups of beautiful trees, and crossed by two alleys lined with very tall cypresses. A beautiful arcade on slender white marble columns covered with a projecting lead roof runs the whole way round. To the left on entering was the Divan, under a gleaming dome; a little further on, there was the great reception hall, preceded by a portico with a great undulating roof resting on six enormous marble columns, the whole – pediments, capitals, walls, roof, doors and arches – carved and inlaid and painted and gilded with such light and delicate workmanship that it resembled a pavilion made of lace embroidered with jewels, shaded

by a group of superb plane trees. On the other sides were the palace
archives, the rooms where ceremonial robes and canopies were kept,
the chief black eunuch's apartments, and the court kitchens. The chief
steward in charge of the kitchens was busier than one of the Sultan's
ministers: he had fifty stewards under him, each of whom in turn
was responsible for an army of cooks and confectioners, who were
helped, for important occasions, by skilled artisans summoned from
all over the Empire. In these kitchens the meals for the viziers were
prepared on the days when a Divan was held, and, on the occasions
of circumcisions and royal marriages, the famous displays of sweet
pastries, storks and falcons, giraffes and camels modelled in sugar,
and whole roasted sheep from which birds would fly out, which were
carried with great pomp into the square of the Hippodrome; here too
confections in a hundred different shapes and colours were created for
the sweet tooths of the harem. Next to the kitchens, on high festival
days, eight hundred workers would be busy getting ready the tents for
the Sultan and the harem which they would erect in the gardens of the
Seraglio or on the Bosphorus hills. When there were not enough tents in
the great storehouses of the palace, ships' sails from the imperial fleet
were used as canopies and cypresses were uprooted from the gardens
of the imperial villas to form poles. The chief eunuch's house nearby
was a small palace between which and the third courtyard there was
a steady toing and froing of black eunuchs, slaves and domestic staff.
Here the ambassadors passed on their way to see the Sultan. On those
occasions all the arches were covered with crimson cloths, the marble
walls gleamed, and the ground was as spick and span as the floor
of a hall. The special Divan guard, made up of two hundred regally
attired and armed janissaries, spahis and *silahtars*, stood to attention
under the cypresses and plane trees, while groups of black and white
eunuchs in spotless perfumed robes stood round the doors. Everything
in this second courtyard spoke of the nearby presence of the *Grand
Signor*: men's voices were hushed, their movements sedate; the beat of
horses' hooves and the noise of men at work were never heard here;
servants and soldiers passed by in silence. The place seemed as quiet
as a sanctuary, its tranquillity only disturbed by sudden snatches of
birdsong in the trees and the resounding clang of the great iron doors
as the *kapıcıs* pushed them shut.

Of all the buildings in this court, I saw only the hall of the
Divan, which remains almost exactly as it was when it was used for

the sessions of the Supreme Council of State. It is a large hall with a vaulted ceiling, lit from above by small Moorish windows, and panelled with marble arabesqued with gold. It is bare of furniture apart from the divan on which the members of the council sat. Above the seat of the Grand Vizier can still be seen the small, gold-latticed window behind which Süleyman the Great and all the Sultans after him listened – or were thought to be listening – to the council sessions, unseen by everyone else present; a secret corridor led from this small hidden chamber to the imperial apartments in the third court. Five times a week the council of ministers met, the Grand Vizier presiding in solemn ceremony. He sat opposite the entrance; next to him were seated the viziers of the Dome, the Kapudan Pasha or Great Admiral of the fleet, and the two Grand Judges of Anatolia and Rumelia, representing the magistrature of the provinces of Asia and Europe. To one side of the room sat the imperial treasurers, while on the other there were the *nişancıs*, the officials who attached the Sultan's seal to his decrees; further back, to the right and left, two throngs of ulemas and chamberlains, and in the corners of the room, *çavuş*, messengers and executioners, keenly watching every gesture and every look.

The bravest of men trembled before such a spectacle, and even the innocent anxiously questioned their consciences. All those gathered together there were the same: their faces impassive, their arms crossed and their hands concealed in their robes. A dim yellow light from above fell on the white turbans, the serious faces, the long beards, the rich furs and jewelled dagger-hilts. At first sight the Council looked like a large group of clothed and painted statues. The rush mats on the floor muffled the steps of those entering and leaving, the air was heavy with the perfumed furs, the marble walls reflected the green of the courtyard trees; birdsong echoed under the golden vault whenever the discussion fell silent; there was an atmosphere of charm and grace in that awesome tribunal. Their voices sounded out one after the other, tranquil and monotonous as the murmur of a stream, while accusers and accused, standing in the middle of the hall, could not identify who was speaking. Fifty pairs of eyes were turned on the individual: his every look was scrutinized, every word weighed, every thought divined from his most fleeting expressions; and the sentence of death was pronounced quite calmly, after long tranquil consultation, and heard in a sepulchral silence, or else declaimed unexpectedly like the fall of a thunderbolt and answered by the terrible cry of a soul in the moment of supreme despair. When that happened, at a given signal the scimitars would fall and hack the accused in two, his blood spurting out onto the walls and carpets. The agas of the spahis and the janissaries would collapse riddled with stabs; governors and kaimakams would struggle and gasp with the rope at their throats and their eyes bulging from their sockets. As soon as the deed was done, their corpses would be laid out under the shadow of the plane trees and covered with a green cloth; in the Divan the blood would be washed away and the air perfumed; the assassins would go back to their stations, and the session would resume, with the row of impassive faces, hidden hands, calm low voices, under the dim light filtering down from the Moorish windows and casting a pale yellow glow on the great turbans and beards. Yet these fierce judges were startled in their turn when Murat IV or Selim II, unhappy with the proceedings, banged furiously on the gilded lattice of the secret chamber! Then, after a protracted silence and the rapid exchange of anxious glances, they resumed their sitting with expressionless faces and solemn voices, but their icy hands went on trembling for a long time under their sleeves, while in their inmost souls they were preparing to meet their maker.

At the end of the second courtyard, which might be called the diplomatic court of the Seraglio, there was a third great door with marble columns on either side and a projecting roof in front of which a company of white eunuchs and a group of *kapıcıs* stood guard night and day, armed with sabres and daggers.

This was the famous Bab-ı Saadet, or Gate of Felicity, which led to the third court; the sacred door which remained closed for almost four centuries to any Christian who did not come in the name of a king or a nation; the mysterious portal on which a thousand illustrious and powerful travellers knocked in vain for admittance; from which so many pleasant tales and sorrowful legends have spread all over the world, so many images of beauty and pleasure, so many dark hints of secret loves and bloodshed, and an inexhaustible atmosphere of sensuous and terrifying poetry; the solemn entrance into the sanctuary of the King of Kings, which people named with an inward sense of terror, like the gate of some enchanted place, where on entering the profane outsider would be turned to stone or witness things beyond human powers of description. Even now the most prosaically minded traveller hesitates and starts with surprise when he sees the shadow of his top hat lengthening upon the half-closed doors.

And yet the roaring tide of military rebellion reached even this solemn portal. It might even be said that this corner of the great court between the hall of the Divan and the Saadet gate was the place where the rebels' fury was boldest and most bloodthirsty. The *Grand Signor* governed with the sword, and the sword in turn held sway over him. The tyranny which forbade access to the Seraglio was the same tyranny which violated its interior. When the scimitars which protected the Sultan were withdrawn, then the fragility of the pedestal on which the menacing colossus stood could be seen. In the middle of the night, hordes of armed janissaries and spahis carrying torches beat down the first and second gates with axe-blows and burst in, waving on the points of their blades petitions demanding the heads of the viziers, and their shouts resounded beyond the inviolable walls, within the sacred precincts of their sovereign, where all was terror and confusion. In vain, bags of gold and silver coin were thrown down from the walls; in vain the frantic sheikhs, muftis, ulemas, and court grandees reasoned and pleaded with them to lay down their arms; in vain the pale wives of the Sultan appeared at the grated windows to display their little children. The thousand-headed monster, unleashed and blind with fury, demanded its prey – living flesh which it could tear to pieces, blood it could spill, heads it could impale. The Sultan, surrounded by his eunuchs and trembling pages, armed with useless daggers, appeared on the battlements and even behind the barricaded gate to plead for pardon for the condemned, for the sake of their mothers, their children, the Prophet, the glory of the Empire, the peace of the world. A yell of insult and menace and a wild waving aloft of torches and scimitars were the only response to their impotent appeals. And then, one by one, from the Gate of Felicity, staggered the victims, the treasurers, the viziers, the eunuchs, the favourites, the generals, and, falling among the wild beasts thirsting for their blood, were, one after the other, hacked with a hundred knives or beaten to a pulp. So Murat III threw Mehmet, his favourite falconer, to the mob and saw him torn to pieces before his eyes; so Mehmet III sacrificed the Kızlar Aga Osman, and the head of the white eunuchs Gazanfer, and was forced to salute the soldiers in front of their two bloody corpses; so a sobbing Murat IV drove out Hafiz, his Grand Vizier, who was quartered and killed with seventeen daggers; and so Selim III surrendered up the whole of his Divan. As the Sultans returned into their apartments, cursing and overcome with rage and shame, the

211

rebels were triumphantly dragging the corpses by torchlight among the drunken crowds in the streets of Stamboul.

Like the Bab-üs Selam, the Gate of Felicity forms a long passageway from which you come out directly into the third secret precinct where the "brother to the sun" can be found. To create a vivid image of the place my words should really be accompanied by low music full of unexpected melodic twists and turns. It is like a small town lying under a spell: mysterious and graceful buildings in bizarre disorder, concealed in groves of towering cypresses and plane trees which stretch their branches over the roofs. Underneath the shadow of the trees there is an intricate maze of gardens full of roses and verbena, little courts with porticoes, narrow paths between Chinese-style kiosks and pavilions, small meadows, ponds surrounded by myrtle trees reflecting white mosques and the silvery domes of temple-like buildings and cloisters connected by covered arcades supported on slender columns. Engraved and painted wooden roofs project over arabesqued porticoes and small outside staircases which lead to balustraded terraces. Everywhere there are shady nooks in which white marble fountains can be glimpsed; between the foliage the arches and columns of more small cloisters can be made out; and from every part, between the pines and the sycamores there are views of the Sea of Marmara, the Bosphorus, the port and Stamboul under the wide sky. It is a small town immersed within a garden, built gradually and haphazardly, as necessity or whim dictated, splendid yet fragile, like a stage set, full of little hiding places and childish quirks. From here everything was seen but it itself remained invisible; it bustled with activity yet seemed deserted, as if the old Ottoman rulers with their pastoral meditative ways were still in charge; a city built of stone which yet, for all its splendour, recalled the encampments of the wandering tribes out of Tartary; a great kingdom scattered about, made up of a hundred miniature palaces hidden from each other, with something of the gloominess of a prison, the austerity of a holy edifice, and the cheerfulness of the countryside about it; a spectacle which is both princely in its ostentation and primitive in its artlessness, where visitors wonder on what planet and in what century they find themselves. This was the heart of the Seraglio, the centre of all the veins and arteries of Ottoman rule and the empire.

The first edifice one encounters on entering the Gate of Felicity is the throne room, which still exists and which I was allowed to visit. It is a small square building, round which runs a beautiful marble portico; you enter by a richly decorated doorway with a wall fountain on either side. The room is covered by a vaulted ceiling decorated with gilded arabesques, the walls are panelled with marble and porcelain tiles in symmetrical patterns, and in the centre there is a marble fountain. The space is lit by tall windows of stained glass, and at one end is the throne, in the form of a large bed, covered by a canopy fringed with pearls on four tall slender columns of gilded copper, ornamented with arabesques and set with precious stones, and surmounted by four golden spheres with four crescents, from which four horsetails are hanging, the emblems of the Padishah's military might. Here the *Grand Signor* would hold public audience in the presence of the entire assembled court; here at his feet were thrown the corpses of his brothers and nephews, murdered to safeguard his rule from conspiracies and treachery. As I entered, I thought of the nineteen brothers of Mehmet III. The same cannon shots which announced to Europe and Asia that their father Murat III had died proclaimed their own death sentence as they lay in prison. The mutes of the Seraglio piled the nineteen corpses in front of the throne. Infants and adults, they were heaped one on top of another, their eyeballs out of their sockets and the marks of their assassins' hands still visible on their faces and throats: the blonde head of a baby lying on a young man's torso, grizzled heads crushed under the feet of their adolescent brothers, rough prison kaftans next to swaddling clothes, twisted among the stiff limbs and deformed faces. These walls with their gleaming porcelain tiles and elegant arabesques have seen blood spurting as Selim II or Ahmet I or Murat IV or Ibrahim raged and exulted at the spectacle of their agonised victims. Here the viziers were felled by *çavuş*, who would trample and crack their skulls against the marble fountains; here the heads of governors brought from Syria and Egypt, hanging from an aga's saddle, would roll along the ground. Whoever entered with an uneasy conscience would turn back on the threshold to say goodbye to the beautiful hills and skies of Asia, and the man who came out alive would greet the sun with all the fervour of a convalescent.

Coming out from the throne pavilion, you pass through various gardens and little courts surrounded by small buildings with marble colonnades and Moorish arches. Here the imperial pages boarded in richly appointed lodgings where they had rooms for recreation and received from the most learned men in the empire the education which prepared them for high offices in the state and in the court. A row of graceful Saracen-style kiosks, with an open peristyle, housed the library: one survives which is chiefly remarkable for its great bronze door, decorated with reliefs in jasper and lapis lazuli, intricately carved with arabesques, stars, leaves and figures of every kind, of miraculous workmanship. A little beyond the library was the Imperial Treasury, gleaming with porcelain tiles, which houses the vast riches, mostly made up of plunder from conquered armies or given to the Sultans or bequeathed by them to conserve their memory – such as Mahmut II, who was an accomplished calligrapher, and proud of the fact, who left his golden inkstand encrusted with diamonds. Today much of this treasure has been exchanged for gold to fill the coffers of the exchequer, but when the monarchy was at its zenith the kiosk dazzled with damascened scimitars with hilts which were clusters of pearls and precious stones, huge pistols with two hundred diamonds encrusting the butt, daggers which alone were worth the annual revenues of some province in Asia, solid silver or steel clubs with heads made from whole lumps of crystal, worked and gilded, jewelled crests belonging to a Murat or a Mehmet, agate cups in which the foaming wines of Hungary were poured during imperial banquets, goblets carved out of a single turquoise which had once belonged to a Persian king or to Tamerlane himself, necklaces with diamonds as large as walnuts from Karaman, pearl-encrusted belts, saddles encased in gold, carpets woven with gems. The room seems to be on fire – one's eyes and one's mind are left dazzled.

Not far from the treasury pavilion, standing in a solitary garden, you can still find the so-called "birdcage" in which from Mehmet IV's reign onwards, any of the Sultan's male blood relations who had offended him were shut up and would remain as though buried alive until a janissary rebellion called them to the throne or the executioner came to strangle them. It is in the form of a small temple, windowless, with thick walls, lit from above, and with one small iron door against which a great stone was placed. Here Abdülaziz was kept immured in the short interval between his fall from the throne and his death. Here Ibrahim, the Ottoman Caligula, met his horrible end: his image is the first to rise up in the visitor's mind on the threshold of that necropolis of the living. The military agas had dethroned him and dragged him to imprison him here. He was incarcerated with two of his favourite mistresses. After the first frenzy of despair had abated, he grew resigned. "This," he said, "was written on my brow. It is God's command." In the whole of his empire and the vast harem where he had indulged his unrestrained desires for nine years on end there remained to him only this prison, two female slaves and a copy of the Koran, but he thought his life was safe and lived in tranquillity, consoled by a ray of hope that his supporters in the barracks and the taverns of Stamboul would succeed in changing his fortunes. But he had forgotten that sentence in the Koran which says: "When there are two caliphs, one should be killed'* – whereas the mufti, from his discussions with the aga and the viziers, remembered it all too well. His last day was spent seated on a mat in a corner of his prison, reading the Koran to his two slave-women, who stood with arms folded on their breasts before him. He was dressed in a black kaftan, tied at the waist with a tattered shawl, and with a red woollen cap on his head. A pale beam of light from the vault shone down on his face, which, though pale and haggard, was calm. Suddenly he heard a low noise and sprang to his feet. The door opened and a group of sinister figures confronted him. He immediately understood why they had come and raised his eyes to a latticed gallery high up on the inside wall, where through the gratings he could see the cold impassive faces of the mufti, the aga and the viziers looking down. He could read his judgement written on them. Terror seized him, and a flood of pleading words poured from his lips: "Have pity on me! Have pity on the Padishah! Grant me my life! If there is one among you who has eaten my bread, let him help me in the name of God! You, mufti Abdul Rahim, take care what you're about to do! Men are blind indeed. Yusuf Pasha told me to have you killed as a traitor, and I spared you, and now you strike at my life! Spare my life, Abdul Rahim! Read the Koran, read the word of God, which condemns ingratitude and injustice. Let me live, Abdul Rahim, I want to live!" The executioner, trembling, looked up at the gallery, but a cold voice issued from the midst of those faces as unmoving as masks: "Kari Ali, do your duty." He took hold of Ibrahim's shoulders, but Ibrahim, with a cry, fled into a corner and took refuge behind the two women. Then Kari Ali and the çavuş fell on him, throwing the slaves aside. Curses and oaths filled the air, followed by a loud scream which subsided into a hoarse rattle, and then silence. It took only an instant for a small silk cord to dispatch for ever the nineteenth sultan of the dynasty of Osman.

Other edifices, besides those already described and those of the harem, were scattered here and there among the groves and gardens. There were the baths of Selim II, made up of thirty-two huge rooms, resplendent in marble and gold and painted decorations; there were circular and octagonal kiosks, with cupolas and roofs of diverse shapes over rooms panelled with mother-of-pearl and decorated with Arabic inscriptions, where gilded cages containing parrots and nightingales hung against the coloured glass of the windows which shed soft bluish and pinkish lights into the interiors. Here the Sultans would go to hear the *Arabian Nights* read to them by aged dervishes, or their sons would be given their first reading lessons. There were small kiosks for meditating and little pavilions for intimate night-time meetings; warm pleasant nests – or prison cells – with views over towards Scutari at sunset and Olympus in the moonlight, freshened by fragrant breezes from the Bosphorus which would make the gilded crescents on their pinnacles gently vibrate. Finally, in the most secret quarters of the harem the temple of relics could be found, the so-called "chamber of the noble garments" imitated from the Golden Room of the Byzantine Emperors and barred by a silver door. Here the mantle of the Prophet was preserved and solemnly displayed once a year in the presence of the assembled court, together with his stick, his bow enclosed in a silver sheath, the relics of the Kaaba, and the venerable and awe-inspiring banner of the Holy Wars, wrapped in forty silk cloths, the mere sight of which would strike blind the infidel who dared to look on it. Everything that was most sacred to the race and precious to the empire, most valued and meaningful to the dynasty, was gathered there in that discreet and shadowy enclosure, that small city which was the focal point towards which the whole vast metropolis seemed to converge, in their desire to bow down and worship.

In one corner of the third courtyard, to the left on entering, under the shadow of the thickest trees, amid the loud murmur of fountains and the twittering of birds, was the harem, like a separate district of the imperial city. It was made up of many small white buildings with lead domes, shaded by orange trees and umbrella pines, divided by small gardens enclosed by walls covered with ivy and honeysuckle, among paths laid down in a bright mosaic of tiny shells which wound their way through rose bushes, ebony and myrtle trees. The whole area is miniature, enclosed, divided and subdivided: the balconies covered, the windows grated and glazed with panes of coloured glass, terraces hidden by pink curtains, the doors barred, the paths leading nowhere, and everywhere a gentle half light, the coolness of a forest glade, an atmosphere of mystery and peace conducive to reverie. Here the great female family of the Seraglio lived and loved, languished and served, and was continually replenished. It was like an immense convent, whose religion was pleasure, and whose God was the Sultan. There were the imperial apartments where the four leading and officially recognized wives of the *Grand Signor* lived; each had her kiosk, her own little court, her important officials, her boats lined with satin, her gilded carriages, her eunuchs, her slaves, and her "slipper money", or the revenue from a province which was allotted to her. The Sultana Valide lived here with all her innumerable retinue of *ustas*, organized into twenty or thirty divisions, each with its own duties. The Sultan's female relations lived here: his aunts, sisters, daughters and nieces, together with the princes while they were still children or youths, forming a court within a court. There were the *gediklis*, from whom the twelve most beautiful were chosen to serve the Sultan, each with her own special title and responsibility; one hundred *şagirds* or novices who were being trained to fill the vacant positions among the *ustas*; dozens on dozens of female slaves – from every country and of every colour of skin and national or tribal dress – who had been selected from thousands and who filled that vast gynaeceum, divided up, like a hive, into countless little cells, with an exuberant youthfulness, a heavy incense of African and Asian voluptuousness which was wafted up to the divine monarch himself and then, steeped in his powerful passions, spread over the entire empire.

What memories there are among these groves and gardens and between the walls of these small white cloisters! How many beautiful daughters of the Caucasus and the Greek Archipelago, from the mountains of Albania and of Ethiopia, the desert and the sea, Muslim, Nazarene, pagan, won in battle by the pashas, sold by merchants, presented by princes, stolen by corsairs, have passed like shadows under those silvery domes! Here are the walls which saw the first Ibrahim –whose reign saw the price of female slaves quadruple in markets all over Asia – wearing a garland of flowers on his head and his beard sparkling with gems, at his crazy antics among his slaves; which witnessed the frenzied sensual fits of Murat III, who fathered a hundred sons; and watched Murat IV, already wasted at thirty-one years of age, burst in and stagger to his notorious couplings, and

EDMONDO DE AMICIS

Selim II indulge in mad orgiastic bouts of sex. Drunk with wine and lust they would come at night and all the slave-girls who were offered up to them by their mothers and viziers and pashas only served to excite their desires even more: they would race from kiosk to kiosk in search of pleasure but achieve only a brief spasm, until they were enraged and their fantasies grew crazed: they would leave the palace and seek out more women among the famous beauties of the gloomy Eski Sarayı. Here those strange nocturnal festivals were celebrated, when the shapes of naval ships made out of burning candles were displayed on the domes and roofs and trees, while thousands of flower vases, lit by countless tapers and reflected in a thousand mirrors, made the place seem like one vast garden ablaze with light. Hundreds of women thronged the treasure-filled bazaars, while eunuchs would raise up the bodies of semi-naked slave-girls who had fainted away in delirious dancing, drunk with the fragrance of a thousand perfumes which, together with the din of a barbarous, warlike music, the breeze from the Black Sea spread over the whole Seraglio.

Let us try to picture what life was like on a beautiful April day, under the reign of Süleyman the Great or Ahmet III. The sky is serene, the air full of springtime fragrance, the gardens gay with flowers. Along the maze of paths still wet with dew, black eunuchs in golden tunics take leisurely strolls and slave-girls, clothed in brightly striped robes, move to and fro between the kitchens and the kiosks carrying trays and baskets covered with green cloths. Under the small Moorish porticoes the Sultana Valide's usta cross paths with the Sultan's *gediklis*, who walk proudly along, followed by novice slaves carrying linen for the imperial household. Suddenly everyone looks in one direction: the youngest of the *gediklis* has just come out of a small door and disappeared up some steps. She is the Sultan's cupbearer, a Syrian girl favoured by Allah and the Sultan – the latter has already bestowed on her the title of "daughter of happiness" and will no doubt give her an ermine mantle as soon as she becomes pregnant. Under the shade of the trees the Sultan's buffoons in harlequin dress and dwarves wearing grotesquely outsized turbans are romping about together. Nearby, behind a hedge, a gigantic eunuch, with an imperceptible gesture of his hand and nod of his head, orders five mutes to go to the Kızlar Aga, who requires their services as torturers for a secret matter. Youths of ambivalent beauty, richly dressed with a feminine attention to detail, are chasing each other round the hedges in a garden under a

218

spreading plane tree. Elsewhere a group of slave-women suddenly stop and divide in two, bowing on either side as the Kiaya, or governess of the harem, passes by, returning their salutation with a sign from her staff of office, a small silver baton with the imperial seal on one end. At the same moment the door of a neighbouring kiosk opens and one of the Sultan's wives – a "kadin" – emerges, dressed in pale blue, and wrapped in a thick white veil, followed by her slave-women. She is going, with the governess's permission, granted the previous day, to play shuttlecock with another kadin. Turning into a shaded alley, she meets and languidly greets one of the Sultan's sisters, who is off to the baths with her children and maids. In front of the kiosk belonging to another kadin at the end of another path, a eunuch is waiting for a sign from his mistress which will allow a Jewess selling gems to go inside. The Jewess has managed, after much intrigue, to obtain a permit to enter the imperial harem (as well as jewellery she will no doubt also be carrying messages from ambitious pashas and audacious lovers). At the other end of the harem the *hanım* whose duty it is to inspect the new slaves is looking for the governess to inform her that the young Abyssinian who has just arrived is in her judgement worthy of being accepted among the *gediklis*, or the Sultan's favourites – so long as one overlooks a small wart on her left shoulder.

Meanwhile, on a small lawn enclosed by myrtle bushes and under a high pergola, the twenty nurses of the princes born during the year are gathered with their charges, while a number of female slaves play guitars and flutes, and a crowd of little girls dressed in blue and red velvet dance merrily to the music, with the Sultana Valide throwing sweets to them from her terrace. Governesses pass by on their way to give lessons in dancing, music and sewing to the *şagirds*; eunuchs carrying great trays of pastries fashioned in the shapes of lions or parrots; slave-girls struggling along clutching huge vases of flowers or rolled-up carpets: gifts from a sultana to a kadin, from a kadin to the Valide, and from the Valide to her grandchildren. The treasuress of the harem arrives, followed by three slaves, looking as if they have important news to impart: the imperial ships that were sent out against the Genoese and Venetian galleys encountered them twenty miles off the port of Syra and have captured their entire cargo of silks and velvets which will all now come to the harem. A eunuch comes running up to tell an anxious sultana that her baby son has been circumcised successfully; shortly afterwards two more eunuchs arrive, one carrying the foreskin on a silver plate to present to the mother while the other holds a gold plate with the blood-smeared knife. Doors constantly open and shut, curtains twitch open and drop, to exchange news, notes, gifts and snatches of gossip. If we imagine we can look down on the whole Seraglio from above and see straight through its walls and domes into the interiors, we might find in one room a sultana standing sadly behind the satin curtains at the window, gazing at the blue mountains on the Asian shore, perhaps thinking of her husband, some handsome pasha, the governor of a remote province, who, as was the custom, was taken away from her six months after their wedding because she had not yet become pregnant; in another small room, with marble walls on which mirrors are hung, a fifteen-year-old kadin is waiting for the visit of the Padishah, and joking with the slave-girls who are adorning her in preparation, praising her most intimate beauties with obsequious marvel and pleasure; young sultanas are running about the gardens, round the goldfish ponds, making the shells on the path crunch under their white satin slippers, while others sit in dark rooms, pale-faced, plotting revenge. There are drawing rooms tapestried with brocade where little children, destined for early death, romp around on gold-striped satin cushions and under tables inlaid with mother-of-pearl; naked princesses in baths of Parian marble; *gediklis* stretched out asleep on carpets; eunuchs and slave-girls standing in groups or bustling about the covered galleries, the hidden staircases, the vestibules and dimly lit corridors; and everywhere faces looking on curiously behind lattices, wordless greetings passed between terraces and gardens, furtive signs behind curtains, brief monosyllabic conversations interrupted by loud and quickly suppressed bursts of laughter, followed by a rapid flight of skirts along the cloistered walls.

But it was not only amorous intrigue and puerile gossip which went on in that maze of buildings and gardens. Politics entered there through the crannies of every door and of every lattice, and the power exercised by women over the affairs of state was no less extensive there than in the kingdoms of the West; indeed their secluded and monotonous life only served to increase the intensity of rivalry and ambition. Those jewelled heads in their small perfumed rooms were the cause of disturbance to the court, the Divan, and the entire Seraglio. The eunuchs served as their means of communication with the muftis, the viziers and the agas of the janissaries. They were allowed to meet, hidden behind a curtain or lattice, the administrators of their assets to discuss issues relating to their property, and from them they learnt everything that was going on in the palace and the city, they heard of the dangers that threatened them, they came to know which ministers they should fear, or in whom they could place their hopes, and they patiently wove mysterious plots to destroy their enemies and promote their protégés. All the various parties of the court and empire had their roots here, in the hearts of the Sultana Valides, the sisters of the Sultan, his wives, and his concubines. There were infinite discussions and manoeuvrings on the education of their sons, the marriage of daughters, their dowries, the order of precedence at banquets, the succession of the young princes to the throne, peace and war. At the whim of the ladies of the harem armies of janissaries and spahis were sent to cover the banks of the Danube with corpses, and fleets of a hundred ships to stain the Black Sea and the Greek Archipelago with blood. The princes of Europe sent secret letters to them so they could help them to obtain a successful outcome for their negotiations. From their small white hands issued the decrees which appointed the governors of provinces and the chief officers of the army. Roxelana's caresses tightened the noose round the necks of the Grand Viziers Ahmet and Ibrahim, and the kisses of Safiye, the beautiful Venetian, "the pearl and shell of the Caliphate", maintained amicable relations between the Porte and the Venetian Republic for many years. The seven kadins of Murat III governed the empire during the last two decades of the sixteenth century. The beautiful Mahpeyker, "like a moon", the kadin who owned two thousand and seven hundred shawls, ruled over the two seas and the two worlds between the reigns of Ahmet I and Mehmet IV. Rabia Gülnuş, the concubine with a hundred silver carriages, directed the imperial divans for ten years in the middle of the eighteenth century, and Şekerpare, "the little sugar lump", made bloodthirsty Ibrahim travel up and down for her pleasure between Stamboul and Adrianople, like a puppet on a string.

That little town, so gracious and so powerful, must have been filled with confused scheming, intricate networks of dangerous espionage and girlish gossip. As I walked along its paths, I seemed to hear women's voices rapidly whispering to each other, questioning and answering, gradually weaving an intimate history of the Seraglio, curiously varied and elaborate. Which kadin would the Sultan take for the summer to his kiosk in the Sweet Waters? What dowry would his third daughter receive, as she was just about to marry the Chief Admiral? Is it true that the herb the mage Süca had given the governess Raziyye had let the third kadin conceive a child after five years of infertility? Had the favourite Canfeda really managed to obtain the governorship of Karaman for the governor of Anatolia? The news went round the kiosks that the first kadin had given birth successfully and that the new Grand Vizier, to outdo his predecessor, had given her a cradle made of solid silver encrusted with emeralds; that the Sultan had chosen as his favourite the slave given to him by the Kiaya and not the girl from the Pasha of Adrianople; that the chief white eunuch was dying and that the ambitious young pageboy Mehmet had had himself castrated in order to take his place. Discreet rumours were circulating that the Grand Vizier Sinan's project to build a great canal in Asia Minor had been cancelled because the labourers were needed instead for the Sultana Baffo's new kiosk; that the kadin Saharay, who was thirty-five, had been crying day and night because she was worried about being relegated to the Old Seraglio; that Ahmet the jester had made the Sultan laugh so much he'd been made aga of the janissaries on the spot. A hundred tales were doing the rounds about the celebrations for the forthcoming wedding of Osman Pasha to the Sultana Ümmetullah – it was said there'd be a bronze dragon breathing out fire in the Atmeydanı; about the Sultana Valide's new dress, all in ermine, with precious gems for the buttons, each costing more than a hundred gold scudi; about the revenues from Wallachia being given as an annuity to the kadin Kamer, "moon of beauty"; about the small blood-red rose displayed round the neck of the çamaşır usta, the keeper of the Sultan's linen; about the beautiful blond ringlets of the new Genoese ambassador, and about the marvellous letter written in her own hand by the Shah of Persia's first wife to the Sultana Hürrem "the cheerful". Rumours from the city, notable incidents in the Divan, noises heard at night – all were grist to the mill of gossip, commented on and conjectured over by a hundred groups of female heads gathered discreetly and inquisitively together all over the gardens. Poems too were passed from hand to hand or recited to each other: the anonymous madrigals written by the Padishah, the melancholy and inventive verses of Abdul Bâkî, known as "the immortal", the brilliant poems of Ebussuud, in which every word was "like a diamond", Fuzuli's songs drunk with opium and wine and Gazâlî's licentious lines.* As Sultans changed, with different characters and ways of life, so too did the

Seraglio. Sometimes an air of tenderness and melancholy filled that little world: a certain gentle dignity was apparent in the way people held themselves, the furies of lust were calmed, manners improved and language became more decorous, there was a new taste for pious reading, a display of religious contemplation and devotion, and while the parties were no less splendid, they were more dignified occasions. But then a Padishah ascended the throne who had been inured to vice and indulgence from childhood onwards: then the goddess of pleasure once more held sway, veils and euphemisms were discarded, raucous laughter was heard and unashamed nudity was seen anew. The buyers of beauty set out once again for Georgia and Circassia and the girls came flooding in. A hundred women boasted they had slept with the *Grand Signor*, the kiosks filled with cradles, the Treasury coffers poured forth gold, wines from Cyprus and Hungary foamed on the dining tables covered with flowers, Sodom and Lesbos triumphed, the beautiful black-eyed faces grew wan: the entire harem was in a state of fever, mad for pleasure, saturated with perfume and vice, until one night a thousand torches would suddenly shake it out of its slumbers and the janissaries' scimitars bring divine judgement down upon it.

Nights of terror and despair were known too in this Babylon hidden among the flowers, for rebellions had no more respect for the third enclosure than they had for the first and second. The soldiery broke in at the Gate of Felicity and invaded the harem. A hundred eunuchs armed in vain with daggers defended the thresholds of the kiosks. The janissaries climbed onto the roofs, broke through the cupolas, and jumped down into the rooms to seize the princes from their mothers' arms. The Sultana Valides, fighting back tooth and nail, were dragged by the feet out of their hiding places and thrown across the knees of the *baltacs* and strangled with the curtain cords. The Sultanas, rushing back into their apartments, screamed in despair at the sight of the empty cradles, while their trembling slaves' awful silence could only mean: "Go and find your children at the foot of the throne". Terrified eunuchs came to tell the favourites, woken by the sounds of tumult in the distance, that their heads were forfeit and they must prepare to die. The three kadins of Selim III, condemned to the executioner and the sack, heard each other's final screams in the night, and gave up their breath in the shadows under the convulsive hands of the mutes. Murderous jealousies and vendettas made the kiosks echo with groans and cries that spread terror through the harem.

Mustafa's Circassian mother tore Roxelana's face with her nails, Şekerpare came to blows with the rival favourites, the Sultana Tarhan saw Mehmet IV's dagger flash over the heads of her offspring, the first wife of Ahmet I choked her rival with her bare hands, and was herself stabbed in the face, and struck down under the feet of the Padishah, howling with grief and rage. The jealous kadins would lie in wait for each other in dark corridors, would scream insults and leap like tigers, poisoned daggers in hand, to stab each other's necks and backs. Who knows how many crimes were committed which will for ever remain unknown? Slave-girls held down in the fountains until they drowned, hacked to pieces in the pavilions, whipped by the eunuchs, crushed between iron doors by ten frenzied rivals. Their veils smother their cries, the flowers hide their blood, two shadows disappear down a dark alley carrying something black between them, the sentinels on the towers hear a splash in the water, and when the following day dawns the harem wakes, as fragrant and lovely as ever, unaware that one of its thousand chambers has been emptied.

All these images came to my mind as I wandered through the enclosure and raised my eyes to the grated windows of the abandoned kiosks, as sad as tombs. And in the midst of these sinister memories, I was also aware of a kind of pleasurable thrill of mingled melancholy and tenderness, when I reflected that the feet of these beautiful and celebrated women had gone down the selfsame steps I was using; that the paths I walked along had heard the rustle of their gowns; that the arcade whose columns I brushed with my hand as I passed had echoed with their girlish laughter. I thought that something of them must have lingered on within these walls and in the air. I felt an impulse to speak their memorable names aloud, to call upon them one by one, and I imagined I would hear some distant voice in reply or see a white form flitting by on the terraces or through the deserted groves of trees. I looked questioningly at the windows and doors. How much I would have given to know where the widow of Alexius Comnenus had been imprisoned, the most beautiful of the captives of Lesbos and the loveliest Greek woman of her time, where the daughter of Erizzo, the governor of Negroponte,* had been put to death for refusing the brutal embraces of Mehmet II, and at which window Hürrem, Süleyman's favourite, had stood with characteristically Persian elegance as she gazed at the Sea of Marmara with her lustrous black eyes, veiled by long silken lashes. Is this the path where the lovely Hungarian dancer, who leapt into Murat III's arms and stole his heart away from Safiye, left the trace of her light feet? Might Kösem, the beautiful and fiercely jealous Greek, with her pale sad face, who lived through the reigns of seven sultans, once have plucked a flower from this flower-bed? The giant Armenian woman whose embraces drove Ibrahim frantic with desire, did she dip her great white arm in this fountain? What about the little favourite of Mehmet IV whose foot was so small that two of her slippers placed heel to toe were no longer than a stiletto dagger, or Rabia Gülnuş, "the springtime draught of roses", who had the most beautiful blue eyes in the Greek Archipelago and whose step was so light she left no prints on the white sand? Who had the softest and fairest hair? Was it Mahfiruz, "the favourite of the evening star" or Melekla, the young Russian concubine, whose charms managed to pacify the ferocious Osman II? What of the Persian and Arab girls who lulled Ibrahim to sleep with their tales? And the forty maidens who drank the blood of Murat? Was nothing left of them, not a single tress of hair, not a thread from their veils, no trace of their fingerprints upon the wall? My reveries ended in a painful and terrible vision. I saw them pass in an interminable procession, far off, among the trees and under the long colonnades, one after the other, sultanas, wives and sisters, kadins, concubines, slaves, pubescent girls, mature matrons and elderly white-haired ladies, shy virginal faces and faces contorted with jealous rage, rulers of empires, favourites of the day, playthings for an hour, from ten generations and a hundred countries, leading their infants by the hand or carrying them, strangled, in their arms or one with a noose at her neck, another with a dagger in her heart, a third dripping with water from the Sea of Marmara; resplendent with gems, covered with wounds, racked by poison, suffering the long death agonies of the Old Seraglio; silent insubstantial ghosts, they passed and were lost in the darkness of the groves, leaving behind them faded flowers and tears and blood: my heart was filled with intense pity.

Beyond the third enclosure stretches a level plot of ground, entirely covered with trees and shrubs, and dotted with little buildings of great charm, among which rises the so-called column of Theodosius, in grey granite, with a handsome Corinthian capital, and on a large pedestal where the last two words can still be made out of a Latin inscription which once read: "*Fortunæ reduci ob devictos Gothos*".* This is the furthest limit of the level terrace on which the great central rectangle of the Seraglio buildings stands. From here to the Seraglio

Point and on all sides between the walls of the three precincts and the outer defensive walls, there was a wood of great plane trees and tall cypresses, rows of pines, groves of laurels and terebinths and poplars wreathed with vines, giving shade to a series of terraced gardens, full of roses and sunflowers, and crossed by broad flights of marble steps leading down to the sea.

By the wall facing Scutari across the water there was the new palace of Sultan Mahmut, which had one great door of gilded copper opening onto the sea. Near the Seraglio Point was the summer harem, an immense semicircular building capable of accommodating five hundred women, with wide courtyards and splendid baths, and gardens where those nocturnal illuminations known as the "Tulip Festivals" were celebrated. In front of this harem, on the shoreline outside the wall, was the famous Seraglio battery, formed of twenty strangely shaped cannon, much carved and ornamented, which were captured from Christian armies in the early European wars. The walls had eight gates, three on the city side, and five towards the sea. Great marble terraces projected from the walls over the shoreline. Tunnels led from the palace to the gates on the Sea of Marmara so that the Sultans could escape secretly in case of attack and reach the refuge of Scutari or Tophane. Nor did the Seraglio end here: on the slopes of the hill and next to the outer walls there were many pavilions in the form of small mosques, fortresses and galleries, which were all reached by paths concealed between two tall hedges from one of the secondary gates in the third enclosure. There was the Yalı Kiosk, since demolished, which was reflected in the waters of the Golden Horn. The New Kiosk is still standing and almost intact – a small circular palace, gilded and painted, from where the Sultans would go to enjoy the view of the port and all its boats at sunset. Near to the summer harem was the Kiosk of the Mirrors, where the peace treaty of 1784 was signed, by which Turkey ceded the Crimea to Russia, and the Kiosk of Hasan Pasha, the walls of which were panelled with mirrors to reflect the nocturnal festivals and orgies of the Sultans. The Kiosk of the Cannon, from which corpses were thrown into the sea, stood near the battery on Seraglio Point. The Kiosk of the Sea, where the Sultana Valide of Mehmet IV held her secret divans, jutted out on a point above the mingled currents of the Bosphorus and the Sea of Marmara. The Rose Kiosk overlooked a level area where the pages did their exercises; it was here that the new constitution was proclaimed in 1839 with the famous Hatti Sherif of Gulhane.* On the other side of the Seraglio the Kiosk of the Vedettes can still be found from which the Sultans could observe unseen all the people going to the Divan; at the corner of the wall near to Hagia Sophia was the Kiosk of Alay, from which Mehmet IV threw his favourite wife Meleki to the rebellious army, together with twenty-nine court officials, who were all torn to pieces before his eyes. At the opposite end of the wall there is the Sepetçiler Kiosk beside which the Padishahs bade farewell to the chief admirals leaving for distant wars. Thus the formidable palace spread from the top of the hill, where its vital parts were concentrated and hidden, down the slopes and along the seashore, crowned with towers, bristling with cannon, garlanded with roses. Its gilded rowing boats set off from every side, it gave off a cloud of fragrance like an altar, its festivals lit by a thousand candles were reflected in the water, gold was thrown to the crowds below its walls and corpses into the sea. Yesterday a slave-girl held power over it, today it is ruled by a madman, tomorrow rioting soldiery will take control. It is as beautiful as an enchanted island and as sinister as a living tomb.

The night is far advanced; the sea reflects the sky burning with stars; the moon silvers the hundred domes of the Seraglio and whitens the tops of cypresses and plane trees, which cast their great shadows over the vast precincts, and one by one the lights in all its many windows go out. The snow-white kiosks and mosques stand out among the dark green groves. Spires and pinnacles and crescents, bronze doors and gilded lattices gleam among the trees, making it seem like a city made of gold and silver. The imperial city sleeps. The three great doors have just been closed: you can still hear the clink of the keys held by the *kapıcıs* under the high ceiling of the vestibules. Another group of them will stand guard at the Gate of Salvation, while thirty white eunuchs will defend the Gate of Felicity, leaning against the walls, still as bas-reliefs, with their faces in shadow. Hundreds of unseen sentinels keep watch from the walls and towers, overlooking the sea, the port, the dark streets of Stamboul, and the vast silent mass of Hagia Sophia. Lanterns can be seen going up and down the stairs in the great kitchens of the first courtyard as the last chores are completed: then the building goes dark. A lamp is still burning in the houses of the *Veznedar* aga and the *Defterdar* effendi. There's a confused movement outside the house of the chief black eunuch in the second courtyard. The last doors are being shut throughout the labyrinth of the harem.

The eunuchs go their rounds along the empty alleys in between the dark kiosks, with only the sudden flight of birds, roused by the sea wind, and the monotonous splash of the fountains to disturb them. The whole palace seems steeped in deep peacefulness. And yet a feverish life is still working away inside its walls. The night thoughts of all the slave-girls, prisoners, and servants who people the palace rise in a confused mass over the palace walls and fly to the four corners of the earth to seek out places which were dear to them and mothers they had to abandon in infancy, and to relive the strange and terrible events of earlier times. Silent prayers and lamentations drift through the dark passages and groves and mingle with plans for revenge and bloodshed and with the overweening desires of secret ambition. The great palace sleeps fitfully or is restlessly awake with doubts and fears. Whispers in a hundred tongues merge with the sound of the breeze and the rustle of the leaves. Only a few walls separate the page who has prostituted himself from the imam who has just given a sermon, the captive prince under sentence of death from the love-struck Sultana who is getting ready for her wedding. Wretched creatures without a penny to their name sleep beside untold riches; the same walls hold divine beauty and scorned deformity, every vice and every misfortune, every form of prostitution of body and soul. The bizarre airy forms of the Moorish buildings among the trees are silhouetted against the starry sky, casting elegant shadows of fringes, festoons and lace on the walls; in the moonlight the fountains seem to spurt forth sapphires and diamonds; all the fragrances of the garden are wafted on the night breeze, to drift and mingle into one overpowering perfume which seeps through the lattices and arouses cries of pleasure and lascivious dreams. This is the hour of night when the eunuchs, sitting under the trees staring at the dim light which flickers from the kiosks, feel their hearts and minds eaten up with rage and finger their daggers with trembling hands; the hour when the wretched young girl, recently abducted and sold, stands at the high window of her cell, gazing with tear-filled eyes at the calm Asian horizons, weeping for the hut where she was born and the valley where her ancestors lie buried; the hour when the chained captive, the mute stained with blood, the despised dwarf see, with a kind of dizziness, the abyss which separates them from the man who rules over everything, and in their agony confront the *hidden power* above which has taken from one his freedom, from the other his speech, from the third his human shape, to bestow them all on one man. It is the hour in which the outcasts weep and the great tremble, uncertain of what the morrow will bring. In the buildings lamps shine on the pale faces of treasurers bent over their papers; on long-abandoned concubines with dishevelled hair, as they toss and turn on their pillows; on the bronzed faces of brawny janissaries, smiling fiercely in their sleep as they dream of massacres. Gasps of pleasure and despairing sobs are heard through the thin walls. In one kiosk, the cursed liquor is poured, foaming in the middle of a circle of semi-naked bacchantes; in a darkened room, a wretched sultana who has just given birth cries wildly into her pillow in order not to see the pool of blood in which her newborn baby lies, for the midwife has been ordered by the Padishah to leave the umbilical cord untied; in the marble niches of the Hümayun gate, the severed heads of the beys executed at dusk are still dripping with blood; and in the highest kiosk of the third precinct, in a room tapestried with crimson damask, on a sable bed, in the middle of scattered cushions embroidered with pearls and velvet blankets threaded with gold, softly lit by an engraved silver lamp hanging from the sandalwood ceiling, there lies a beautiful dark-skinned girl swathed in a great white veil. Only a few years before she was leading a flock of sheep across the plains of Arabia Felix; now she leans close above the pale face of Murat III, who dozes at her feet, and murmurs to him in a sweet timid voice: "Once upon a time in Damascus there was a merchant named Abu Ayub who had accumulated much wealth and was respected by all who knew him. He had a son, who was handsome and knowledgeable and was called Slave-of-Love, and a beautiful daughter who was named Heart's-Strength. Abu Ayub passed away and left all his goods wrapped up and tied in bundles; on each was written: 'For Baghdad'. Slave-of-Love asked his mother: 'Why is "For Baghdad" written on all the goods which belonged to my father?' And his mother replied: 'My son...'"* But the Padishah has fallen asleep and the slave-girl gently leans back against the pillows. All the doors of the harem are closed, all the lamps have been extinguished, the hundred domes are silvery in the moonlight, the gilded crescents and windows gleam among the trees, the splash of the fountains is loud in the silence of the night: the whole Seraglio sleeps. And has slept for thirty years, abandoned on its solitary hill. The verses of the Persian poet which Mehmet the Conqueror uttered on first stepping over the threshold of the desecrated palace of the Eastern Emperors can be spoken again here: "The filthy spider weaves its web in the halls of kings, and from the proud heights of Afrasiab the raven croaks its sinister song."*

## Final Days

At this point the clear and detailed recollections of my stay in Constantinople, which have enabled me to describe what I saw at length, come to an end. I remember nothing more than a series of hurried trips from one shore of the Golden Horn to the other, from Europe to Asia and back, after which, in the evening, I saw, passing like a dream, illuminated cities, vast crowds, groves and fleets and hills, while the thought of my approaching departure tinged everything with sadness, as if those visions were already only memories of a distant country.

## The Mosques

And yet, out of the midst of that rush of people and things, some images remain which I see whenever I think back to those final days.

I recall the lovely morning when I visited most of the imperial mosques, and as I think of them once more I sense around me a vast emptiness and a solemn silence. The memory of Hagia Sophia in no way diminishes the wonder you feel when you first enter the titanic walls of these mosques. There, as elsewhere, the religion of the conquerors appropriated the religious art of the conquered. Almost all the mosques are copied from the Basilica of Justinian;* they have the great dome, the half-domes beneath, the courts and porticoes; some even have the form of a Greek cross. But Islam has spread its own colour and light over everything so that the familiar features seen as a whole take on the appearance of a new structure, in which the horizons of an unknown world are glimpsed and the presence of another God is felt. They are enormous naves of austere and grandiose simplicity, completely white, and lit with a soft and equal light from numerous windows, a light in which the eye can discern every object from one end of the building to the other and rests, almost sleeps – together with the mind – in a gentle tranquillity which permeates everything, like that of a snowy valley under a white sky. Only the echo of your footsteps tells you you are in an enclosed place. There is nothing to distract the mind, which moves straight across that emptiness and clarity to the object of worship. There is nothing which arouses melancholy or fear; there are no illusions, or mysteries, or dark corners with dimly gleaming images of a complicated hierarchy of supernatural beings to confound the senses; there is nothing but the clear, sharp, dazzling and overwhelming conception of a single God, who loves the austere bareness of desert places flooded with light and allows no other image of himself than the sky. All the imperial mosques of Constantinople present the same appearance of grandeur which elevates the mind and of simplicity which concentrates it on a single thought, and they differ so little in detail that it is difficult to recall them individually. The exterior of the Mosque of Ahmet is enormous, yet also light and graceful, like some airborne construction; its dome rests on four massive round pillars of white marble enclosing an area wide enough for four small mosques, and it is the only mosque in Stamboul that is gloriously crowned by six minarets. The Mosque of Süleyman is a holy city more than a temple, where visitors can lose their way; it is formed of three naves, and its dome, higher than that of Hagia Sophia, rests on four marvellous columns of rose-coloured granite which remind one of the trunks of the famous giant redwood trees in California. The Mosque of Mehmet is another Hagia Sophia, white and cheerful in atmosphere; that of Beyazit is the most elegant in form; that of Osman is entirely of marble; that of Şehzade has the two most graceful minarets in Stamboul; Aksaray is the finest example of the Turkish Renaissance style; the Selimiye is the most serious and Mahmut's the most inventive, the Mosque of the Sultana Valide the most decorated. Each has its own peculiar beauty, or legend, or privilege. Sultan Ahmet has the custody of the Prophet's Standard; Beyazit is always full of flocks of pigeons; Süleymaniye boasts the inscriptions of Karahisari;* Sultana Valide has the false golden column that cost the life of the conqueror of Khaniá;* Sultan Mehmet sees "eleven imperial mosques bow their heads around him, as the sheaves of his brothers bowed in a circle round Joseph's sheaf". In one are the columns of the Palace of Justinian and of the Augusteon, which bore the statues of Venus, Theodora, and Eudoxia; in others are found marble blocks from the ancient churches of Chalcedonia, columns from the ruins of Troy, pillars from Egyptian temples, precious glass plundered from Persian palaces, remains of circus and forum, aqueduct and basilica; all merge under the enveloping white light of an all-conquering religion.

Inside, the differences are even slighter than they are externally. At the back there is a marble pulpit; the Sultan's loggia faces it, closed in by a gilded lattice. Next to the mihrab there are two enormous candelabra with torches as tall as palm trees; and all about the nave innumerable lamps in large glass globes are hung, in a curious arrangement which looks more like the preparations for a ball than for a solemn religious rite. The great sacred inscriptions that run round the pillars, the doors and the windows of the domes, and a sort of imitation frieze painted to resemble marble, and glass coloured and ornamented with floral motifs are the only decorative elements to stand out against the bare white of those monumental walls. Precious types of marble are everywhere – in the pavements of the vestibules and porticoes round the courtyards, in the fountains for ablution and the minarets, but they in no way alter the gracefully austere and sober character of the edifice: white, surrounded by trees, and crowned by domes glittering against the blue sky. The mosque occupies only a small part of the enclosure, which includes a labyrinth of courtyards and houses. There are auditoriums for the reading of the Koran, depositaries for the safe-keeping of private property, libraries and academies, schools of medicine and schools for children, dormitories for students, kitchens for the poor, asylums and infirmaries, hospices for travellers, and baths; a small town, hospitable and benevolent, clustered round the lofty mass of the temple as at the foot of a mountain, and under the shade of enormous trees. But all these objects are now dim in my memory; I see nothing but the small black mark made by my own person, like an atom, almost lost in those enormous buildings, among long rows of tiny figures of prostrate Turks at their prayers. I am dazzled by the light and overwhelmed by the vastness; I shuffle in tatty slippers over the floor, as my pride in my powers of description is cut down to size. Each mosque seems to merge into another – I am lost in an endless sequence of pillars and vaults through which moves an endless crowd of white-robed figures.

## The Cisterns

The reminiscences of another day are all dark, and full of mysteries and ghosts. I entered the courtyard of a Muslim house, went down a damp and gloomy staircase by the light of a torch to find myself under the vault of Yerebatan Sarayı, the great Cistern Basilica of Constantine, the extent of which, or so the common people of the city believe, has never been ascertained. The greenish water is lost to sight under the black arches, illuminated here and there by a ray of pale light which only accentuates the horror of the surrounding shadows. The torch threw a fiery gleam upon the arches near the door and revealed dripping walls and endless rows of columns wherever one looked, like tree trunks in a dense flooded forest. With a pleasurable sensation of terror the imagination wanders off down those long sepulchral porticoes, hovers above the gloomy waters and loses itself in giddying circles among the innumerable columns, while the dragoman, in a low voice, tells fearsome tales of those brave enough to explore those subterranean solitudes in a boat, hoping to discover how far they extend, only to return after many hours of frantic rowing, with their hair standing on end and their faces transfixed with horror, while the distant vaults echo with loud laughter and shrill whistling; and as for others who never came back, who knows what became of them? Perhaps they were driven mad with terror, or died of starvation, or were carried away by some mysterious current far from Stamboul. This lugubrious vision vanished immediately in the broad daylight of the Atmeydanı square. A few minutes later I was again underground among the two hundred pillars of the dry cistern called Binbirdirek, where, lit by some feeble rays that filter down through the arches, a hundred Greek workmen were weaving silk and chanting some warlike song in high-pitched voices. I could hear the confused noise of a caravan passing overhead. Then once more the sunshine and the open air, followed again by darkness – under ancient arches and among more columns, in a tomb-like silence broken only by a faint sound of distant voices – and so on until evening, a mysterious, thought-provoking pilgrimage, after which I was haunted for a long time by the image of an underground lake, into which the metropolis of the Byzantine Empire had sunk and vanished, and where the gay and heedless city of Stamboul would one day disappear in her turn.

## Scutari

The darkness gives way to the bright picture of Scutari. Whenever Junck and I took the crowded ferry to Scutari, we would debate whether the Asian shore or that of the Golden Horn was the most beautiful. Junck preferred Scutari whereas I held out for Stamboul.

But Scutari delighted me with the sudden changes of view as you approach it from the sea – almost as if it wants to play a game with you... From the Sea of Marmara it looks like a large hilltop village, but seen from the Golden Horn it already starts to look more like a town. Yet as the steamboat rounds the most advanced point of the Asian shore and heads straight for the harbour, Scutari seems to rise and expand; the hills covered with buildings emerge one behind the other; suburbs suddenly appear in the valleys, villas crowd the heights; the shore with its rows of brightly painted houses stretches away as far as the eye can see. It is huge, grand, theatrical – where could it have been hiding? In the space of a few minutes it is revealed as if a huge curtain has been raised and you remain astonished by the spectacle, waiting for it to disappear again. You go down the gangplank, from the ferry into a crowd of boatmen, horse-traders and interpreters, and walk up the winding main street, which rises gently between little red and yellow houses covered in ivy and vine leaves, alongside garden walls, under high pergolas and the shade of huge plane trees, whose trunks almost block the way. You walk on in front of Turkish cafés full of idlers reclining and smoking and staring into space. You meet herds of goats and heavy country carts pulled along by buffaloes with garlands of flowers between their horns, peasants wearing fezzes or turbans, Muslim funeral processions, and groups of Turkish ladies on holiday, carrying flowers and branches. It's like another Stamboul, less majestic but livelier and more cheerful than the metropolis on its seven hills. It is like a city in a rural setting: the countryside is everywhere. The narrow streets are lined with houses straight out of a scene from a Christmas nativity crib, wind up and down the valleys and the hills, and are lost to sight in the green gardens and orchards. Higher up in the town you find deep rural tranquillity; lower down there is all the bustling life of a busy seaside resort. A noise of shouting and singing and drums comes from the large barracks which are located round about. Birds hop about the empty lanes. We follow a funeral cortège and find ourselves outside the town; we enter the famous cemetery and lose our way in a large forest of tall cypress trees which stretch down the hill on one side towards the Sea of Marmara and on the other towards the Golden Horn. Wherever one turns one can see white tombstones in groups or in long rows in the middle of wild flowers and shrubs; paths wind about, and through the dense groves of trees the glittering trembling horizon of the sea can just be glimpsed. We walk

on aimlessly through the gilded and painted tombstones, upright and
fallen, past the gates of family plots, the small mausoleums belonging
to pashas and the rough-hewn columns for commoners, looking at
withered bunches of flowers and skulls appearing through the newly
dug earth, hearing the doves cooing in the trees on every side. It
gradually seems as if the forest is growing larger, the tombstones more
thickly crowded, the paths more numerous, the light of the horizon
more distant, the kingdom of the dead nearer with every step. We start
to wonder how we'll find our way out when we suddenly find ourselves
on a wide road leading to the huge open plain of Haydarpaşa where
Muslim armies used to assemble before going off to wage war in
Asia. From there we can take in with one sweeping glance the Sea of
Marmara, Stamboul, the entrance into the Golden Horn, Galata and
Pera, all covered by a morning mist dappled with heavenly colours: the
view makes us gasp with astonishment and the joy of arrival.

## Çırağan Palace

On another day we took a tram, seated between two giant black
eunuchs who had been assigned to us as guides by one of Abdülaziz's
aides-de-camp, for a tour of the Çırağan Palace, built on the shore of
the Bosphorus at the foot of the district of Beşiktaş. I remember the
indefinable mixture of curiosity and distaste I felt as I stole a sidelong
glance at the eunuch sitting next to me, who towered over me by a
whole head, with his huge hands spread out upon his knees. Each time
I turned in his direction I caught the fragrance of bergamot from his
clean and formal apparel. When the tram came to a halt I reached in
my pockets to pay the fare, but one of those monstrous hands seized
me by the arm in an iron grip, and his great black eyes looked into
mine, as if to say: "Christian, do not offend me, or I'll dislocate your
bones!" We came to a small door decorated with arabesque carving,
went down a long corridor, where a number of servants in livery came
to meet us, and exchanging our boots for slippers, climbed a wide
staircase that led into the royal apartments. Here there was no need to
evoke the memories of the past in order to make the place come alive
for the air was still warm with the presence of the court. Only a few
weeks earlier, the ladies of the harem had lounged on the broad divans
covered with velvet and satin that ran along the walls. A faint sense

of that soft and luxurious existence still pervaded the air. We walked through many beautiful rooms, decorated in a mixed European and Moorish style, but of such a pure and fastidiously simple design that we spoke in hushed tones. The eunuchs muttered some incomprehensible explanations while pointing out corners and doors with discreet gestures as if indicating something secretive. The silk hangings, the colourful carpets, the inlaid marble tables, the fine oil paintings hung out of the light, the elegant ogee arches of the doors divided by little Arabian columns, the tall candelabra like trees made of crystal which tinkled loudly as we walked by – all these impressions merged and sank into our imagination, intent on catching sight of some kadin in hasty retreat. Only the Sultan's bath, however, remains clear to my mind's eye: made of the whitest marble, sculpted and carved with such a profusion of hanging flowers and pendants and fringes and lacelike ornaments that you were frightened to touch them in case they broke off. The arrangement of the rooms reminded me vaguely of the Alhambra. We hurried along soundlessly, almost furtively, on the thick carpets. Every now and then, a eunuch would pull a cord, a green curtain rose and we would see through a large window the Bosphorus, Asia, a thousand ships, a great light; then it all suddenly vanished again, and our eyes remained dazzled as by a flash of lightning. From one window we caught a glimpse of a small garden closed in by a high wall, neat and well-tended, like a convent garden, suggesting to us a whole secret world of melancholy beauties yearning for love and liberty, until the curtain fell back. The rooms seemed never-ending: as each new door appeared we hastened our steps to enter unannounced, but silence reigned throughout and we never caught so much as a fleeting glimpse of a dress disappearing quickly. The concubines were all gone and the rustle which made us turn expectantly was only the heavy brocade curtains falling back across the door. The tinkling crystal prisms of the candelabra seemed to mock us like the silvery laughter of some hidden observer watching us. At last we grew weary of that endless toing and froing through that silent palace and its lifeless splendours, of seeing reflected in large mirrors the black faces of our guides and of the silent servants who accompanied us, together with our own bemused and travel-weary expressions; we left the building almost at a run, thankful to find ourselves again in the open air, surrounded by the dilapidated houses and noisy, ragged inhabitants of Tophane.

Tophane Mosque

The hill of Eyüp on the Golden Horn

Dancing dervishes

## *Eyüp*

How could I forget the necropolis of Eyüp? We went there one
evening at sunset, and it remains in my memory as I saw it then, lit
by the last rays of the sun. A caique had brought us to the end of the
Golden Horn and we climbed up to the Ottoman "Holy Land" along
a steep path bordered with tombs. At that hour all the stonemasons
who work during the day on the gravestones, making the place echo
with the sound of their tools, had gone home and it was empty. We
walked on cautiously, looking about us for the severe face of an imam
or a dervish, since here of all places the profane curiosity of a *giaour*
is least tolerated. But we came across no conical hats or turbans.
In some trepidation we arrived at the mysterious Mosque of Eyüp,
which we had so often seen from the hills of the opposite shore and
the inlets of the Golden Horn, with its glittering domes and slender
minarets. In the courtyard, shaded by a great plane tree and lit by a
circle of lamps which burn perpetually, there is the mausoleum of
the famous standard-bearer of the Prophet, who died with the first
Muslims in front of the walls of Byzantium. His body was found eight
centuries later by Mehmet the Conqueror, who built a tomb for it on
this shore. The mosque is consecrated to him, and here the Padishah
comes to gird on the sword of Osman; it is the holiest mosque in
Constantinople just as the surrounding cemetery is the holiest of the
city. Sultans, viziers and court grandees are buried here in turbehs
which are surrounded with flowers, resplendent with marble and
gold arabesques, and decorated with florid inscriptions. Standing a
little apart is the mortuary temple of the muftis, surmounted by an
octagonal dome, where the high priests are laid to rest in enormous
black catafalques, with tall muslin turbans placed upon them. It is a
city of tombs, white and shadowy; it inspires in one both religious
melancholy and a feeling of social diffidence, as if one were walking
through an aristocratic district of town, pervaded by a haughty
silence. One walks alongside white walls and delicate wrought-iron
gates, down which lush vegetation hangs and through which branches
of acacia, oak and myrtle protrude; while through the gilded iron
bars which close the arched windows of the turbehs you can see the
marble mausoleums inside, bathed in a soft light and tinted with
the green reflection of the foliage outside. There is no other place
in Stamboul where one appreciates quite so clearly the Muslim

capacity to soften the image of death and allow one to contemplate it without terror. It is a necropolis, a palace, a garden, a pantheon, full of melancholy and grace, which evokes in the visitor both a prayer and a smile. On every side there are cemeteries, shaded by centuries-old cypress trees, crossed by winding paths, white with tombstones which look as if they're about to topple in a cascade down the slope into the sea or are crowding to the edge of the paths to watch ghosts pass. From hundreds of shady nooks, if you push the branches aside, you can dimly make out Stamboul in the bluish distance on the right, like a series of separate towns one after the other; below there is the Golden Horn gleaming in the last rays of the setting sun; facing you the suburbs of Sütlüce, Halıcıoğlu, Piripaşa, Hasköy, and in the far distance the large district of Kasımpaşa and Galata's vague outline, all indistinct with soft fading colours, like some unearthly vision.

## The Janissary Museum

All these images vanish, and I now find myself walking through long bare halls, between two motionless ranks of sinister figures, looking like corpses nailed to the walls. I have never been so repelled since my visit to the last room of the Tussaud exhibition in London where I could half make out in the gloom the effigies of all the most horrible murderers in England. It is like a museum of ghosts, or an open tomb containing the mummified bodies of the most famous personages of Turkey as it once was: splendid, extravagant and fierce, and now surviving only in the memories of the old and the imaginations of the poets. There are hundreds of large wooden figures, painted and dressed in old costumes, erect in stiff and haughty poses, with their heads held high and their eyes staring, and their hands on their sword-hilts, as if waiting for the signal to draw their weapons and fall on their enemies, as in the good old days. First comes the household of the Padishah; the chief eunuch, the Grand Vizier, the mufti, chamberlains and high officials, wearing turbans of every colour and shape, pyramidal, spherical, square, extravagant and extraordinary, with brightly coloured and brocaded kaftans, tunics of white and crimson silk, tied at the waist with cashmere scarves, and with their chests covered in gold and silver breastplates, and armed with princely weapons: two long rows of bizarre and splendid scarecrows, which show to perfection what the old Ottoman court was like in all its brazen splendour and barbaric pride. Then come the pages who carry the *Grand Signor*'s fur mantles, his turban, his footstool and his sword. Then the guards of the gates and the gardens, the Sultan's bodyguard, white and black eunuchs looking like idols or magi, glittering and plumed, their heads covered with Persian caps, metal helmets, strange turbans shaped like crescents, cones and inverted pyramids, and armed with steel rods, huge poniards and whips, like a horde of brigands or executioners. One looks at you with contempt, another gnashes his teeth, the bloodshot eyeballs of a third are bulging, and a fourth has a devilish smile. Finally, the janissary corps, with its holy patron, Emin Baba* – nothing more than a skeleton dressed in a white tunic – and officials of all grades, each symbolized by a different kitchen chore, and soldiers of every rank, with all the uniforms and insignia of that insolent army wiped out by Mahmut's rifles. The most unbridled imagination could not invent the crazy confusion of dress – of king, priest, brigand, minstrel – as in some wild carnival crowd. The "water-carriers," the "preparers of soup," the "head cooks," the "heads of the scullions" – soldiers with a host of different responsibilities follow on row by row, with brushes and spoons in their turbans, with bells attached to their tunics, carrying water jugs and the famous stewpots which were used to give the signal for rebellion, with large leather caps, wide loose tunics like sorcerers' capes from the neck down to the waist, broad belts made of chiselled metal disks and gigantic sabres, with staring eyes, huge torsos and faces contorted in expressions of scorn, menace and insult. Last of all come the mutes of the Seraglio, carrying silken nooses, and dwarves and buffoons sporting burlesque crowns above their repulsive faces, full of malice and stupidity... The great glass cases which enclose all these figures give the place the look of an anatomy museum, an impression which is only increased by their cadaverous appearance and makes you shudder with horror. When you reach the end you feel as though you've walked through a hall in the Old Seraglio and seen the whole court, frozen in terror at some threat just uttered by the Padishah. And when you come out onto the square of the Atmeydanı and see the pashas in their black coats and the nizams modestly dressed in Zouave costume, you think "Ah, what a mild and amiable lot the Turks of today are!"

And after this, there are more tombs as I continue to wander among the imperial turbehs of the city, which are such fine expressions of

Muslim art and philosophy. With a firman we gained access to the mausoleum of Mahmut the Reformer, located not far from the Atmeydanı within a garden full of roses and jasmine. It is a beautiful white marble temple, hexagonal in shape, with a lead dome resting on Ionic pillars and lit by seven grated windows, some of which look onto one of the main streets in Stamboul. The interior walls are ornamented with bas-reliefs and hung with carpets of brocaded silk. In the centre there is the sarcophagus covered with beautiful Persian shawls, and on it a fez has been placed, the emblem of the Reform, decorated with a glittering diamond feather. Around the sarcophagus is a charming balustrade inlaid with mother-of-pearl, which encloses four silver candelabra. A further seven sarcophagi belonging to seven sultanas are placed against the walls. Finely woven mats and colourful carpets cover the floor. Precious Korans written in gold are placed upon elegant lecterns. In a silver casket there is a long roll of muslin cloth completely covered in minute Arabic script. Before he inherited the throne, while still a prisoner in the Old Seraglio, Mahmut patiently transcribed a large part of the Koran onto the cloth. When he was dying, he gave orders that this memento of his youth should be placed on his tomb. From inside the turbeh you can see, through the gilded gratings on the windows, the green garden outside, and smell the fragrance of the roses. Light fills the interior; noises from the city echo as if from under an open portico; women and children stop to look through the windows and whisper a prayer. In all this there is something primitive and tender which touches the heart. It's as if Mahmut's soul, not his corpse, is enclosed within those walls, watching over his people and listening to them as they still pass by and greet him. When he died he simply moved out of one kiosk in the Seraglio to this new one, as pleasant as the one he lived in before, still in sunlight, in the middle of Stamboul's bustle, near his sons – in fact even nearer to them – on the edge of the road, under the eyes of every passer-by, who can see his glittering plumage just as they used to when he went in procession to the mosque, radiating life and majesty, to pray for the prosperity of the Empire. Almost all the imperial turbehs are like this: Ahmet's, Beyazit's – where the Sultan rests his head on a brick made from the dust of his clothes and slippers – Süleyman's, Mustafa's and Selim III's, Abdülhamit's and Sultana Roxelana's. They are in the form of small temples resting on columns of white marble and porphyry, gleaming with amber and mother-of-pearl. In some a hole is left in the dome for the rain to enter and water the flowers and plants placed round the sarcophagus, which is covered with velvet cloth and lace. Ostrich eggs and gilded lamps hang from the side vaults to light the tombs of the princes which are arranged in a circle round their father's sarcophagus and on which the handkerchiefs which were used to throttle them in their infancy or youth are placed, perhaps to remind the onlooker, full of pity for the victims, of the unavoidable necessity for the crime. I recall that after I had seen several of these tombs I felt my heart and mind beginning to assent to the monstrous *raison d'état* which sanctioned these murders, just as something inside me, after seeing the name of one man recorded and glorified everywhere – in mosques, on fountains, in turbehs, and in a thousand other images – began to submit to his absolute and supreme power. In a similar way, after wandering for so long through cemeteries gazing at tombs, I started to look on death in a new, almost untroubled light, to have a greater sense of equanimity and lack of care about my existence, to yield myself up to some unstrenuous philosophy of life, a meandering reflectiveness, a new state of mind in which it seemed to me that the best thing to do is to pass one's time in dreaming, and allow what is destined to take its course. And in this tranquil state of mind a wave of depression and aversion would wash over me whenever I thought of our own bustling cities, gloomy churches, walled-off and deserted cemeteries.

## The Dervishes

Among the images of those final days in Constantinople there are also the dervishes. The most famous of their thirty-two orders, the Mevlevi,* have a celebrated tekke in Pera. I went prepared to see the luminous visages of saints, rapt in visions of Paradise. But I was in for a severe disappointment, for even among the dervishes the flame of faith "flickers on a burnt-out wick".* The famous divine dance seemed to me nothing more than a routine theatrical performance. They are certainly curious to behold, as they enter the circular mosque, one behind the other, wrapped in large dark cloaks, their heads bent, their arms concealed, accompanied by primitive music, monotonous and sweet, which sounds like the wind moaning in the cypresses in the cemetery at Scutari and sends you into a hypnotic reverie. And when they whirl round and bow two by two before the mihrab, their movement is so languid and majestic you suddenly wonder if they are in fact men. It is also a fine sight when they throw off their mantles with a striking gesture, and, appearing in their long white woollen tunics, open their arms as if for an embrace and throw back their heads, and then one after the other begin to spin as if turned by an invisible hand; and when they spin all together in the middle of the mosque, keeping equal distance from each other, not straying an inch from their positions, like automata on a pivot, white, light and rapid, with their skirts billowing and waving around them and their eyes half closed, and when they fall to the floor as if they've been knocked down by some supernatural apparition, with a great cry of "Allah!" as they fall; and when they rise and bow to each other and kiss each other's hands, and move along the walls of the mosque with a graceful, half-walking, half-dancing gait. But I did not witness the ecstasy, the transfigured and rapt faces that so many travellers have seen and described. I saw only agile and tireless dancers going through their business with supreme indifference. Indeed I caught sight of some stifled laughs, and noticed one young dervish who didn't seem at all displeased to be the object of an English lady's fixed stare from the public gallery. I also saw several of them biting rather than kissing their neighbour's hand, who in his turn retorted with a pinch. Oh, the hypocrites! What I did find and appreciate among these men – and they were of all ages and physical appearance – was a grace and elegance of movement that might well be envied by some of our drawing-room dancers, and which is certainly a natural gift of the oriental races, owing to their particular physiques. I observed it again on another day when we were allowed to enter a cell of the tekke, and see a dervish in the act of dressing for the ceremony. He was a tall, slender, beardless youth, with a girlish face. He smoothed his white skirt over his hips, standing at the mirror, and turning to smile at us; he felt his slender waist; he prepared hurriedly, but with care and with an artistic eye, seeing to every part of his dress, like a lady giving the last touches to her costume. Seen from behind with his trailing gown, he was not unlike a girl dressed for the ball who checks her appearance in the mirror before leaving... and he was a monk! "'Tis a strange truth," as Desdemona says to Othello.*

* * *

# Çamlıca

But the most precious memory from those final days in the city is our climb to the top of Mount Çamlıca behind Scutari. From its summit I said farewell to the city and it was the last and most splendid panorama of the place which I saw. We set off at dawn in the midst of fog, which still lingered on the summit when we reached it, although the day promised to be fine. It concealed everything below us. It was a very strange sight: we were above an immense level blanket of grey covering Scutari, the Bosphorus, the Golden Horn, the whole of Constantinople. Absolutely nothing could be seen. It was as if the entire city with all its neighbourhoods and all its ports had vanished. The summit of Çamlıca emerged like an island in the middle of a vast grey sea. Junck and I imagined we were two poor pilgrims who had come all the way from remotest Asia Minor and had arrived at that spot in the fog before dawn, unaware that the great capital city of the Ottoman Empire lay beneath us. It was enjoyable to imagine their increasing astonishment and amazement as the sun rose and gradually revealed under the blanket of fog the marvellous and entirely unexpected sight of the great metropolis. The fog did indeed begin to lift here and there as we watched. Parts of the city began to emerge like small islands: an archipelago of little towns, set wide apart from each other, floating in the mist, the tops of Scutari and the seven hills of Stamboul, of Pera, and the high-lying districts on the European shore of the Bosphorus, the peak of Kasımpaşa, an indistinct glimpse of the furthermost towns along the Golden Horn, towards Eyüp and Hasköy. Twenty miniature Constantinoples, pink in the sun's rays, afloat, glittering with white and green and silvery pinnacles. Then each one started to expand and grow, as if they were rising up from the sea of fog, and it looked as if a great throng of roofs, domes, towers and minarets were gathering and hurrying to find their proper positions before the sun was fully up and revealed them. Now the whole of Scutari could be seen, and facing it, almost all of Stamboul. The higher areas on the other shore of the Golden Horn stretching from Galata all the way to the Sweet Waters were visible, as were Tophane, Fındıklı, Dolmabahçe and Beşiktaş on the European shore of the Bosphorus, and so on, as far as the eye could see, town after town, great terraced slopes of buildings, and towns even further off, the façades of whose buildings were tinged with the most delicate shade of coral red. But the waters of the Golden Horn and the Bosphorus and the sea itself were still hidden. The two pilgrims would have jumped, mistakenly, to the conclusion that the huge city at their feet was built over two deep and connected valleys, where the fog lingered all day long, and they would have wondered what was at the mysterious bottom of them. But after a few minutes, the last grey drifts of mist disperse, grow lighter, turn bluish, start to glow: water – a jetty – a channel – a sea – two seas – the whole of Constantinople lies stretched before them in a sea of light, of blues and greens, like a new creation. Even though you've gazed on this beauty from a hundred vantage points and examined it in all its details and given voice to your amazement and wonder in a hundred different ways, you still exclaim and cry out in astonishment. The thought that in a few days' time we will see it no more, that it will become a fading memory wrapped by a fog that will never lift, that the moment has come to say farewell for ever – it is as if we were going into exile, as if a light were going out of our lives.

And yet... even in Constantinople, even in those final days, we were bored. Our minds were tired and couldn't take in new sights. We crossed the bridge and didn't bother to look around. Everything seemed monotonous. Like vagabonds with nothing to do, we yawned and wandered about aimlessly. We spent endless hours sitting in front of a Turkish café studying the cobblestones, or at the hotel window looking at the cats climbing over the roofs of the houses across the road. We were sated with the Orient; we felt the need to take stock and to start work. Then it rained for two days, turning everything grey, and the city became a swamp. That was the last straw. Our mood turned black, we cursed the place, became rude and boorish about it, full of European pretensions and condescension. Who would have thought it when we first arrived! And what a pass it brought us to! Even to celebrating on the day we emerged from the Austrian Lloyd shipping agency with two tickets for Varna and the Danube! Yet even as we celebrated we were still sorry to have to leave our friends in Pera; we spent all our last evenings in their convivial company. How sad it is to have to keep saying goodbye, to break one's ties, to leave bits of one's heart behind everywhere one goes. Is there really nowhere in the world some magic wand to be found which I could wave to summon up round one dinner table all my good friends scattered across the globe – you, Santoro, in Constantinople; you, Selam, from the shores of Africa; you, Ten Brink, from the dunes of Holland; you, Segovia, from Gualdaquivir, and you, Saavedra, on the Tagus – and let them know they are for ever in my heart? But alas, there's no such magic wand: the years go by and our hopes fade.


## The Turks


Now, before I go on board the Austrian steamer that lies in the Golden Horn opposite Galata ready to leave for the Black Sea, it only remains for me to set down modestly, from a mere traveller's point of view, some general observations that will try to answer the question: "What did you think of the Turks?" Spontaneous observations, for the rest, free from any consideration of current events, set down here just as I remember them from my impressions of those days. When I hear that question – "What did you think of the Turks?" – I remember immediately how struck I was throughout my stay by the appearance of the male population of Stamboul. Even if you take no account of the physical differences, it is an impression quite different from that produced by the people of any other country in Europe. One seems to be looking at people – I cannot find a better way of expressing the notion – who are all perpetually thinking the same thing. An inhabitant of southern Europe might think the same at the sight of a northern European population – but there is a great difference. Northerners have the serious and self-contained expression of people who are busy about their own affairs, while the Turks look as if they're thinking about remote and indeterminate matters. They look like philosophers with an *idée fixe*, or sleepwalkers who are unconscious of the place they're in or of the objects around them. They all look straight ahead into the distance, as if they're used to scanning the wide horizons, and an indefinable sadness hovers round the mouth and eyes, like people who are accustomed to living shut up within themselves. All have the same gravity, the same composure, the same reserve in speaking, in looking and gesticulating. From the pasha down to the shopkeeper, all are gentlemanly and courteous in the same manner, endowed with a certain dignified and aristocratic air, so that at first sight, were it not for the distinctions of dress, you would think there was no such thing as the working class in Constantinople. Their faces are inexpressive, revealing nothing of their souls or their minds. It is exceedingly rare to find among them one of those open countenances that are so common among us and which reflect the owner's temperament – kindly or passionate or curmudgeonly as may be – and which allow the observer to make a rapid and confident judgement of his character. In every face there is an enigma; their glance questions but makes no response; their lips betray no movement of the heart. It is impossible to express the deadening weight produced upon the visitor by these silent masks, this cold reserve, these rigid postures and staring eyes that say nothing. Sometimes you feel an almost irresistible impulse to shout: "Stir yourselves for once, for Heaven's sake! Tell us who you are, what you're thinking about, what you're looking at in front of you, with those glassy eyes!" It is all so strange that you almost begin to wonder if it's natural, and imagine for a moment it might be the result of some agreement amongst themselves, or the passing effect of some spiritual malady common to the Muslims of Stamboul. However, despite the uniformity of manner and behaviour, there is a notable distinction in the appearance of different parts of the population. The original physical type of the Turkish race, which is robust and handsome, is now only to be found among the lower orders, who, by necessity or from religious feeling, still preserve their forefathers' sobriety of life. Among this class you can still find vigorous and slender bodies, well-formed heads, aquiline noses, shining eyes and prominent jaws, as well as an air of strength and boldness in the whole person. Turks from the higher social classes, however, in whom corruption is more rooted and the mingling of foreign blood is greater, have for the most part small skulls, low foreheads, dull eyes, pendent lips and flabby bodies. And to these physical differences there corresponds an equally prominent – perhaps even greater – moral difference between genuine Turks and that ambiguous, colourless, insipid being known as the reformed Turk. This makes it difficult to study the Turkish people, since, with those who have preserved the original character of the race there is no possibility of association or understanding, whereas the others, whom it is very easy to observe and to enter into social intercourse with, represent neither the real character nor the authentic conception of the nation. But even corruption and the new colouring of European civilization have not yet sufficed to take away from upper-class Turks that austere and vaguely melancholy air which is seen among the ordinary people, and which, if you take the general population as a whole, produces an undeniably favourable impression. Indeed, to judge from appearances alone, the Turkish inhabitants of Constantinople are the most upright and civilized people in Europe. In the most solitary streets of Stamboul a visitor will always wander unmolested; he may visit the mosques, even during prayers, with much greater confidence he'll be treated with respect than a Turk could in our churches; among the crowd, no one looks at you, not even inquisitively, much less insolently; brawls are almost unknown, and noise and disturbance among the people very uncommon; there is no open prostitution or public indecency of any kind; the market is only a shade less dignified than the mosque; everywhere there is a great sobriety of words and gestures; no singing, no raucous laughter, no rowdiness, no riff-raff disturbing the public streets; faces, hands and feet all quite clean; ragged clothes are rare, and soiled ones even rarer; there is a universal and reciprocal manifestation of respect between social classes. But this is only on the surface. The rottenness lies within. The corruption is hidden by the separation of the two sexes, idleness is masked by calm, dignity conceals pride, the composed gravity of countenance – which seems to indicate thoughtfulness – is only the effect of a deadly intellectual inertia, and their apparent temperance is nothing but an absence of life in its true sense.

The nature, the philosophy, the entire existence of this people can be summed up by a particular condition of the mind and body which is called "*kef*", which represents their supreme pleasure. To have eaten sparely, to have drunk a glass of pure water, to have said your prayers, to feel the body at rest and the conscience at peace, and to be in a place from where, under the shade of a tree, a wide horizon can be contemplated, following with the eye the flight of doves from the cemetery on the hillside below, ships in the distance, insects close at hand, clouds in the sky and the smoke of the narghile, vaguely ruminating upon God, on death, on the vanity of earthly things, and the sweetness of eternal rest; this is *kef*. To be an idle spectator in the great theatre of the world: this is the Turk's highest aspiration. To this he is naturally inclined, as a result of his former condition as a shepherd, contemplative and slow, by his religion which ties his hands and leaves all things up to God, by his traditions as a soldier of Islam which teach him that there is no more important or essential act than that of fighting and conquering for his faith, and once the battle is over, every duty has been fulfilled.

All is fatality for him; man is only an instrument in the hands of Providence; it is futile for him to try and direct human affairs, which are already foreordained in heaven; earth is merely a great caravanserai; God created man to travel through the world praying and admiring His works; therefore let us leave all things to God; let that which will befall, befall, and that which is to pass, pass; let us not tire ourselves either to renew or to preserve. Thus the Turk's one supreme desire is tranquillity, and he takes care to shield himself from each and every commotion that might disturb the placid harmony of his existence. As a consequence, he has no thirst for knowledge, or fever of gain, or desire to travel, or feels the vague unappeasable passions of love and ambition. The absence of so many intellectual and physical needs which we struggle continually to satisfy, makes the Turk incapable of understanding why we exert ourselves. He regards it as a morbid aberration of mind in us since for him the ultimate aim of every effort is the attainment of that tranquillity which he seeks as the highest good. He therefore thinks it wiser and more practical to reach it by the shortest and easiest route, and the intellectual and manual labour of the European races are to him only childish exertions, because he does not see how they would help him to increase his ideal happiness. Since he doesn't work, he has no sense of the value of time, and so he neither desires nor attaches any importance to all those inventions of human genius which tend to accelerate the pace of life and human progress. He is capable of asking what the use of a railway is if it doesn't take you to a city where you can be happier than you are in the one you're leaving behind. His fatalism, which regards taking thought for the future as futile, makes him prize nothing which does not contribute to his immediate enjoyment. Thus, the European, who anticipates and plans, who lays the foundations of a building the completion of which he will not live to see, consuming his strength and sacrificing his peace for an uncertain and remote end, is for him an idle dreamer, belonging to a frivolous, mean-spirited, presumptuous and disinherited race, whose only achievement is an overweening science of material matters, which the Turk regards with utter disdain so long as he does not feel obliged to draw some advantage from it in order not to remain the underdog. And he despises us. This seems to me to be the dominant sentiment which we Europeans inspire in genuine Turks, who still constitute the majority of the nation. Perhaps it is difficult for my readers to believe this, but no one who has lived even a short time among them can deny its truth.

There are various reasons for this feeling of contempt, the first of which holds great importance for them: namely, that for more than four centuries, although comparatively few in number, they have ruled over a large part of Europe holding a different faith to their own, and that they remain its rulers, despite everything that has happened in the past and is happening today. Only a tiny minority of them sees that the survival of Ottoman domination depends on the mutual jealousies and discords among European states; the majority attribute it to the superiority of their strength and to our own debased condition. It never crosses the mind of any ordinary Turk that the Muslim part of Europe could ever be subjected to the affront of Christian conquest from the Dardanelles to the Danube. To our boasts of civilization they oppose the fact of their domination. Proud by nature, and fortified in their pride by the habits of imperial rule, accustomed to telling themselves, in the name of God, that they belong to a victorious race, born to fight and not to labour, indeed accustomed to living off the labour of the defeated, they cannot even begin to comprehend how a people subject to their sway can claim any right whatever to civil equality. For them, possessed of a blind faith in the evident sway of Providence, their conquests in Europe were the fulfilment of God's decree. God Himself, as a sign of His favour, has invested them with this earthly sovereignty; and the fact that they manage to preserve it, in the teeth of so many hostile forces, is an incontestable proof of their divine right and at the same time a luminous argument in favour of the truth of their religion.

Against such a feeling all arguments of civilization, legal rights and equality are futile. Civilization for them is merely a hostile force that seeks to disarm them without fighting, by stealth, little by little, in order to bring them down to the level of their subjects and despoil them of their rule. Thus they not only despise European civilization as vacuous, they fear it as hostile; and since they may not subdue it by force, they oppose it with the intractable resistance of their inertia. They realize that to transform themselves, to become civilized, to equal their subjects' attainments would mean entering into competition with those who think and labour and study. The idea of acquiring a new form of superiority, of forging afresh through intellectual effort the conquest they have accomplished with the sword is opposed not only by their material interests as rulers, but also by their religious disdain for the infidel, their military pride, their by now ingrained indolence, the very nature of their character which never initiates but prefers to slumber in the immobility of those five traditional ideas which form the entire intellectual patrimony of the nation. And on the other hand they do not find any incentive to undertake such a transformation in the example set by their fellow Turks who belong to the social class which, so they believe, accepts European civilization and represents the condition to which Europe would like to see all the sons of Osman reduced – their fellow citizens who wear overcoats and gloves, who stammer a little French and who refuse to go to the mosque. How does this part of the Ottoman nation represent European civilization? On this most of us can agree: the new Turk is not worth the old Turk. He has adopted our clothes, our comforts, our vices and vanities, but he has not – not yet at least – assimilated either our sentiments or our ideas; rather he has lost, in this partial transformation, what was good in his authentically Ottoman nature. At present, as old-fashioned Turks see it, all that the progress of Europeanization has produced is an ever-increasing plague of red tape with an interminable army of bureaucrats who are idle, inept, rapacious, brazenly hypocritical, and scornful of every national tradition, together with a corrupt and insolent *jeunesse dorée* who will turn out a lot worse than their fathers. To dress and to live after this fashion, is, according to the way of thinking of the old Turk, to be "civilized"; and he in fact describes all those actions which not only his conscience as a Muslim but all upstanding men of whatever race would condemn, as behaving, living and thinking "like a European". He considers the so-called "civilized" ones not as Muslims who are more advanced than others along the road of general progress, but as fallen, gone astray, little less than apostates and traitors to the nation. He distrusts novelty and rejects it outright, as far as he can, if only because it comes to him from that quarter where he witnesses every day its fatal effects. Each European innovation is for him an assault on his character and on his interests. The government is radical, the people are conservative; the seeds of the new ideas fall on stony ground that is incapable of fertilizing them; the hand that holds the sword grasps and shakes the hilt, but the blade merely turns in the handle.

These are the reasons why the attempts at reform which have been going on for fifty years have not yet penetrated beneath the skin of the nation. The names have changed, but the things behind them remain the same. What little has been done has been forced through and the people attribute to this the growing audacity of the infidels, the corruption that is seated at the heart of the empire, and all the misfortunes of the nation. Why change our institutions, they ask, if with these selfsame institutions we have succeeded in conquering and ruling other peoples for centuries? The whole being and way of life of the Turks, with their traditions, are those of a victorious army encamped in Europe; it exercises the authority, enjoys the privileges and conveniences, and feels the pride of such an army, and like all armies, it prefers a discipline of iron – which gives it power over the defeated – to a milder rule which would set limits to its will as a conqueror. The hope that such a state of affairs, unchanged for centuries, can be transformed in the space of a few years is a mirage. The fleet-footed vanguard of civilization may proceed as rapidly as it likes, but the bulk of the army, still weighed down with its heavy medieval armour, is either motionless or follows slowly and a long way behind. Blind despotism, the janissaries, the severed heads on the Seraglio gate, the sense of Ottoman invincibility, the belief that a Christian rayah is an inferior being, the French ambassadors clothed and fed on the threshold of the throne room to symbolize the shameful poverty of the infidel in the presence of the *Grand Signor* – it has to be remembered that all these things were still true only yesterday. But upon this argument, there is not, I think, a great disparity of opinion between the Europeans and the Turks themselves. Real differences of judgement – and hence the difficulty an outsider faces in forming an independent opinion – lie in the assessment of the Turks' inner qualities, since if you question the rayahs you will hear nothing but the diatribe of the oppressed against the oppressor, and if you appeal to the free Europeans in the colonies, who have no reason either to hate or fear the Ottomans, but on the contrary can feel contented with the actual state of affairs, you will usually obtain a possibly conscientious, but certainly excessively favourable opinion. Most agree in pronouncing the Turks to be honest, open, loyal and sincerely religious. But as far as religious sentiment is concerned, the preservation of which can be seen as highly meritorious, it should be noted that their religion does not oppose itself to any of their inclinations or interests: it can even be said to comfort their sensuality, justify their inertia, and confirm their domination. They hold to it tenaciously, for they feel that in its dogma lies their sense of nationhood, and in its faith their destiny. With regard to their probity, many individual incidents cited

EDMONDO DE AMICIS

as proofs of it could find a parallel even among the most corrupt
European peoples. But it should also be borne in mind that ostentation
plays no small part in the probity which the Turk shows in his dealings
with Christians, since he will often do out of pride what he would not
do from a simple impulse of conscience, as he is reluctant to appear in
any way less worthy than the people to whom he holds himself
superior in terms of race and moral principle. And the same reason
lies behind other qualities, all praiseworthy in the abstract, such as
straightforwardness, pride, dignity – qualities which perhaps might
not have been maintained had the Turk been the oppressed instead of
the oppressor. The Turkish sense of charity, however, the only balm for
the grievous disorders which afflict their society, cannot be denied,
although it encourages thriftlessness and leads to poverty; nor other
sentiments which belong to a certain nobility of spirit, such as the
gratitude which is felt for even the smallest favours, the respect shown
for the dead, the courtesy displayed towards guests, and the kindness
with which animals are treated. Their feeling for the equality of all
social classes is admirable; and a certain severe moderation in their
character is undeniable, which finds expression in innumerable
proverbs full of wisdom and prudence. There is a certain patriarchal
simplicity about them, an inclination for solitude and melancholy
which precludes vulgarity and existential despair. Nevertheless all
these qualities float, so to speak, on the surface of the Turkish soul, in
the undisturbed tranquillity of his day-to-day existence; while beneath
them his violent Asiatic nature lies dormant, his fanaticism, his
military bloodlust, his barbarian ferocity, which on provocation break
out and transform him into another being. There is a saying that Turks
are the mildest of men when they're not engaged in chopping other
people's heads off. The Tartar is crouched half asleep within him. His
native vigour remains unmodified, almost preserved by the very
indolence of his outward life, and only comes to his need on supreme
occasions. In the same way the courage which intelligence can
undermine – by refining one's sense of life and making human
existence even more precious because of its possibilities – remains
intact in him. Religious and warlike passions hold claim to a field
unmarred by doubts or spiritual rebellion, or by the shock of ideas; a
wholly and instantaneously inflammable substance; a man made all of
one piece who springs into action with mind and body and soul; a
blade forever sharpened, on which only the names of God and the

252

Sultan are incised. Social life has barely softened in him the ancient man of the steppe and the hut. He still lives in the city more or less as he once lived among his tribe, surrounded by people but alone... Indeed a true social life cannot be said to exist among them. The lives of men and women are like two parallel rivers, which never mingle except occasionally through underground channels. Men meet among themselves but enjoy no real intimacy, no exchange of thought; they associate but do not form ties; each prefers to any extroversion of his self what a great poet once called the "silent growth of ideas".* Our spirited and varied conversations – jesting, arguing, teaching, stimulating – our need to exchange ideas and feelings, this reciprocal outgoing of our being which refreshes the intelligence and warms the heart, are scarcely known among them. Their talk is in general confined to material and necessary matters. Love is excluded, literature is the privilege of a few, science is a myth, politics a question of personalities, business occupies only a very small part of most people's lives. The nature of their intelligence abhors abstract discussions. They understand well only that which they can see and touch – as their own language shows, for when they wish to express an abstraction, educated Turks must have recourse to Persian or Arabic, or a European language. In any case they do not feel the need to make the effort to understand things which lie beyond the circle of their desires and almost of their existence. When faced with something unfamiliar, Persians are keen to investigate and Arabs are inquisitive, but a Turk will remain supremely indifferent. He is not interested in the exchange of ideas with Europeans because he has no ideas to exchange; he takes no pleasure in them or in their endless subtle discussions. There can never be complete familiarity between Turks and Europeans, since one will always hide a part of himself: his private affections, his home life, his enjoyments, and, what is most important, his true attitude towards the other, which is an insuperable feeling of distrust. The Turk tolerates the Armenian, despises the Jew, hates the Greek and distrusts the European. On the whole he puts up with them, just as a horse or cow endures a swarm of flies on its back, only giving them a quick flick of its tail every now and then when they sting too much. He lets them all busy themselves around him; profits from Europeans when he thinks they might be useful to him, accepts material innovations for which he can see an immediate benefit, listens impassively to the sermons on civilization he is given, changes laws, customs and ceremonies, learns

to repeat word for word our philosophical opinions, allows himself to
be improved, embellished and made to wear a mask; but within he
remains – immutably, invincibly – the same. Yet reason finds it hard to
accept the idea that the gradual and persistent advance of civilization
will not one day ignite a new spark in this Asiatic giant stretched out
asleep across two continents, this soldier who only rouses himself to
wield his sword. However, when you think of the efforts which have
been made so far and the paucity of the results which have been
obtained, such a day still seems far off, too far off to meet the urgent
needs of the Christian populations in the East. Any hope that the
Eastern question which preoccupies the European powers today can
be resolved by a progressive westernization of the Turkish people is
quite unfounded. This is the conclusion I came to during my brief stay
in Constantinople. It will be asked: how else can the issue be resolved?
But here I can quite properly decline to give an answer since it would
look as if I were advising Europe what to do and that is something my
sense of modesty strictly forbids. Besides… haven't I already mentioned
there's an Austrian steamer waiting on the Golden Horn opposite
Galata ready to set off in the direction of the Black Sea? My reader
can easily guess what route it's going to take on the journey home!

## The Bosphorus

We had hardly gone on board our vessel when a screen, painted with
the mountains of Moravia and Hungary, and the Alps of lower Austria,
seemed to descend over Constantinople. The scene always seems to
change rapidly when you embark on a boat full of the faces and accents
of the country for which it's bound. We are imprisoned in a circle of
German faces which fill us with a sense of the cold and tedium of the
North long before we actually arrive there. Our friendly rowers have
left us; we can only see three white handkerchiefs waving from a distant
caique among a throng of black boats in front of the custom house.
We are at the very same point where our Sicilian steamer docked on
the day of our arrival. It is a lovely autumn evening, warm and bright.
Constantinople has never looked grander or lovelier. For the last time
we strive to fix in our memories the immensity of her outline against
the sky and her soft enchanting colours, like some city in a fairy tale,
and once more we gaze down the wondrous Golden Horn, which in

Praying dervishes

The Golden Horn

A caique

a moment will be hidden from us for ever. The white handkerchiefs have disappeared. The vessel moves, and everything changes place. Scutari advances, Stamboul retreats, Galata wheels round as if to see us depart. Goodbye to the Golden Horn! A sudden movement of the ship snatches away the district of Kasımpaşa, and another Eyüp, and another the sixth hill of Stamboul; the fifth disappears, the fourth hides away, the third vanishes, the second is gone; only the hill of the Seraglio remains, and, thank heaven, we shall not lose that for a while. We are steaming rapidly down the very middle of the Bosphorus. We pass the neighbourhoods of Tophane and Fındıklı; the white sculpted façade of the Dolmabahçe palace flies past; and for the last time Scutari unfurls her amphitheatre of hills, brimming with gardens and villas. Goodbye Constantinople! Great and beloved city, which I dreamed of as a child and longed for as a youth, and is now an indelible memory for the rest of my life! Goodbye lovely and immortal queen of the East! May your beauty remain undiminished despite the passage of time and may my children one day see you with the same fervour of youthful enthusiasm with which I saw you and now take leave of you!

The sadness of farewell, however, lasts only for a moment, because another Constantinople, ampler and livelier and more beautiful than the city we are leaving behind now stretches before us along the two loveliest shores in the world.

The first village on the left, or European shore of the Bosphorus is Beşiktaş, a large Turkish village – or rather suburb – of Constantinople, set around a small harbour at the foot of a hill. Behind it there is a pretty valley, the ancient valley of Stephen's laurels, the Valley of Constantinople, which climbs towards Pera; among the houses there is a group of plane trees which cast a shade over the tomb of the famous corsair Barbarossa; a large café, packed with people, juts out over the water on numerous wooden piles; the harbour is full of boats and caiques; the quay thronged with people, the hill covered with trees, and the valley full of houses and gardens. But the place no longer looks like a typical suburb of Constantinople. Things are smaller, the foliage is thicker, the colours more gaudy. It's like a nestful of cottages, fit for lovers and poets, placed there on a whim between sea and land, on a beautiful summer night, soon to be dismantled. There is already the air of gaiety and gracefulness which characterizes the villages along the Bosphorus. We have scarcely looked at it when it has already gone by, and we are passing the Çırağan Palace, or rather a row of palaces built of white marble, simple and magnificent, with long rows of columns, crowned with parapets, along which, like a living crenellation, innumerable flocks of white birds from the Bosphorus perch in bold relief against the vivid green of the hills behind. But now a pleasant torment begins of seeing a hundred beautiful sights slip by as you fix your admiring attention on a single one. While we contemplate Çırağan and Beşiktaş, the Asian shore on the other side is speeding by unseen, with exquisite villages, pretty enough to buy and put in your pocket like jewels. Thus Kuzguncuk goes by, tinted like an iris flower, with its little harbour, where tradition says Io as a heifer landed after swimming across the Bosphorus to escape Juno's gadflies,* and Istavros with its beautiful mosque and two minarets; the Imperial Palace of Beylerbeyi appears and disappears, with its conical and pyramid-shaped roofs, and its grey and yellow walls, looking strange and mysterious, like a convent for princesses; and then the village of Beylerbeyi, reflected in the water, with Mount Bulgurlu rising behind it; and all these villages – clustered or scattered at the foot of small green hills and immersed in lush vegetation – are connected together by strings of villas and small houses, and long lines of trees running along the shore or in zigzags down the hill-slopes to the sea, through a patchwork of terraced gardens and orchards and meadows in infinite shades of green.

So there is nothing for it but to resign ourselves to seeing everything as it moves, turning our heads continually to right and left with clockwork regularity. A little beyond Çırağan the large village of Ortaköy is seen on the left, on the European side, above which can be seen the gleaming dome of the Mosque of the Sultana Valide, the mother of Abdülaziz, while the elegant roofs of the palace of Rızapaşa can be made out at the bottom of a hill, the summit of which is crowned with the white walls of the imperial kiosk known as "the star". Ortaköy is where many Armenian, European and Greek bankers have their homes. As we passed, the steamboat from Constantinople was just mooring: a crowd of passengers was disembarking while another throng stood upon the quay waiting to get on. There were Turkish and European ladies, officers, monks, eunuchs, dandies, fezzes, turbans, caps, top hats, all mixed together, in a display that can be seen at all the twenty landing stages along the Bosphorus, especially towards evening. Opposite Ortaköy, on the Asian shore, stands the village of Çengel, which means anchor, from an old iron anchor discovered there by Mehmet II; behind the village there is the notorious white kiosk, where Murat IV looked out on cheerful passers-by singing to themselves as they wandered through the fields and in his savage envy had them put to death. Turning again towards Europe, we find ourselves looking at the pretty village and graceful harbour of Kuruçeşme, the ancient Anaplos, where Medea disembarked with Jason and planted the famous laurel; and, turning back again towards Asia, we find the two pleasant villages of Kuleli and Vaniköy, on either side of a vast barracks looking like a royal palace, mirrored in the water. Behind the two villages is a hill, on the top of which there is a large garden where there is a white kiosk, almost hidden by trees, in which Süleyman the Great lived in hiding for three years in a small tower, to protect him from his father Selim's spies and executioners. While we're trying to make out the tower among the trees the ship passes in front of Arnavutköy, the village of the Albanians, which is now inhabited by Greeks, in the form of a crescent round a small bay. But it is impossible to see them all: one village replaces another, a fine mosque distracts us from a beautiful landscape, and, while we gaze at the villages and the harbours, the palaces of viziers, pashas, sultans, chief eunuchs, great dignitaries glide past. Looking as if they're floating on the water, there are houses painted yellow or blue or purple, covered in ivy and liana, with flower-filled terraces, half hidden among groves of cypress, laurel and orange trees. We pass buildings with Corinthian porticoes and marble columns, Swiss chalets, tiny Japanese-style houses and Moorish villas, Turkish kiosks with three floors projecting one above the other, with steps and gardens leading down to the water's edge, and the latticed balconies of the harems suspended above the current; all of them small short-lived constructions built to mark their owner's good fortune: a young beauty's celebrity, some intrigue which has ended successfully, a promotion to high office which will be lost tomorrow, glory which will end in exile, wealth which will all be squandered, greatness waiting for its inevitable fall. There is hardly a stretch of the two shores not covered by houses. It is like the Grand Canal of some vast rural Venice. Villas, kiosks, palaces rise up one behind the other, with all their façades visible, looking as if the building above rests upon the roof of the one below, while around and stretching far above them oaks, sycamores, poplars, pines, plane trees and fig trees sway in the breeze, and white fountains and the small domes of mausoleums and solitary mosques can be glimpsed.

Looking back towards Constantinople, we can still just make out the Seraglio hill and the huge dome of Hagia Sophia silhouetted against the clear golden sky. Arnavutköy, Vaniköy, Kuleli, Çengel and Ortaköy have vanished and there's a completely new scene. We seem to be in a very large lake. A small bay opens to the right on the Asian shore, another to the left. On the European side the pretty Greek town of Bebek lies in a semicircle under the shadow of large trees, with a fine ancient mosque and the imperial kiosk of Hümayun Habat where the Sultans held secret audiences with European ambassadors. Part of the town is quite hidden by trees in a small valley; the rest is scattered over an oak-covered hillside, on the top of which is a grove celebrated for its resonant echo which answers the beat of a single horse's hoof with the noise of an entire cavalry squadron. It is a sweet and amiable landscape, but on turning back to the Asian shore it is immediately eclipsed: here is a terrestrial paradise. On a broad promontory curving out into the sea stands the village of Kandilli, as gaily painted as a Dutch village, with a white mosque and a cluster of cottages gathered round it. Behind it there is the hill of Icadiye, with a crenellated tower on the summit from where watch is kept for fires along the shore. To the right of Kandilli the two valleys of the so-called great and small "celestial streams" open to the sea; in the short distance between them stretch the beautiful meadows of the Sweet Waters of Asia, full of sycamores, oaks and plane trees, the main feature of which is the splendid kiosk which belongs to Abdülmecit's mother, designed like a smaller version of Dolmabahçe, surrounded by rose gardens. Beyond the larger of the "celestial streams" there is the village of Anadoluhisar and then on a hill the slender towers of the castle of *Yıldırım** Beyazit, facing the castle of Mehmet II on the opposite shore. The whole of this beautiful stretch of the Bosphorus was at that time of day full of life and colour. Hundreds of boats were leaving the European shore; sailing vessels and steamers were passing on their way to Bebek; Turkish fishermen were casting their nets, from a kind of large airy cage supported in the water on tall interlinked wooden beams; from the ferry on the European side Greek ladies, Lazarists, students from the American Protestant college, and numerous large families carrying packets and bundles of clothes were disembarking, while on the other shore you could see through binoculars groups of Muslim women strolling under the trees of the Sweet Waters of Asia or seated in groups on the banks of the stream. Caiques and boats with awnings, full of Turks, jostled each other along the shore. It looked as if a festival were in progress and had an air of Arcadia, that made me want to dive overboard, swim to the shore, plant myself right in the middle of them and declare: "Come what may, I never want to leave. I shall live and die here in this Muslim paradise."

But again the spectacle changes and all these fancies take flight. The Bosphorus now extends straight before us and has a vague resemblance to the Rhine, but with the rich warm colouring of the East. To the left a cemetery in the shade of a forest of pines and cypresses breaks the line of houses until then unbroken, and on the slopes of the small rocky hill of Hermaion rise the three great towers of Rumeli Hisar, the Castle of Europe, ringed by the remains of battlemented walls and smaller towers, descending in picturesque ruin to the waterside. This is the famous fortress built by Mehmet II in the year before the conquest of Constantinople, in spite of the remonstrances of Constantine, whose ambassadors were driven back with threats of death. Here the current is at its fiercest – called by the Greeks "the great current," and "Satan's current" by the Turks – and it is also the narrowest stretch of the Bosphorus, with the two shores no more than five hundred metres apart. It was here that Mandrocles of Samos constructed his bridge of boats, over which passed the seven hundred thousand soldiers of Darius, and here too the Ten Thousand returning from Asia are said to have crossed the Bosphorus.* But no trace is left either of the two columns of Mandrocles, or of the throne cut in the rock from which the Persian king watched the passage of his army. An idyllic little Turkish village perches secretively at the foot of the castle, and the Asian shore stretches away, ever greener and livelier, in a constant procession of cottages belonging to boatmen and gardeners, small lush valleys, deserted little inlets shaded by the trees on the shore, by the side of which white-sailed fishing boats drift slowly past. There are flowery meadows sloping gently down to the water's edge; small garden rockeries covered in ivy; tiny cemeteries glimpsed at the top of steep hills. Suddenly the lovely village of Kanlıca emerges on the Asian shore, on two rocky promontories against which the waves beat noisily. We can see the minarets of the local mosque above the cypresses and umbrella pines. Then the land begins to climb again: the gardens are terraced like belvederes and the villas become more frequent. Among them you can see the enchanting palace which belonged to Fuad Pasha, the vain, pleasure-loving and kind-hearted diplomat and poet who was known as the Ottoman Lamartine.* A little further on, on the European side, there appears the pleasant village of Baltalimanı, at the entrance to a small valley, in the middle of which a stream runs down to the harbour, and overlooked by a hill covered with villas including the old palace of Reşitpaşa. Then comes the little bay of Emir Günoğlu Bahçe, green with cypress trees, in the middle of which there is a solitary mosque at the water's edge, with a large golden globe as a pinnacle on the dome representing the sun and its rays. The steamer approaches now one and now the other shore, and as it does, a thousand details of the grand landscape come into view: here the vestibule of the selamlik of some rich Turk's house, overlooking the sea, in which a stout major-domo is smoking, stretched at ease on a divan; there a eunuch is assisting two veiled ladies to step into their caique from the marble steps of a villa; further on, a small garden surrounded by hedges and almost entirely covered by the branches of a single plane tree, at the foot of which an old white-bearded Turk sits cross-legged, meditating upon the Koran; families of holidaymakers gathered on their terraces; flocks of sheep and goats grazing in the meadows above; horsemen galloping along the shore and trains of camels passing over the hills, with their strange shapes silhouetted against the sky.

Suddenly the Bosphorus widens, the scene changes, we are again in a vast lake between two bays. To the left round a narrow deep bay lies the Greek town of Istenia, called Sosthenium from the temple and winged statue which the Argonauts built there in honour of the tutelary genius who had given them victory in their struggle against Amycus, king of Bebryces. The steamer turns its course slightly in the direction of the European shore and so we can see quite clearly the cafés and little houses along the quay, the small villas among the olive trees and vines, the valley behind the harbour, the waterfall and the famous Moorish white marble fountain in a circle of great sycamore trees, with fishing nets hung on the branches, and Greek women coming and going carrying jugs to fill. Opposite Istenia on the Asian side, the Turkish village of Çubuklu emerges among the trees. Here was once the famous monastery of the Sleepless Monks, who prayed and chanted continually night and day. From one sea to the other the shores of the Bosphorus are full of the memories of these fanatical coenobites and anchorites of the fifth century, who wandered about the hills, stooping under the weight of chains and crosses, tormented by hair shirts and iron collars, or sitting for weeks and months motionless on the tops of columns or trees, while all around them princes and soldiers, judges and shepherds came to kneel and fast and pray and beat their breasts in the hope of receiving a blessing or counsel, as a favour from God. Yet the Bosphorus has a peculiar effect on travellers who visit its shores for the first time: it always manages to turn their thoughts away from the past. All the memories and all the images of those places made famous by history or legend, however grand or beautiful or sad, are overcome, as if submerged, by the sight alone of the extraordinary lushness of vegetation, the dazzlingly vivid colours, the bold, exuberant and youthful presence of a benign and festive natural world. It is hard to believe that in these waters, in the midst of all this enchanted beauty, the ships of Bulgars, Goths, Herulians, Byzantines, Russians and Turks clashed and fought and shed their soldiers' blood. Even the castles on top of the hills do not arouse the poetic shiver of foreboding which comparable ruins do in other places; they seem more like architectural follies to adorn the landscape than real defensive constructions, under the walls of which men were killed. Languor and gentleness hold sway, lulling the mind with tranquil thoughts and a yearning for repose.

Beyond Istena the Bosphorus widens again and after a few minutes the steamer arrives where the most spectacular view we have seen so far can be enjoyed. Turning back towards Europe, we see in front of us the little Greek and Armenian village of Yeniköy on the slopes of a high hill covered with vine groves and pine woods and curving out over a rocky shoreline against which the strong current breaks into powerful waves. A little further on there is the beautiful bay of Kalender, full of rowing boats, little holiday houses surrounded by green foliage, and, up above, the airy terraces of some imperial kiosk. Turning again, the bend of the Asian shore now presents a marvellous amphitheatre of hills and villages and harbours. This is Incirköy, the village of fig trees, full of orchards. Next to it, there is Sultaniye, nestling in a wood, and after Sultaniye, the large village of Beykoz, surrounded by orchards and vineyards under the shade of great walnut trees, reflected in the most beautiful inlet on the Bosphorus, where Pollux vanquished the king of Bebryces, and where the miraculous laurel tree grew which made all those who touched its leaves mad. In the distance beyond Beykoz, there is the village of Yalı, the ancient Amea, which has the appearance of a heap of red and yellow flowers on a large green carpet. But all this is merely an attempt to sketch the grand canvas we see. Only imagination can capture the slopes of the hills which are so gentle one would like to reach out and stroke them; the innumerable little villages which seem to have been placed there by a painter's hand; the trees and plants from every clime, the buildings in the style of every country, the terraced gardens, the waterfalls and shadows and glinting mosques, the blue water dotted with white sails, the sky rose-pink with the setting sun.

Yet once we had arrived there I felt, as almost everyone feels, sated with the Bosphorus. The procession of gentle slopes and bright colours at last grows wearying; the prettiness and gracefulness become monotonous and lull the mind to sleep. One wants to see some huge misshapen rock suddenly breaking the shoreline or a gloomy deserted stretch of beach scattered with the remains of some shipwreck. But when such a mood comes all one can do for distraction is to look at the waters of the Bosphorus itself. It is like one long port: you pass by splendid battleships from the Ottoman fleet, merchant vessels from every nation, with different-coloured flags and curiously carved sterns from which strange-looking people look down on you. There are old-fashioned vessels from the Asian ports on the Black Sea and small elegant corvettes belonging to ambassadors; yachts belonging to the wealthy race each other watched by lines of spectators from the land; at the hundreds of small landing stages along both shores there is a continual traffic of boats of every kind, full of people of every race, embarking and disembarking. Caiques being towed along dart through long lines of goods barges, while launches hung with pennants weave across the paths of fishermen's rafts, pashas' gilded caiques, and the ferries from Constantinople, their decks crowded with turbans and fezzes and veils, which zigzag their way up and down the channel to the landing stages on either side. And since our own steamer is busy weaving in and out it seems as if the whole spectacle is revolving around us: the promontories shift, the hills suddenly change shape, villages disappear and then reappear looking quite different, while ahead of us and behind, the Bosphorus itself changes, sometimes closed off like a single vast lake, sometimes opening on to a distant view of further lakes and hills. Suddenly the hills around join in a circle and you seem to be in some enclosed basin with no obvious way out. No sooner have you remarked on this to the person standing next to you than the ship moves on and new hills and towns and harbours come into view.

We are between the bay of Therapia – the ancient Pharmacia, where Medea gathered her poisons – and the bay of Hünkâr Iskelesi, the Sultans' harbour, where the famous treaty which closed the Dardanelles to foreign vessels was signed in 1833. Here the Bosphorus almost but not quite attains the zenith of its beauty, for Therapia is the loveliest village on its shore after Büyükdere, and the valley which opens behind the bay of Hünkâr Iskelesi is the greenest, most captivatingly and hauntingly beautiful valley between the Sea of Marmara and the Black Sea. Therapia stands partly along a straight stretch of the shore at the foot of a large hill and partly round a deep bay which serves as the harbour and is always full of ships and boats. Behind the harbour there is the valley of Krio Nero, where another part of the village nestles among the trees. The shore is lined with picturesque cafés with terraces built out into the water, grand hotels and splendid residences, groves of tall trees which lend shade to little squares and fountains. Behind these there are the summer residences of the French and British and Italian ambassadors and further up the hill an imperial kiosk. All around and extending up the hillside there are terraces and gardens and villas and woods. People dressed in bright colours sit in the cafés and round the harbour, stroll along the shore or the paths leading up the hill, as if on some public holiday. On the Asian side, in contrast, everything is still. The little village of Hünkâr Iskelesi, much frequented as a resort by wealthy Armenians from the city, sleeps under the cypresses and plane trees round its small harbour crossed by a few discreet rowing boats. Towering beyond and above the village at the top of a steep terraced hillside is the lonely yet magnificent Kiosk of Abdülaziz, hidden behind which there is the Sultans' favourite valley, indescribably lush with tropical vegetation, a place of mystery and dreams.

But all this beauty is as nothing a mile further on when we arrive in sight of the bay of Büyükdere. This is the crowning splendour and beauty of the Bosphorus. Whoever has wearied of its loveliness and spoken dismissively of it will now uncover his head and ask for pardon. We are in the middle of a huge lake surrounded with marvels that make one want to spin round like a dervish on the prow of the ship in order to see all the shores and all the hills at once. On the European side, round a deep bay where the fierce current breaks into gentle waves, upon the slopes of a hill dotted with innumerable villas, lies the town of Büyükdere, vast and varied in colour like an immense parterre. The town extends to the right as far as a small inlet, like a bay within the bay; around this is the village of Kefeliköy. Behind this a wide valley opens, green with meadows and white with houses, which leads to the great Aqueduct of Mahmut and to the Belgrad Forest. It is the same valley where, according to tradition, the army of the first Crusade set up camp in 1096, and one of the seven gigantic plane trees for which the place is famous is called the tree of Godfrey of Bouillon.*

Beyond Kefeliköy there is another bay and beyond that you can still make out Therapia, lying at the foot of its dark green hill. When your eyes turn back towards Asia, a feeling of amazement comes over you. There facing you is the highest hill along the Bosphorus, the "Giant", in the form of an enormous green pyramid, where there is the tomb famous in three legends as the "bed of Hercules", the "tomb of Amycus", and the "grave of Joshua, Judge of the Hebrews". It is now guarded by two dervishes, and is visited by the sick who leave scraps of their clothing upon it. The mountain pushes its green and flowery slopes down to the very shore, where between two promontories there is the lovely bay of Umuryeri, with the gaily coloured houses of a Muslim village dotting the shore like flower petals tossed at random. Directly ahead the Black Sea glitters, and if we turn towards Constantinople, we can still make out, beyond Therapia, in the dim purple distance, the bay of Kalender, Kaniköy, Incirköy, Sultaniye, unreal, like imaginary views of some remote world. The sun is setting; bluish-grey shadows begin to veil the European shore; on the other side the shore of Asia is still golden; the surface of the water gleams; swarms of boats carrying husbands and sweethearts back from Constantinople approach the European side, crossing and threading their way among other boats filled with women and children from the villas; from the cafés of Büyükdere come intermittent sounds of musical instruments and singing; eagles circle over the Mountain of the Giant, halcyons skim the water, dolphins dart about our vessel, the fresh breeze from the Black Sea cools our cheeks. Where are we? Where are we headed? In a moment of intoxication and illusion, everything we've seen in the past two hours along the Bosphorus expands into the vision of one enormous city, ten times the size of Constantinople, inhabited by people from all over the world, bestowed with all the beauty God can give, its streets filled with perpetual festival – the sight leaves us melancholy and envious.

* * *

But this is the last vision. The ship steams rapidly away from the bay of Büyükdere. We see on the left the village of Sarıyer surrounded by cemeteries, with a small bay in front, formed by the ancient promontory of Simas, where the temple of Venus Meretrix once stood, a place of particular worship for Greek sailors; then the village of Yenimahalle; then the fort of Telli Tabya, opposite another small fort on the Asian side, at the foot of the Mountain of the Giant; then the castle of Rumeli Kavaği, the severe outline of its walls silhouetted against the last gleams of twilight. Opposite this is another fortress, crowning the promontory, where the temple of the twelve gods once stood, built by the Argive Phryxus, near that of Jove, "distributor of propitious winds", established by the Chalcedonians, and converted by Justinian into a church consecrated to the Archangel Michael. This is the point where the Bosphorus narrows for the last time, between the foothills of the mountains of Bithynia and the very end of the Haemus range: this was always considered to be the main entrance to the channel, to be defended against northern invasion, and the theatre, therefore, of bitter struggles between Byzantines and barbarians, Venetians and Genoese. Two ruined Genoese fortresses facing one another, between which an iron chain was thrown to close off the entrance, can still be seen.

From this point the Bosphorus widens to the sea; the shores are high and steep, like two enormous bastions, on which only a few groups of mean-looking houses, a solitary tower, the ruins of a monastery, or the remains of some ancient jetties and breakwaters can be seen. For a long time we can still see the lights of the village of Büyükliman twinkling on the European side, while on the other there is the lantern of a fortress which overlooks the promontory called "the Elephant'; then, on the left, the great rocky mass of ancient Gypopolis, where the palace of Phineus once stood, infested by the Harpies; and on the right the fortress of Cape Poyraz, like a dark stain upon the greyish sky. Here the shores are far apart and the channel has already become a gulf; night falls, the sea wind moans through the ship's rigging, and the pale shifting horizon of the gloomy Mare Cimmerium stretches endlessly before us. But the imagination cannot yet detach itself from those shores so full of poetry and history vying with natural beauty; it flies to the foot of the Balkans to seek out the tower of the exiled Ovid, and the marvellous wall of Anastasius, and on the right, towards Asia, wanders off over a vast volcanic land, across forests where wild boars and jackals roam, inhabited by a primitive and unfamiliar race whose bizarre shadows we seem to see watching us from the high shoreline, wishing us an unlucky voyage along the "*fera litora Ponti*".* Two fiery points like the eyes of two Cyclopes set to guard the enchanted straits break the darkness for the last time; the Anadolu Feneri, or Asian lighthouse on one side, the Rumeli Feneri, or European lighthouse on the other, below which we can dimly make out in the shadows of the shoreline the jagged outlines of the rocks of the fabled Symplegades.* Then the two coasts are only two dark lines, and then, "*quocumque adspicio, nihil est nisi pontus et aer*",* as poor Ovid sang. But I can still see her, my Constantinople, behind those black shores, larger and more luminous than she ever appeared from the Sultana Valide bridge or from the heights of Scutari. I speak to her and greet her and pay homage to her, for she is the last and most precious vision of my youth now drawing to its end. But a sudden splash of salt water drenches my face and knocks my hat off. I wake up and look round: the prow of the steamer is empty, the sky is misty, a bitter autumn wind chills me to the bone, my good friend Junck is feeling seasick and has gone below. I can hear only the rattling of the ship's lamps and its creaking as it moves along, buffeted by the waves, into the dark night.

My beautiful dream of the Orient is over.

## Note on the Illustrations

The illustrations contained in this volume are a selection from the nearly two hundred images created by Cesare Biseo (1843–1909), an artist well-known for specializing in oriental subjects, for the first illustrated edition of *Costantinopoli* in 1882. On his trip, De Amicis had actually been accompanied by the young painter Enrico Junck (1849–78), to whom there are frequent references in the text, but Junck fell ill and died from tuberculosis after their return, presumably before he had time to work on the illustrations for the volume. After the book had come out, in a text-only version, the publisher Treves sent Biseo, who had already worked with De Amicis on an earlier travel book on Morocco, to the city to prepare the illustrated edition. Biseo has followed De Amicis's text closely but not slavishly, succeeding in creating a parallel evocation of the city which reflects the relationship between writer and artist during the visit itself.

## Notes

p. 1, *Amigos... Egipto*: "Friends, here is my final travel book; from now on I will only listen to the inspirations of the heart" (Spanish). Neither the author nor the work could be identified: they may be De Amicis's invention.

p. 3, *my friend Junck*: The painter Enrico Junck (1849–78) travelled with De Amicis to Constantinople in 1874.

p. 4, *Pertusier... such a high opinion*: Charles Pertusier was an aide-de-camp to the French ambassador of Constantinople and published *Picturesque Promenades in and near Constantinople, and on the Waters of the Bosphorus* in three volumes from 1815 to 1817. Joseph Pitton de Tournefort (1656–1708) was a famous French botanist who visited Constantinople some time between 1700 and 1702. François-Charles-Hugues-Laurent Pouqueville (1770–1838) was a French doctor who was captured by Turkish pirates and published an account of his travels in 1805. The Vicomte de Marcellus was a French diplomat who made an official trip to Constantinople to acquire the Venus de Milo in 1820 and later published his memoirs, *Souvenirs de l'Orient*. Sieur de La Croix (*d*.1704) published a survey of the churches and peoples of Turkey in 1695. Alphonse de Lamartine

(1790–1869) travelled to Constantinople in 1832 and published his *Voyage en Orient* in 1835. Théophile Gautier (1811–72) published *Constantinople* in 1853, the year after his trip to the city. François-René de Chateaubriand (1768–1848) travelled to Constantinople in 1806 and there is a section devoted to the city in *Itinéraire de Paris à Jérusalem* (1811). Lady Mary Wortley Montagu (1689–1762) lived in Constantinople from 1716 to 1718. Her letters, first published in 1763, contained vivid and witty accounts of the city.

p. 5, *Zavegorod*: This is possibly a corruption or mishearing of *Tsaregorod*, an Old Russian name for the city.

p. 6, *Umm al-Dunia... upon the sea*: De Amicis's references are misleading: *Umm al-Dunia* ("Mother of the World") usually refers to Egypt, not Constantinople, and the description of the city he quotes is not from the Koran.

p. 6, *Mehmet II... Adrianople*: In Chapter 68 of Edward Gibbon's (1737–94) *History of the Decline and Fall of the Roman Empire* (1776), Mehmet II describes to his vizier how the prospect of conquering Constantinople has kept him awake all night. Adrianople (modern-day Edirne) was the capital of the Ottoman Empire from 1365 to the conquest of Constantinople in 1453.

p. 11, *Chalcedon... Megarians*: Chalcedon may actually have been founded in 676 BC by the Megarians – i.e. settlers from the Greek city of Megara.

p. 14, *Wonderful, quite wonderful*: In English in the original.

p. 18, *faldetta*: A type of hood typically worn by Maltese women.

p. 20, *Hottentot Venus*: The Hottentot Venus was the famous stage name of Saartjie Baartman (1789–1815), a South African woman who, because of her prominent buttocks, was exhibited as a sideshow attraction in France and England.

p. 21, *Candia... The Pomak*: Candia is the ancient name for the city of Iráklion, Crete. The Druze are a small middle-eastern religious community in Lebanon, Israel, Syria, Turkey and Jordan. The Pomak, a Muslim group speaking a Bulgarian dialect, are concentrated along the border with Bulgaria.

p. 23, *Madame de Staël... pleasures*: From Chapter 2 of *Corinne, or Italy* (1807) by Madame de Staël (1766–1817).

p. 27, *Sublime Porte*: The term "Sublime Porte" – a French translation from the Turkish "*bâbiâli*" – also refers to the Ottoman court and government in general.

p. 28, *janissaries*: The janissaries were an elite army corps of the Ottoman Empire, originally consisting of former Christian prisoners and founded in the late fourteenth century. They were massacred in 1826 under the orders of Sultan Mahmut II, as they were becoming too powerful and resisting the modernization of the Ottoman army.

p. 28, *the descendants... took place*: The Comneni and Paleologi were important Byzantine dynasties. On 22nd April 1821, Mahmut II had the Patriarch Gregorios V and three other bishops executed in order to try to quell Greek rebellion across the empire.

p. 28, *Constantine Porphyrogenitus*: Constantine VII Porphyrogenitus ("purple-born") was the Byzantine emperor from 913 to 959.

p. 29, *Abdülaziz*: Abdülaziz (1830–76) was the reigning Sultan of Turkey when De Amicis visited the country in 1874.

p. 30, *the eighth gift of the Holy Spirit*: There are only seven gifts of the Holy Spirit: De Amicis jokingly refers here to the man's talents as a womanizer.

p. 31, *Je suis... l'aventure*: "I am adventure's child" (French).

p. 31, *Neue Freie Presse*: The *Neue Freie Presse* was an important independent liberal Viennese newspaper from 1864 to 1938.

p. 32, *Je suis... enfant*: "I am happy to see you happy, my dear child" (French).

p. 32, *talika*: A type of light carriage, usually decorated and colourful.

p. 32, *Karagöz*: Karagöz (literally meaning "black eye") is both the name of a famous traditional shadow-puppet play and its popular protagonist, known for his streetwise wit and irreverent antics.

p. 33, *Maison Dorée*: A fashionable nineteenth-century Parisian restaurant in the ninth *arrondissement*.

p. 33, *Bursa*: Bursa was the capital of the Ottoman Empire before the conquest of Constantinople in 1453.

p. 35, *The Turkish porter shouted... Watch out*: *Sakın ha* actually means "don't you dare" in Turkish – De Amicis has probably confused it with *Savulun*, which does mean "clear the way". *Var mi su* means "do you have any water" in Turkish. *Krio nero* means "cold water" in Greek; *burada* is Turkish for "here"; *neologos* may be a malapropism for "newspapers".

p. 36, *West End*: In English in the original, referring to the West End of London.

p. 37, *La Dame aux camélias... ma femme*: *La Dame aux camélias* was written by Alexandre Dumas *fils* (1824–95) in 1852; *Madame Bovary* by Gustave Flaubert (1821–80) in 1857; *Mademoiselle Giraud ma femme* (*My wife, Miss Giraud*) by Adolphe Bolet (1829–90) in 1870.

p. 47, *Aida*: Famous 1871 opera by Giuseppe Verdi (1829–90).

p. 50, *Ventre de Paris*: Émile Zola (1840–1902) published *Le Ventre de Paris* (*The Belly of Paris*) in 1874.

p. 50, *Lüfer... kingfishers*: *Lüfer* and *istavrit* mean bluefish and horse-mackerel respectively. *Falianos*, or *fokena*, is a small species of dolphin which is now rare and used to flourish in the Aegean Sea.

p. 55, *the fires... silver pipes*: De Amicis here is adapting a quotation from the Koran, *al-Tawba* 34–35.

p. 56, *Golconda... as it appeared*: Golconda was an ancient south-central Indian city, famous for its diamonds; Hormoz is an island off the coast of Iran; Jamshid – or Takht-e Jamshid in full – is the Persian name for the ancient city of Persepolis, former capital of the Achaemenian kings of Iran.

p. 56, *Croesus*: Croesus was the last king of Lydia, an ancient country in present-day north-west Turkey, from circa 560 to 546 BC, and was famous for his vast fortune.

p. 56, *Ophir*: Unidentified region which is mentioned in the Old Testament and is renowned for its gold.

p. 56, *tesbih*: Rosary beads.

p. 59, *Tamerlane*: Tamerlane, or Timur (336–405), was a Turkic warrior who brutally conquered vast territories ranging from India to Russia and the Mediterranean. His dynasty was also remembered for its cultural achievements.

p. 60, *Georgiana*: Possibly a reference to Georgiana Spencer, fifth Duchess of Devonshire (1757–1806), who was renowned for her beauty.

p. 61, *Skanderbeg*: Skanderbeg (a corruption of Iskander Beg) is another name for George Kastrioti (1405–68), an Albanian military leader and national hero who fought off several Turkish invasions and notably killed Firuz Pasha in a duel.

p. 69, *Brancovan*: Constantine Brancovan (1652–1714) was prince of Wallachia. He formed an alliance with Russia against his sovereign Sultan Ahmet III, and was therefore accused of treason and beheaded, along with his brothers, in 1714.

p. 70, *Bouillon's soldiers*: Godfrey of Bouillon (*c.*1058–1100), the Duke of Lower Lorraine, was a famous crusader who took part in the siege of Nicaea (in Asia Minor) in 1097 and became ruler of Jerusalem after playing a prominent role in the city's conquest in 1099, inspiring several medieval epics.

p. 70, *Jalal al-Din*: Possibly a reference to Jalal ad-Din ar-Rumi (*c.*1207–73), a great Persian mystic, poet and scholar, who did not come from Bursa but ended up settling in Konya, Turkey.

p. 70, *Urban's cannon*: Also known as the Basilic, or Ottoman Cannon. It was a giant cannon (which could shoot a distance of 2 km) built by the Hungarian engineer Urban and used by the Ottomans during the siege of Constantinople in 1453.

p. 70, *Fighani*: Baba Fighani is a Persian poet (*d.*1519).

p. 77, *Gazanfer Aga*: Chief white eunuch who died in 1603.

p. 78, *the poor black eunuch... into the bath*: De Amicis here refers to an episode described in Letter 9 of the *Persian Letters* (1721) by Charles-Louis de Montesquieu (1689–1755).

p. 79, *the massacres in Bulgaria*: The Ottoman military's brutal reprisal against the Bulgarian nationalistic uprising of 1876 sparked controversy throughout Europe, precipitated the 1877–78 Russo-Turkish War and remained an incendiary issue up to the First World War.

p. 82, *kalpaks*: A type of hood.

p. 83, *Rumelia... victorious sword*: Rumelia was an area of the Balkans which roughly corresponds to modern-day Bulgaria. Dulkadir was a principality named after a Turkoman dynasty, which was annexed by the Ottomans in the sixteenth century. Diyarbakir is a city in south-eastern Turkey. Ajem was a former Persian kingdom. Shaam was the name of a large region which encompassed modern-day Syria, Palestine, Lebanon, Jordan and parts of Saudi Arabia and Iraq.

p. 87, *Cambronne's word*: As famously mentioned in *Les Misérables*, French General Pierre Jacques Étienne Cambronne (1770–1842) is said to have uttered the word "*merde*" ("shit") on the battlefield in 1813.

p. 89, *the Crusca*: The leading learned academy for the study of the Italian language, founded in Florence in 1583. They published the first important dictionary of the language in 1612.

p. 89, *puote... puossi*: Old Italian words and phrases, meaning "he can", "because", "at every turn", "there is" and "one can" respectively.

p. 90, *divine Tuscan tongue*: A reference to line 11 of the 1798 sonnet 'On the capital sentence proposed by the Cisalpine Council against the Latin language' by Ugo Foscolo (1778–1827).

p. 102, *Praxiteles or Lysippus*: Famous Greek sculptors who flourished in the fourth century BC.

p. 104, *mellahs*: A mellah is a Jewish quarter in a Turkish or Moroccan city.

p. 104, *quid valeant humeri*: "How much my shoulders can bear", taken from Horace's *Ars Poetica*, l. 40.

p. 105, *Arethusa's lover*: As described in the Fifth Book of Ovid's *Metamorphoses*, the naiad Arethusa – and not her lover, as De Amicis claims – was transformed into a river by Artemis in order to escape the attentions of the river-god Alpheus.

p. 107, *pure and ready to see again the stars*: This is a reference to the final line (XXXIII, 145) of Dante's *Purgatory*.

p. 109, *Victor Hugo's Oriental Poems*: A collection of poems by Victor Hugo (1802–85), published in 1829.

p. 109, *before the noble subject*: Possibly a reference to John Milton's *Paradise Lost* I, 24.

p. 114, *suspended… heaven*: Possibly a reference to Paul the Silentiary's (6th century AD) long poem 'The magnificence of Hagia Sophia'.

p. 114, *mihrab… ratib*: One of the two types of imam – khatib and ratib – who officiate in a mosque. The ratib reads out from the Koran and leads the five daily prayers, while the khatib preaches the Friday sermons.

p. 115, *like an abyss suspended over one's head*: From Chapter 3 of *Corinne, or Italy* (see note to p. 23).

p. 115, *Deus in medio… vultu suo*: "God is in the midst of [the Earth], it shall not be moved; God will help it in the early morning", Psalms 46:5.

p. 118, *colossal sepulchre*: Possibly a reference to Théophile Gautier's poem 'Seule!'

p. 120, *Anthemius of Tralles and Isidore of Miletus*: Sixth-century Greek architects who helped rebuild the dome of Hagia Sophia.

p. 120, *House of Wisdom*: Sophia means "wisdom" in Greek.

p. 126, *the trembling joy of a great purpose*: From the 1821 poem 'The Fifth of May' by Alessandro Manzoni (1785–1873).

p. 127, *You are nothing but a cursed dog*: From the poem 'The Dervish', contained in Victor Hugo's *Oriental Poems*.

p. 138, *Harpagon*: Harpagon is the protagonist of Molière's 1668 play *The Miser*.

p. 139, *Tommaseo… hieroglyphical women*: Niccolò Tommaseo (1802–74) was an Italian poet and critic. The quotation is taken from 'The Young Man' (ll. 15–16) by Italian poet Giuseppe Giusti (1809–50).

p. 150, *nefanda voluptas*: "Unspeakable pleasures" (Latin).

p. 151, *Madame de Sévigné's expression*: Madame de Sévigné (1626–96) was a French marquise whose vast correspondence achieved posthumous literary fame.

p. 156, *La Mode illustrée*: Popular Parisian fashion magazine which ran from the 1860s to the 1920s.

p. 156, *kokona*: The term *kokona* means an overdressed and excessively made-up woman in Turkish.

p. 158, *Bayram*: Bayram – *Kücük Bayram* ("Minor Festival") in full – is the Turkish name for the Muslim *Eid-ul-Fitr* festival, which marks the end of Ramadan.

p. 158, *Le Bourgeois gentilhomme*: *Le Bourgeois gentilhomme* (*The Bourgeois Gentleman*) was a famous 1670 play by Molière.

p. 161, *Menelaus*: As implied by the reference to Menelaus, whose wife Helen was stolen from him by the Trojan Paris, *kerata* means "cuckold" in Turkish.

p. 166, *The Betrothed*: *The Betrothed* by Alessandro Manzoni was published in 1827 and is considered by many to be the first modern Italian novel.

p. 166, *Superga*: Superga is a hill overlooking Turin, which is famous for its monastery.

p. 166, *Yangın var*: "There's a fire" (Turkish).

p. 166, *four years previously*: There was a great fire in Constantinople on 5th June 1870 – four years before De Amicis visited the city – which killed around 900 people.

p. 166, *Doré*: Gustave Doré (1832–83) was a famous and prolific French painter, illustrator and engraver.

p. 179, *Be quiet, cursed wolf*: Here De Amicis amusingly quotes Dante's *Inferno* VI, 27 and VII, 8 to refer to his hunger.

p. 181, *John Grant*: John Grant was a British engineer (although some sources claim that he was German and named Johannes Grant), whose expertise helped destroy the tunnels that the Ottomans tried to dig to enter Constantinople.

p. 182, *Antonio and Troilo Bocchiardo*: The Bocchiardo brothers were Genoese soldiers who fought for the Byzantines.

p. 182, *at the end of spring in 1453*: The Ottomans set up camp outside Constantinople in early April 1453, and attacked and conquered the city on 29th May.

p. 183, *Elepolis*: An ancient type of mobile fortified tower used for sieges, also called Helepolis or helepole.

p. 184, *Marshals Saint-Arnaud... Pelissier*: Famous *Maréchaux de France* under Napoleon III.

p. 184, *Eugène Saccard... 1854*: "Eugène Saccard, corporal in the 22nd light infantry regiment, 16th June 1854" (French).

p. 185, *Giustiniani or Don Francisco of Toledo*: Giovanni Giustiniani Longo was a young Genoese nobleman who, along with his 700 troops, fought for the Byzantine emperor in 1453. Don Francisco of Toledo was a Castilian soldier who also fought against the Ottomans.

p. 188, *Ali of Tepelenë*: Ali Pasha of Tepelenë (1744–1822), whose father was the deposed governor of Tepelenë in southern Albania, became governor of the Ottoman province of Janina, before gradually expanding his dominion across Albania and north-western Greece and gaining increasing autonomy. He was assassinated by the Turks since he had in their eyes become too powerful and dangerous due to his association with the Greek independence movement.

p. 189, *Lion of Epirus... Vassiliki*: "Lion of Epirus" refers to Ali Pasha of Tepelenë (see note to p. 188). "Arnaut" was a former word for "Albanian" and a "palikar" was an Albanian soldier of the time. Kyra Vassiliki was Ali Pasha's wife.

p. 191, *Narses*: Narses (*c*.480–574) was an Armenian eunuch who rose through the ranks to become a general of the Byzantine army and successfully fought against the Ostrogoths in Italy from 552 to 554.

p. 192, *when the war in the Morea broke out*: In 1715, the Ottomans invaded the Morea (Peloponnese) and recaptured it from the Venetians, an event which reignited the conflict between the Ottoman and the Austrian Empires.

p. 195, *passes away as in a dream*: This refers to Giacomo Leopardi's (1798–1837) poem 'The Evening of the Holiday' (1820).

p. 204, *karakulak*: Literally, "Black Ear" (Turkish).

p. 204, *Charles V... Francis I*: Charles V (1500–58) was the Holy Roman Emperor from 1519 to 1556 and King of Spain (as Charles I) from 1516 to 1556; Francis I (1494–1547) was King of France from 1515 to 1547.

p. 215, *When there are two caliphs, one should be killed*: This saying is not from the Koran, but has been attributed to the Prophet Mohammad by various Islamic scholars.

p. 222, *Bâkî... Gazâlî's licentious lines*: Bâkî (1526–1600) – Mahmut Abdülbâkî in full – and Mehmet bin Süleyman Fuzuli (1495–1556) were both lyric poets of the Divan and are widely considered as the most important figures in the classical school of Turkish literature. Ebüssud is a more obscure poet who died in 1646. Mehmet Gazâlî (1466–1535) – also known as Deli Birader, or "Mad Brother" – was a famous poet from Bursa whose writing has been compared to Rabelais.

p. 224, *Erizzo... Negroponte*: In 1470, under Mehmet II, the Turks conquered the island of Negroponte (Eubea), which had been under the control of the Venetians and their local governor Paolo Erizzo.

p. 225, *Fortunæ reduci ob devictos Gothos*: "To our Good Fortune, who has returned because of the defeat of the Goths."

p. 227, *Hatti Sherif of Gulhane*: The Hatti Sherif of Gulhane was proclaimed on 3rd November 1839 by the Sultan Abdülmecit I, following the advice of his Grand Vizier Mustafa Resid Pasha. It heralded the so-called "Tanzimat" period of fundamental military, social and economic reform, which lasted until 1876 and aimed to modernize the Ottoman Empire.

p. 229, *Once upon a time... My son*: The girl has just told the beginning of the tale of "Ghanim Ben Ayub the Slave of Love" from the *Arabian Nights*.

p. 230, *The filthy spider... its sinister song*: De Amicis slightly misquotes a verse by the Persian poet Firdausi (940–c.1020), which according to Chapter 68 of Edward Gibbon's *History of the Decline and Fall of the Roman Empire* was indeed quoted by Mehmet the Conqueror.

p. 230, *the Basilica of Justinian*: In Sabratha, modern-day Libya.

p. 231, *Karahisari*: Ahmet Karahisari was a famous sixteenth-century calligrapher.

p. 231, *Khaniá*: Ahmet Koprülü, Grand Vizier under Ibrahim I, conquered Khaniá – ancient Canea – from the Venetians in 1645.

p. 239, *Emin Baba*: Probably a reference to Hacı Bektaş (*c*.1248–1337), a mystic and philosopher who lived in Anatolia.

p. 241, *the Mevlevi*: Also known as the Whirling Dervishes, the dervishes of the Mevlevi order are followers of Mevlana Jalal ad-Din ar-Rumi (see second note to p. 70).

p. 241, *flickers on a burnt-out wick*: De Amicis adapts a phrase from line 2 of the poem 'On the Death of Lorenzo Mascheroni' (1801) by Vincenzo Monti (1754–1828).

p. 242, *as Desdemona says to Othello*: This phrase, which De Amicis mistakenly attributes to Desdemona, is from *Othello*, Act v, Sc. 2, and is actually used by Gratiano, just after Desdemona's death.

p. 253, *silent growth of ideas*: De Amicis may have translated the expression "*végétation sourde*", which can be found in Charles Baudelaire's (1812–67) story '*La Fanfarlo*' (1847).

p. 256, *Juno's gadflies*: After having been transformed into a heifer by Zeus, Io was chased by a gadfly sent by the jealous Hera (also known by the Romans as Juno) over the Bosphorus (which literally means "cow ford").

p. 258, *Yıldırım*: "Thunderbolt" (Turkish).

p. 258, *It was here... crossed the Bosphorus*: As described by Herodotus, Mandrocles of Samos was an engineer who constructed the first floating pontoon bridge over the Bosphorus for the Persian emperor Darius in 490 BC. The Ten Thousand were an army of Greek and foreign soldiers assembled by Cyrus the Younger to conquer the Persian Empire from 401 to 399 BC.

p. 259, *the Ottoman Lamartine*: Fuad Pasha (*d*.1869) was a Turkish statesman renowned for his wit and his pro-European diplomatic efforts.

p. 264, *Godfrey of Bouillon*: See first note to p. 70.

p. 266, *fera litora Ponti*: "The wild shores of Pontus", from Ovid's *Tristia* (I, 2, 83).

p. 266, *the fabled Symplegades*: The fabled moving cliffs that Jason's *Argo* had to pass through in order to reach the Hellespont.

p. 266, *quocumque... et aer*: "Wherever I look, there is nothing but sea and air", also taken from Ovid's *Tristia* (I, 2, 23).

# Glossary

aga: Title of rank; military commander/head of a household

*azab*: Infantryman

*baltacı*: Halberdier/guard

bey: Title of rank; governor of a province or district

*başi*: Head, chief

*bostancı*: Palace gardener

*çavuş*: Sergeant, executioner

*defterdar*: Head of the treasury

dervish: Muslim friar

Divan: Privy council of the Ottoman State

dragoman: Interpreter

effendi: Title of rank; mainly used for officials and men of learning

firman: Edict issued in the Sultan's name

*gedikli*: Concubine favoured by the Sultan, maid-in-waiting

Grand Vizier: Chief Minister of the Sultan

*hanım*: Lady of rank

hatti sherif: Irrevocable decree personally signed by the Sultan

janissary: Member of former elite corps of Sultan's personal infantry

*kadıasker*: High judicial authority

kadin: Wife/favourite of the Sultan

kaimakam: Deputy of the Grand Vizier/deputy-governor of a province

*kapıcı*: Palace gatekeeper

kavass: Constable/armed servant

Kiaya: Minister of the interior or governess of the harem

Kızlar Aga: Chief black eunuch

logothete: Byzantine high official

mufti: Title of head of state religion (also Grand Mufti) or of his deputies

musellim: Lieutenant of a pasha

*müderris*: Professor at a madrasah, or Muslim university

*nisancı*: General secretary to the Sultan

nizam: Turkish regular soldier

*Padishah*: Sultan of Turkey

pasha: Title of high rank; military commander or governor of a province

*peyk*: Lackey

*pişkeş*: Present from a subordinate to a superior

protospathaire: Byzantine captain of the guards

rayah: Non-Muslim subject, liable to pay poll tax

*şagird*: Apprentice/disciple

*silahtar*: Sultan's swordbearer/armourer

solak: Sultan's attendant, guardsman

spahi: Horseman

Sultan: Sovereign of the Ottoman Empire

Sultana Valide: Mother of the reigning Sultan

tekke: Dervish lodge

timariot: Holder of a timar, or parcel of land obtained through military conquest

turbeh: Monument erected over Muslim tomb

ulema: Community of legal and religious scholars

*usta*: Master in a craft

*veznedar*: Treasurer

vizier: High official/minister

*yasakçı*: Guard for foreign ambassadors

*zülüflü baltacı*: Palace guard

# RECENT TITLES FROM ALMA CLASSICS

To order any of our titles and for up-to-date information about our current and forthcoming publications, please visit our website on:

# www.almaclassics.com